Fun Web page

with

JavaScript

2nd Edition

Other Titles of Interest

Titles in italics are by John Shelley

Fun Web pages
with
JavaScript

2nd edition

by

John Shelley

BERNARD BABANI (publishing) LTD
THE GRAMPIANS
SHEPHERDS BUSH ROAD
LONDON W6 7NF
ENGLAND

www.babanibooks.com

PLEASE NOTE

Although every care has been taken with the production of this book to ensure that any projects, designs, modifications and/or programs, etc., contained herewith, operate in a correct and safe manner and also that any components specified are normally available in Great Britain, the Publishers and Author(s) do not accept responsibility in any way for the failure (including fault in design) of any project, design, modification or program to work correctly or to cause damage to any equipment that it may be connected to or used in conjunction with, or in respect of any other damage or injury that may be so caused, nor do the Publishers accept responsibility in any way for the failure to obtain specified components.

Notice is also given that if equipment that is still under warranty is modified in any way or used or connected with home-built equipment then that warranty may be void.

First Published - March 2000
Reprinted - September 2000
Reprinted - March 2001
2nd edition Published - January 2002
Reprinted - March 2002
Reprinted - November 2002

British Library Cataloguing in Publication Data

A catalogue record for this book is available from the British Library

ISBN 0 85934 520 3

Cover Design by Gregor Arthur

Printed and Bound in Great Britain by Cox & Wyman Ltd

Preface

It is a truism to say that one learns by one's own mistakes. During some thirty years of having to learn and use and, then, to teach programming to thousands of students, this is something with which I wholeheartedly agree. Of course, it applies to many walks of life and not just computing. Just think of how you managed to pass your driving test, capture that girl or boy of your dreams, cook a 'perfect' Yorkshire pudding?

As an author of a programming text, just what does one include? Well, I am reminded of what one of my College lecturers once said. He bounced into the lecture hall one day claiming to know a secret.

> "A lecturer passes through three stages. During the first he teaches everything he knows about a subject. During the second he teaches all that he did not know during his first stage. Finally, and this is when he is of greatest value to his students, he teaches what they need to know."

The lecturer was Charles Davis who taught Theology.

I am not too sure one should say that about Theology, but it is certainly apposite for Computing.

I have aspired to this approach, as best I can, by working from practical examples. There are over 40 practical exercises. Each one is followed by an examination and discussion about the JavaScript used. As one progresses through the examples, one should build up a practical, working knowledge of how to use the language.

JavaScript has gone through several versions, but there remains a large basic core which can never change. As later versions emerge, new tweaks are bolted onto this immutable core. This core is what is taught in this text. Once mastered, new additions can be quickly learnt.

Finally, there are two qualities one needs to have in order to master the skill or art or craft (take your pick) of programming. One is 'attention to detail' - dotting the i's and crossing the t's. You will very quickly know what this means once you start to write your own programs.

The second is logical thinking. Getting things done at the right time and in the right order. Both are maddeningly difficult to achieve. But persevere because on your journey, Lady Programming will bestow upon you a rare gift, one which is sadly lacking in our times - *humility*.

Only those who truly know themselves can be humble - *meek*. After all, are they not the ones to inherit the earth rather than the wind?

Well that is enough of that. Now let's get down to some other business.

I would like to thank Mari-Elena Shelley for the helpful comments she made whilst this text was in progress. I would also like to thank the originators of JavaScript in all its versions for their imaginative construction of the syntax. They certainly know how to present a challenge. ☺

There are various *Tests* set at the end of most chapters. I would encourage you to try them since they are designed to emphasise certain material. There are *Answers* to the Tests at the back of the book which occasionally provide some additional points not raised in the Chapters.

About the Author

John Shelley took his postgraduate Diploma and, later, his Masters degree in Computing at Imperial College, London, where he has worked as a lecturer in the Centre for Computing Services for over thirty years, providing training in programming, operating systems, Web design, HTML and a wide range of application packages to both students and staff.

This is his latest text which he hopes will prove useful to those who wish to learn JavaScript.

Trademarks

Microsoft, MS-DOS, Internet Assistant, Internet Explorer are registered trademarks of Microsoft Corporation. PhotoShop is the trademark of Adobe. AskJeeves is the service mark of AskJeeves, Inc. Java is a trademark of Sun Microsystems.

All other trademarks are the registered and legally protected trademarks of the companies who make the products. There is no intent to use the trademarks generically and readers should investigate ownership of a trademark before using it for any purpose.

I also acknowledge the following where Netscape pages are shown:

"Copyright 1998 Netscape Communications Corp. Used with permission. All Rights Reserved. This electronic file or page may not be reprinted or copied without the express written permission of Netscape."

"Netscape Communications Corporation has not authorized, sponsored, or endorsed, or approved this publication and is not responsible for its content. Netscape and the Netscape Communications Corporate Logos, are trademarks and trade names of Netscape Communications Corporation. All other product names and/or logos are trademarks of their respective owners."

Similar acknowledgements apply to all other screen shots.

The clipart used in some illustrations has been taken from the Clipart Gallery of Word 97.

Contents

ONE

Introduction

What is JavaScript?
JavaScript was developed by Netscape as a simple programming language to be used for enhancing Web pages. It was originally called *LiveScript*, but due to the growing popularity of the Java language, it was called JavaScript on its release and was included in Netscape Navigator 2.0. JavaScript programs can run on all major browsers. In this text, all programs have been tested on both Netscape 4.5 and Internet Explorer 5.0.

Microsoft brought out their own implementation of JavaScript, officially known as JScript. Fortunately, both are more or less compatible. So all programs in this text will run on either of the two major browsers.

Why Learn JavaScript?
A plain Web page using just HTML tags will be displayed by a browser in exactly the same way each time that page is loaded. It cannot change. But by adding JavaScript to that Web page, it is possible to make changes to the page. Suppose we have a conventional Web page which contains an <IMG> tag. That image will be displayed in exactly the same way each time the page is loaded. But with JavaScript, we could change the image when a user passes a mouse over the image and change it back to the original when a user moves the mouse to some other part of the page. That is, in part, what is meant by enhancing Web pages.

1: <u>Introduction</u>

Here are some of the other things JavaScript programs allow us to do:

- you can create pop-up boxes to provide crucial information to a user
- via a cookie, inform a user that the page has changed since it was last viewed
- create simple animation
- invite the user to choose the colour for the Web page background
- compute the cost of items being ordered by a user and then display the result
- determine the age of a user provided he/she enters a date of birth
- include the current date and time each time the page is loaded
- display different content according to which browser is being used
- change the colour of image buttons
- open new document pages and control their size and content
- interact with users by getting them to click various FORM buttons
- validate the entry of data typed into FORMs before sending the information back to the server

The following is more technical. If you wish, you can move on to the next Chapter to see what JavaScript looks like and return to the following at a later stage.

JavaScript is not Java
Many people confuse JavaScript with Java but they are different. Although they are both related, their connection is somewhat frail. Java is the product of Sun Microsystems, whereas JavaScript is the product of Netscape. In fact, as mentioned above, it was not even called JavaScript to begin with but *LiveScript*.

Java is a *general purpose* programming language in the sense that programs can be written to perform almost any task that can be programmed. It was originally used to write programs to control washing machines and the like. But Java cannot be used to control Web pages.

Although JavaScript can also be used as a general purpose language, one of its main attractions is that it can work directly with Web pages using the HTML <SCRIPT> tags, something Java cannot do. In this way, JavaScript can be placed in our Web pages, whereas Java cannot.

What is Covered in this text
There are three ways of using JavaScript:

- purely as a programming language
- as a client-side programming language
- as a server-side programming language

Not many people would use JavaScript purely as a programming language. They would use one of the standard languages such as Java, C or C++. We shall look at the programming aspects of JavaScript, but it is not the main purpose of this text.

So that leaves *client-side* versus *server-side* JavaScript. The JavaScript language has been given some additions which enable it to manipulate the browser, for example, to swap one image or another or to look at and validate something a user has typed into a text box. This is called client-side JavaScript where *client* refers to the browser.

Netscape has also extended JavaScript for working with Web servers, those computers which store Web pages at given sites. These extensions are referred to as server-side JavaScript and are not the same as client-side JavaScript.

1: <u>Introduction</u>

To work with server-side JavaScript, one needs a knowledge of not only JavaScript but also of the server being used. This is beyond the scope of this or, indeed, of many texts since the servers and the systems they run on are frequently far too server dependent. This aspect of JavaScript is really for systems programmers. The problem gets worse because Netscape and Microsoft have different techniques for writing server-side programs.

So, in this book, we shall be looking at the programming and the client-side features of JavaScript. We begin by assuming absolutely no knowledge of JavaScript. But by the end of the book, you will have learnt sufficient to enable you to become competent Web designers.

Client-side v. Server-side

The *client* is the browser program resident on our home and office PCs. Typically, a user wanting a Web page types in the address in the browser's *location/address* box.

The browser now requests, over the Internet, a copy of the desired page from the site holding the page - *step 1* in the following illustration. This site acts as a service provider (a *server*) and will submit the page to the client end - *step 2*. Assume this page has a form which the user has to fill in.

Having filled in the form, and let us suppose it contains errors, the browser has to send it back to the server - *step 3*. The server now has to validate the form's data and if errors are found, inform the client (browser) - *step 4*. The user reads the error messages, fills in the form again and re-submits the form - *step 5*. The server has to validate the form's data again; etc., etc.

It takes time for the client to send forms to the server, and for the server to check and return error messages. However, if the validation of a form can take place at the client-side, it is clear that the whole process will be faster. There should be a need for only *one* submission, namely, once the form is found to be correct.

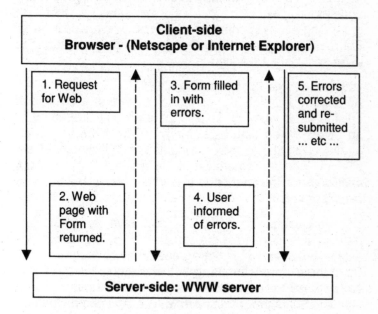

Form validation at the client end is one of the main attractions of JavaScript. JavaScript can be processed by the browser. There is no need for the constant *to*-ing and *fro*-ing between client and server. It involves only two trips over the Internet rather than at least five in the above scenario, reducing the amount of Internet use. With the increasing use of the WWW, it makes sense to rely on JavaScript for client-side processing of data.

Versions of JavaScript
JavaScript is evolving all the time. At the time of writing, the latest version is JavaScript 2 but is not available for

general use. Version 1.5 is available, but you need the latest versions of the two main browsers.

In this book we look at JavaScript 1.2. Provided you understand this version, you will have a thorough grounding in JavaScript and a version which works on all the main browsers. You will then be ready to learn the extra and more advanced features.

Object-Oriented Programming (OOP)

Amongst the JavaScript community, there is a division of opinion as to whether JavaScript is an object-oriented or an object-based language. Many regard it as the latter, others claim it has object oriented capabilities. But we shall not become embroiled in the argument, at least not until we have the chance to see what *objects* are all about (see Chapter 16).

OOP languages, such as C++ and Java, are the latest rage, designed to make the construction of large programs easier. But even this is not agreed on by all programmers. So, if the experts cannot agree, why should we try at this early stage? Let us keep an open mind. The main point is that JavaScript programs work with *objects* and by the end of the book, you will know all there is to know about OOP.

It may be encouraging to point out that people who have never programmed before often find OOP languages easier to understand than the more traditional ones such as Fortran, Cobol or C.

How to Use this Text

In general, each section will begin with an example illustrating something we may want to do using JavaScript. The JavaScript code, that is the program instructions, is then listed and the code explained so that you can understand the various features used. You may wish to experiment by making slight alterations to the original code to suit your own requirements. As we progress, we shall gradually build up a working knowledge of JavaScript.

Unhappily, a complete JavaScript reference is beyond the scope of this text. As an example, one of the references given in the Bibliography, devotes some 300 pages alone, out of 800, to an alphabetical listing of the features of JavaScript. It contains little explanation and few examples. What we are attempting in this text, is to provide a fairly comprehensive coverage which will supply much of what many Web page designers use on an everyday basis. It is after this has been digested that such reference material will become meaningful.

When you run your own JavaScript code, you should run it on *both* Netscape and Internet Explorer. You may become frustrated, as I and many others before you have, in that it works fine on one browser, but not on the other.

One of the 'joys' of writing programs is that they seldom work first time around. Internet Explorer pops up a little error box, indicating the line number and some vague error message as to why your program failed. In Netscape, if the page does not work as you expect, type in `javascript:` in the location box. (Typing the colon is essential.) You will get a little bit more advice.

Jargon
client-side: the client is the browser being used by a user on his/her personal computer - and is referred to as the client-side

code: a term used for JavaScript program instructions

Java: an *OOP* language not to be confused with JavaScript

1: **Introduction**

JScript: Microsoft's implementation of JavaScript and compatible with Netscape's version

OOP: object-oriented programming, supposed to make the writing of large programs easier

server-side: refers to the *WWW* server, the site holding the Web pages a user wishes to view. Programs can be written so that the server can process data which a user has typed into a form and which has been sent back to the server by the browser (client). For example, to check the server's database for details about a client's credit worthiness, etc.

TWO

What Does JavaScript Look Like?

In this section, we shall look at a simple example, namely,
how to get JavaScript to write out a few words on a Web
page. This will introduce us to how we write JavaScript
programs.

Exercise 1: *Getting JavaScript to write out a Message.*

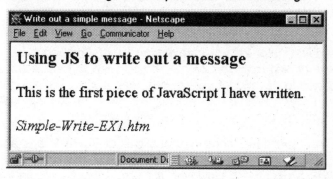

```
<HEAD>
<TITLE>Write out a simple message.</TITLE>
</HEAD>
<BODY>
<H3>Using JS to write out a message </H3>

<SCRIPT  LANGUAGE="JavaScript1.2">
document.writeln("This is the first piece of
JavaScript I have written.");
</SCRIPT>
<ADDRESS> Simple-Write-EX1.htm </ADDRESS>
</BODY>
```

Notes:

1. Everything is standard HTML except for the pair of <SCRIPT> ... </SCRIPT> tags and what they contain. The first thing to notice is that JavaScript code is enclosed in a pair of <SCRIPT> tags:

```
<SCRIPT  LANGUAGE="JavaScript1.2">
  .. our JavaScript code
    (frequently called a 'script') ......
</SCRIPT>
```

This tag can take the LANGUAGE attribute to specify which version of JavaScript is being used. Note that the attribute value (JavaScript1.2) is enclosed in double quotes and that there is no space between the version number and JavaScript.

You can use the default value of just "JavaScript", in which case Navigator 2.0 will infer version 1.0 of JavaScript. Later versions will infer version 1.1. If you wish to use features specific to JavaScript version 1.2, then it must be included as shown above. In this text, we frequently use `LANGUAGE="Javascript"` or omit it altogether.

2. You can have more than one pair of SCRIPT tags and they can be placed within the <HEAD> or the <BODY> of the web document. However, the browser will execute the scripts in the order in which they are placed in the HTML source code. We shall see the impact of this in later examples. In the above code, the content between the HTML <H3> tags will be displayed first, secondly the *script code* and finally the <ADDRESS> to show the following:

Using JavaScript to write out a message

This is the first piece of JavaScript I have written.

Simple-Write-EX1.htm

However, if the SCRIPT tags were placed in the HEAD or, indeed, between the HEAD and the BODY, or even before the <H3> tag in the BODY, the script message would then come *before* the H3 heading!

This is the first piece of JavaScript I have written.

Using JavaScript to write out a message

Simple-Write-EX1.htm

It is important to place script code in the correct position within an HTML document just as we have to with our <IMG> and <FORM> tags.

3. Let us now look at the actual JavaScript code which consists of just one instruction. Notice the semi-colon (;) used to mark the end of an instruction:

```
document.writeln("This is the first piece of
JavaScript I have written.");
```

JavaScript works with *objects*. At the heart of object-based and object-oriented programming languages, such as Java, Visual Basic, C++ and JavaScript, lie objects. These are the basic 'things' programmers work with. Objects have *properties* and *methods* and, if you are like me when I first began to learn JavaScript, this is where you begin to wonder if you ought to quit.

At the beginning, I felt I had to understand these terms before I could continue. But it was only by *using* them that I gradually began to appreciate what they meant. So do not give up yet! As we progress and look at JavaScript in more detail, these strange terms will become clearer. For the masochists amongst you, you can have a quick look at Chapter 16, where these terms are discussed in some detail. For the moment we shall have to accept the jargon. So, here it goes.

The word `document` is one of many JavaScript objects we can manipulate. It simply refers to the Web page currently being displayed. We want to do something to the current web document (the currently displayed page). But what do we want to do to this page?

That is the purpose of the second word `'writeln'` (pronounced 'write line'), typed in lowercase. It is called a *method*. Most objects have one or more methods. They specify what we want to do to an *object*.

Right now, we want to write a message in the current Web page, so, we need to refer to the *document object* and use its *writeln method*. It is really a special built-in program (like a *function*) which does something to its object, in this case 'to write a line of text to the web document'. Note that the JavaScript syntax requires a period (full stop) between the *object* and its *method*: `object.method`

But what do we want to write out? That is what we place inside the brackets in double quotes. (If you are trying this out, do not press the Enter key at the end of a line. We explain why on page 19.) We can now interpret this line of code as follows:

"In the currently displayed document - Write out the phrase - 'This is the first piece of JavaScript I have written'."

The message in double quotes is more formally called an *argument*. The argument is put inside round brackets and surrounded by double quotes.

Why bother to use a script, why not simply type the text using standard HTML? We could, but we need to know that we can use JavaScript to type text on to a web page.

Make sure you appreciate that the <SCRIPT> tags are part of HTML rather than JavaScript. They notify the browser that some JavaScript code is enclosed. The browser has to be *JavaScript enabled*, otherwise it will not be able to read the code inside the <SCRIPT> tags.

When it comes to using JavaScript code (as opposed to writing HTML) *case* is significant. The C language, on which JavaScript is based, is case sensitive, that is why we need to be careful when writing JavaScript code.

C and the other languages use lowercase for the code and sometimes a mixture of upper and lower. If you do not abide by the case, then the script will *fail* (a term for *will not work*). If you doubt me, then try this out.

```
DOCUMENT.writeln("A Message")
```

Internet Explorer and Netscape (provided `javascript:` is typed into Netscape's location box) would give an error message saying that DOCUMENT is not defined, meaning that it would understand `document` but not DOCUMENT. So, be warned! (The text within the double quotes can be in any case, of course.)

Exercise 2: *Writing out two messages*

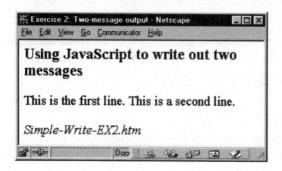

- 13 -

2: JavaScript

We shall expand the above exercise to print out *two* messages and then explain how to get each one on a separate line.

```
<HEAD>
<TITLE>Exercise 2: Two-message output</TITLE>
</HEAD>
<BODY>
<H3>Using JavaScript to write out two messages
</H3>
<SCRIPT Language="JavaScript">
document.writeln("This is the first line.");
document.writeln("This is a second line.");
</SCRIPT>
<P>
<ADDRESS>Simple-Write-EX2.htm</ADDRESS>
</BODY>
```

Notes:
1. Notice the semi-colon after the first and second `document.writeln`. This is how one instruction is separated from another. The semi-colon is used to mark the end of an instruction, frequently referred to as a *statement*. (Yes, I know that new jargon is popping up all the time, but programming has been around for a very long time and it is littered with jargon. It is something we just have to put up with.)

We should emphasise a policy on the use of semi-colons right at the start. The original version of JavaScript required semi-colons, but the popular browsers do not require them any more. As a result, it is becoming common practice not to include them **provided** that each statement goes on to a new line. If you type more than one statement on a single line, then you **must** include semi-colons otherwise the script may fail for no obvious reason.

Should semi-colons be used or not?

This will depend upon which school you want to go to. Some experts say 'do not bother' - the *relaxed* school; other experts say that you should include them because it is good programming practice - the *strict* school! You must make up your own mind. I shall borrow from both schools throughout this text just to remind you that both exist.

2. Notice, too, that the two messages displayed on the Web page are not separated, they flow on from each other. In Exercise 3 we shall see how to force them on to separate lines. (Using JavaScript is not quite the same as using a word processor.)

3. There is another form - the *write* method:

```
document.write("Type out some text")
```

It is identical in behaviour to `writeln`, except that the latter will append a new line **after** it has output its message whereas `write()` appends a second message to the previous one. So why were the two messages output by the *writeln()* method not put on two lines? I had to ask this at first until it dawned on me that what `writeln()` does is to write the message into the Web page *source code*. It does not affect how it is displayed in the browser window.

To understand this, let us look at the source code which the *Netscape* browser will generate for Exercise 2. You can see this if you use the *View>>Page Source* command from within Netscape. Click *View*, then select *Page Source*. This opens a new window with the HTML source code shown for whatever page is currently being displayed by the browser. This is what Netscape shows:

```
<HEAD>
<TITLE>Exercise 2</TITLE></HEAD>
```

```
<BODY>
<H3>Using JavaScript to write out two
messages</H3>

This is the first line.
This is a second line.

<P>
<ADDRESS>Simple-Write-EX2.htm </ADDRESS>
</BODY>
```

`writeln()` was used. Now, substitute `write()` for the two `writeln()` statements. You will see that the messages flow on one line, as follows, when viewing the *page source* in Netscape:

```
<BODY>
<H3>Using JavaScript to write out two messages
</H3>
This is the first line. This is a second line.
<P> .. etc. ..
```

Notes:

1. You see neither the SCRIPT tags nor the JavaScript code when viewing the source code in Netscape. In other words, there is no difference between write() or writeln() except when viewing the source code in Netscape.

2. Internet Explorer also shows the source code (under *View* with the single word *Source*), but IE displays the source code in the Notepad editor and, consequently, displays the original source just as you typed it, complete with <SCRIPT> tags and the JavaScript code.

3. The above is one of the subtle differences between the way the two main browsers operate and underlines the need to have both browsers on your machine so that you can begin to make comparisons. (Do not worry, it will only get worse! There are some other annoying discrepancies

between the two browsers which we shall see in due course.)

So, how do we force a browser to put the second line of text on a separate line? That is what we look at next and it does not matter whether we use `write()` or `writeln()`.

Exercise 3: *Forcing Text to appear on Separate Lines*

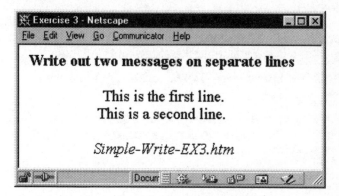

How would you get a second line to appear on a separate line in HTML? You would use either the <BR> or the <P> tag, thus: `Line one. <P> Line 2.`

Well, not only can you get the *write()* and the *writeln()* methods to type out text, but you can also get them to type out HTML tags. So, if we include a <P> tag or a <BR> after the first piece of text in the first *write()* method, it will write out that tag in the source code and force the argument of the next *write()* to appear on a new line. Let us look at the code for this:

```
<BODY>
<CENTER>
<B>Write out two messages on separate ines</B>
<P>
```

```
<SCRIPT>
document.write("This is the first line.<BR>");
document.write("This is a second line.");
</SCRIPT>
<P><ADDRESS>Simple-Write-EX3.htm</ADDRESS>
</CENTER>
</BODY>
```

Notes:

1. The <BR> tag has been included as part of the argument. In other words, it must go within the two double quotes. It is equivalent to the following HTML code:

```
This is the first line. <BR> This is the
second line.
```

and the above is exactly what you would see if you examined the *source code* in Netscape.

```
<HEAD>
<TITLE>Exercise 3</TITLE>
</HEAD>

<BODY>
<CENTER>
<B>Write out two messages on separate ines</B>
<P>

This is the first line.<BR> This is a second
line.

<P>
<ADDRESS>Simple-Write-EX3.htm</ADDRESS>
</BODY>
```

Note the <BR> tag has been written out as well as the text argument in the source code.

If we had used `writeln()` instead, the result would be exactly the same when displayed by a browser, but the actual *source code* in Netscape would look like this:

```
<BODY>
<B> Write out two messages on separate lines
</B>
This is the first line.<BR>
This is a second line.
<P>
<ADDRESS>Simple-Write-EX3.htm</ADDRESS></BODY>
```

The `writeln()` will create a new line *in the source code* after it has written out the first argument, so that the second `writeln()` argument will begin on a new line.

So, what have we learnt? We now know that we can generate pages of HTML code using JavaScript. What is so marvellous about that, why not merely write the HTML code in the first place? As we shall see fairly soon, we can give a user a choice of buttons to click. Depending on which one is chosen, one of several scripts can be generated, each with its own unique HTML code. In this way, an web-author can interact with the reader.

> **Warning:** *Before we finish this chapter, there is one important point to make.*

When using either the *write()* or the *writeln()* method you must not press the Enter key in your editor between the double quotes. For example, in this long piece of text:

```
document.write("Here is a long piece of text to
type out. I must resist the temptation to press
the Enter key at the end of a line which I
would normally do in my word processor.")
```

it is tempting to press the Enter key in your editor after the word 'to' on the first line. However, JavaScript takes Enter to mean the end of that statement and in our example, this would mean that the argument does not end with a double quote. The syntax would be incorrect. There are two ways to overcome this. Either, simply keep on typing and let your editor word wrap, or, and this is the better approach, use *multiple* arguments as follows:

```
document.write("Here is a long piece of text",
               " to type out. I must resist",
               " the temptation to press the",
               " Enter key at the end of a",
               " line which I would normally",
               " do in my word processor.")
```

See how the write() method takes more than one argument each surrounded by double quotes and a comma separating one from another? The arguments' text will, of course, not be on separate lines when *displayed* in the browser window because we have not included any HTML tags. We do so below:

```
document.write("<HR> Here is a long piece of",
               " text to type out. <BR>",
               " I must resist the temptation",
               " to press the Enter key at the",
               " end of a line which I would",
               " normally do in my word",
               " processor. <HR>")
```

Now, the browser will display the text on separate lines.

(Due to the page size of this book, it is not always possible to use multiple arguments in the examples. Where that occurs, you must assume that word wrap has taken place.)

2. Out of interest, both Netscape and IE refused to display anything for the version which had the Enter key pressed between the quotes. But they both came up with an error message complaining about an *"Unterminated string constant"* and gave the line number where it had occurred. (Blank lines are included in line counts.)

So what is a *string constant*? The text within double quotes is called a *quoted string*, *string* or *string constant*. A string constant is anything enclosed within double quotes. *Unterminated* means that the closing double quote is missing.

3. Finally, notice in the following:

```
document.write("Here is a long piece of text",
               " to type out and it will",
               "spread over another line.")
```

that a space occurs between the opening double quote and the word to in the second line. If a space had not been included, the last word of the first quoted string would join with the first word of the second string, without a gap. This is what has happened in the third string which has no space before spread and would result in "willspread over another line." being displayed. So, you need to take spacing into account when using multiple arguments.

Jargon used in this chapter:
argument: in programming, arguments are the data on which methods work. In the examples we have used so far, the arguments contain text-strings and HTML tags which have been written to the Web page via the *write()* and *writeln()* methods. These methods form part of the client-side JavaScript language and their arguments must be enclosed in round brackets.

code: a term used for JavaScript instructions. In general, the terms *code, scripts, statements* and *programs* can be used interchangeably to refer to a block or group of JavaScript instructions.

2: <u>JavaScript</u>

JavaScript enabled: choose this option in your browser so that it will be able to execute any JavaScript code within SCRIPT tags.

method: in object based languages, a *method* is similar to a function, a short program, which does something to an object. Most objects have one or more methods. `document` is an object which has the *methods* `write()` and `writeln()`.

objects: we have met one, *document,* and we shall meet others later. Objects are the building blocks for the scripts we wish to create. (It took me some time to become a little clearer in my own mind about these terms - objects and methods. Let us not worry too much about them just yet.)

quoted string: a string of characters enclosed in double or single quotes. A character string may consist of simple text and/or HTML tags.

script: a term used for a block of JavaScript code.

statement: each piece of programming code is known as a statement or, indeed, an instruction. It is akin to a complete English sentence or command. In JavaScript, each statement can end with a semi-colon.

syntax: the rules or syntax for constructing JavaScript code. Including a full-stop between an object and its method, the correct use of case and the correct use of quotes are some examples of JavaScript syntax.

What you have learned
We have covered a few of the basics in this chapter.

JavaScript code is placed within a pair of HTML <SCRIPT> tags. The positioning of the tags will determine where they will take effect on the displayed page, just like the placement of <IMG> tags.

We can have multiple <SCRIPT> tags and they may be put in the <HEAD> or <BODY> tags, or even between the two. But, we need to give careful thought to where we actually place them.

We have seen that JavaScript can write out text to a Web page and more importantly can write out pure HTML code upon which the browser will act, just as though we had written pure HTML in the first place.

We can use either the `write()` or the `writeln()` methods. They both have the same effect on the actual display of the Web page, but in Netscape, their difference is seen in the *source code*.

Some methods can take more than one argument. However, when a string constant argument is used, it must not contain an *Enter* code within its double quotes.

Case becomes significant when using JavaScript code, whereas case is not significant when writing HTML code. We now have two things to think about as we embed JavaScript into our Web designs. The HTML itself and the syntax of JavaScript.

Test: Chap. 2

2.1 What are the <SCRIPT> tags used for and where can they be placed?

2.2 Do the <SCRIPT> tags form part of JavaScript or HTML?

2.3 Is `document` an object or method?

2.4 Is `writeln()` an object or method?

2.5 What is the main difference between `write()` and `writeln()`?

2: <u>JavaScript</u>

2.6 Can you have more than one pair of <SCRIPT> tags in the same HTML document?

2.7 What would the following display on a Web page:

```
document.write("Hallo there.",
              "My name is Joe.")
```

2.8 What is the formal term for what is enclosed within the round brackets in the above code?

2.9 When would you need to add:

LANGUAGE="Javascript1.2" to an opening <SCRIPT> tag?

2.10 How are multiple arguments separated?

Forms & Pop-Up Boxes

In this section we shall see how to use Forms to interact with our readers. We shall also see how to add more HTML code via the *write()* and *writeln()* methods.

User Interaction
A normal HTML Web page is static. Each time it is called up and displayed by a browser the page will look exactly the same as it did on any previous occasion.

One of the reasons people use JavaScript is to create some form of interaction with a user. For example, allowing the user to buy some of our goods and to display the total cost; to replace one image for another such as a photograph of different views of the progress of some disease. One of the main mechanisms for creating user interaction is via Form buttons. We shall begin with a simple interaction whereby we invite a user to click a button to display an *alert* box.

Exercise 4: *Using a Form to make an alert box pop-up.*
Here is some simple HTML which creates a Form button with some text on it.

```
<FORM>
<INPUT TYPE="button"
       VALUE="Click this button">
</FORM>
```

3: <u>Forms & Pop-Up Boxes</u>

But how do we go about getting the button to display an
alert box when it is clicked? We can do this by adding just
one more attribute to the <INPUT> tag. The *onClick*
attribute as shown below.

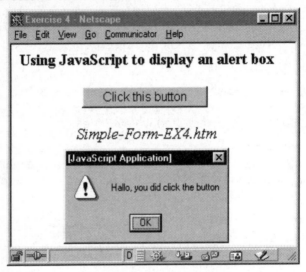

Figure 3.1

```
<HEAD>
<TITLE>Exercise 4</TITLE>
</HEAD>
<BODY>
<H3>Using JavaScript to display an alert box
</H3>
<FORM>
<INPUT   TYPE="button"
         VALUE="Click this button"
         onClick="alert('Hallo, you did click the
button')">
</FORM> <P>
<ADDRESS>Simple-Form-EX4.htm</ADDRESS>
</BODY>
```

The *onClick* attribute was originally a Netscape extension added to the <INPUT> HTML tag. Now, it has become standard in HTML version 4.0. Figure 3.1 shows what happens when a user does click the Form button.

Notes:

1. The first point to appreciate is the syntax for the *onClick* attribute. This applies to all the other variations we shall encounter later.

```
onClick = "... some JavaScript code ..."
```

The HTML attribute *onClick* is not case sensitive - but it is conventional to write it as shown with a capital C and the rest in lowercase. By contrast, the *value* this attribute takes is JavaScript code and as such *is* case sensitive.

```
onClick = "alert('Hallo, you did click the
button')"
```

Therefore, `Alert(..)` or `ALERT(..)` would be wrong, it must be in lowercase. (Just to remind you, should you use this example, you must not press the Enter key after `the`, keep on typing and allow word wrap to take effect.)

2. The value of the attribute *onClick* is a piece of JavaScript code enclosed in double quotes with the equals symbol between the attribute and its value, just like other attribute values in HTML. When the button is clicked, it causes the value of the *onClick* attribute to be executed. In our example, this is a call to the *alert()* method to display whatever message is inside the brackets.

3. `alert()` is a method of the *window* object which automatically causes an alert dialogue box to pop up with whatever message has been typed inside the brackets. But note how the message is in *single* quotes. We cannot use a double quote within a double quote since the second double quote would finish off the first one.

3: Forms & Pop-Up Boxes

Since the entire JavaScript code must be contained within a pair of double quotes, the *alert()* function's message must be in single quotes so that these do not interfere with the main outer double quotes. I hope that makes sense. It is something which will crop up time and again. Beginners frequently forget this and wonder why their scripts do not work. Consequently, we have to type the code as follows:

```
onClick="alert('message to be displayed')"
```

4. `alert` must be in lowercase, otherwise when a user clicks on the button, nothing will happen. Netscape simply sits there totally dumb, whereas IE will tell you that an error has occurred - "Object expected". Not very helpful but at least you can concentrate on the spelling and/or case of the *alert()* method by looking at the line number given. But why would the mis-spelt *Alert* be called an object rather than a method?

To begin with, IE does not recognise your mis-typed *Alert()* as a call to the *alert()* method of the window object. It has not a clue what it is. More often than not, an error checking program has to guess at what the programmer intended. A good guess is object, because it assumes that the *Alert()* method should belong to an object. It cannot find one associated with *Alert()* and is trying to tell you that it cannot find it.

5. We now have another piece of jargon to learn. Clicking on the button is formally known as an *event,* something which the user has to do. Other types of events can be: moving a mouse over a hyperlink; moving a mouse out of an image map; clicking a submit button; changing the text in a text field, etc. We shall be looking at all these and other events in more detail later.

The *onClick* value is called an *event handler.* It defines what has to be done when the event occurs.

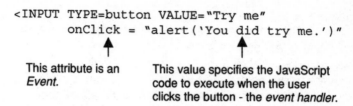

```
<INPUT TYPE=button VALUE="Try me"
      onClick = "alert('You did try me.')"
```

This attribute is an *Event*.

This value specifies the JavaScript code to execute when the user clicks the button - the *event handler*.

6. Note that our JavaScript code has been written without any <SCRIPT> tags. We now know *two* ways of writing JavaScript code, using <SCRIPT> tags and using FORM buttons with an event attribute such as *onClick*. (*See page 57 if you use Word 97 to write your scripts.*)

Here is another example of user interaction:

Exercise 5: *Getting the User to choose the bgColor*
Interaction with your Web page readers is one of the main attractions of using JavaScript. In this example, we shall use a <TABLE> to display the colour names and buttons. The user is invited to click one of the buttons to set the background (bgColor) to his/her choice of colour.

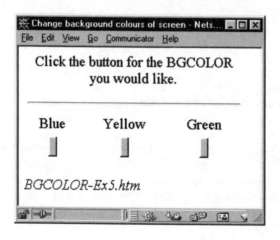

```
<HEAD>
<TITLE> Change background colours of the screen
</TITLE> </HEAD>

<BODY><FORM>
<TABLE WIDTH=100%>
<CAPTION>Click the button for the BGCOLOR you
          would like.</CAPTION>
<TR>
<TD COLSPAN=3> <HR>
<TR ALIGN=center>
<TD>Blue <TD>Yellow <TD> Green
<TR ALIGN=center>
<TD>
<input type="button"
       onClick="document.bgColor='lightblue'">
<TD>
<input type="button"
       onClick="document.bgColor='lightyellow'">
<TD>
<input type="button"
       onClick="document.bgColor='lightgreen'">
</TR>
</TABLE></FORM>
<ADDRESS> BGCOLOR-Ex5.htm </ADDRESS></BODY>
```

Notes:
1. When one of the buttons is clicked, the relevant JavaScript code is executed and will change the background colour of the Web page.

```
onClick="document.bgColor='lightblue'"
```

The *onClick's* value (in double quotes) assigns the *bgColor* of the currently displayed document to a `'lightblue'` colour. Again, because the *onClick* value must be in double quotes *and* the syntax requires a quoted string for the actual colour value, we have to use *single* quotes for the latter.

2. We have already seen that the *document object* can take two methods, `write()` and `writeln()`. But here we are making use of *bgColor*. It is not a method so what is it? It is called a *property*.

> *(If you wish, you could now look at Chapter 16 for a discussion about objects and their methods and properties. It is not yet essential, but some amongst you may be curious. If not, just leave it until we have come across a few more examples. For the time being, just try to appreciate that objects have* methods *which can do something to the object, such as generate an alert box or write out some text, and that objects also have* properties *which affect the appearance of the object.)*

3. We could have used the RGB (red, green, blue) hexadecimal numbers instead of the colour words - thus:

```
onClick="document.bgColor='DE6633'
```

4. Do note the case for *bgColor*. Any other variation would not work. (I shall stop repeating the importance of case soon, so please make sure that you keep to the correct case when writing your own code.)

5. The term *assign,* in Note 1 above, is another jargon word and requires some explanation for those new to programming.

In mathematics: $x = 4$ means the letter x takes on the value of 4, that is, x equals 4. In programming, although it looks the same, it means something different, namely that x *is to be replaced by* (assigned) the value 4. To be more precise, we should read it as:

"whatever is on the right-hand side of the assignment operator (=) is to replace whatever is contained on the left-hand side."

What is the difference? Well in programming we could write this: x = x + 1

Mathematically, this is not possible, x cannot be 1 greater than itself. But this is not mathematics, it is a perfectly valid *programming* statement and means that whatever value the right-hand side 'x' currently has, add 1 to it and replace the left-hand side 'x' with the new value.

What use is that? It happens to be one of the commonest statements in programming as we shall discover when we come to discuss the programming aspects of JavaScript.

For the moment, we just need to remember that an assignment statement replaces whatever is on the left with whatever is on the right. It is best, right from the start, to get into the habit of saying: x *is to be replaced by* 4 (or whatever) rather than saying x *equals* 4.

Exercise 6: *More HTML code using* `document.write()`

This exercise is merely to show how we can use the document's *write()* method to generate HTML code and to introduce another way of writing arguments.

```
<BODY>
<H3 ALIGN=right>Writing HTML to a Document</H3>

<SCRIPT>
document.write("<HR WIDTH=50%>"
            + "<FONT COLOR='#0000FF'>"
            + "<CENTER>"
            + "This is some coloured text."
            + "</CENTER>"
            + "</FONT>"
            + "<HR WIDTH='90%'>")
</SCRIPT>
<ADDRESS>Write-HTML-Ex6.htm </ADDRESS>
<SCRIPT>
document.write("<P> This document was last"
            + " Modified on <BR>"
            + document.lastModified)
</SCRIPT>
</BODY>
```

Notes:

1. Notice that the `document.write()` uses the *concatenate* operator (+). These will join each quoted string into a single argument. This new operator is discussed below. We could have used commas instead but then we would be using *multiple* arguments.

2. Since we are using <SCRIPT> tags, as opposed to event handlers, we can use double quotes to surround each string.

3. For the sake of clarity, we have put each string on to a new line. But there was no need to do so. However, it makes it easier to find any errors in our scripts, such as missing operators, missing quotes, etc.

3: <u>Forms & Pop-Up Boxes</u>

Concatenate

Concatenate means 'to join together'. The concatenate operator is used to join two or more quoted strings together to form a *single* argument. If we had used commas, then we would have been using *multiple* arguments. (*Do not confuse the concatenate operator with the arithmetical addition symbol. They both look identical but have to be interpreted from the* context *in which they are used.*)

We shall see more of this operator in the next chapter, but for now simply appreciate how we can use the concatenate operator or multiple arguments to overcome the problem of writing long strings of text without worrying about whether we have pressed the Enter key or not.

lastModified

We have also included the lastModified property of the document object, note the use of interCapping. It returns the date (mm/dd/yy hh:mm:ss - American) the document was last modified. We shall see in Chapter 11 how to convert to English style. Note that because we are using a property, we must not use quotes to enclose the object.property. (As an exercise, why not use an alert box to show the date last modified?)

```
<SCRIPT>
document.write("<P> This document was last"
            + " Modified on <BR>"
            + "<FONT color='red'>"
            + document.lastModified
            + "</font>")
</SCRIPT>
```

Some Horrors

If you have been experimenting with your own scripts, you may have come across some really weird things. Here are some of the ones I have met.

When I began writing JavaScript, I kept having to puzzle out what was happening when using `document.write`, or rather, why things were not happening. My reference books were not too helpful.

1. Do not press the Enter key anywhere between a string in single or double quotes. Allow word-wrap to take place if the string flows onto a new line. Better still, employ commas or concatenate operators. The reason for this is that JavaScript assumes the Enter key means the end of a statement. So, if you do press Enter within a quoted string argument, that string has no ending quote mark! The syntax is incorrect.

What happens when the page is displayed will depend on which browser you are using. Netscape will simply ignore the script, do nothing more and give you no warning unless you type `javascript:` in the location box. Internet Explorer will also fail but will automatically display an error message and give the line number (blank lines are included in the line count) of where the error occurred. The error messages in both browsers are somewhat cryptic, but at least you can begin to examine the code where the error occurred.

2. When using multiple arguments, make sure each argument, except the final one, has a comma separator, otherwise the arguments which follow will not be recognised. Remember that programming languages have very strict rules of behaviour (the syntax). Breaking the rules will always cause errors to occur.

3. A real surprise with Netscape, version 4 at least, is that should you resize a window after loading a web page, it re-reads the source code from its cache memory. It uses a cache memory to speed up the display, especially when

images are involved. However, the real surprise occurs if this cached version contains JavaScript code.

Imagine that you load a page and spot a mistake in your code once the page is displayed. You go back and correct the error in the source code, save the page and re-load it in Netscape. But, if you now resize the window, the source code which Netscape uses may be an earlier cached version which still contains the original mistake!

4. Do not use `document.write()` or `writeln()` with an event handler, at least not until we discuss opening new windows in Chapter 8. For the time being, it is safer to use `document.write` only within <SCRIPT> tags. The browser will then write out the arguments to the *current* window.

If you do use it as the value of an event attribute, such as onClick, browsers will open a new window and display the arguments of `document.write()` in that window. This can be useful in some situations but we need to know a bit more before we can safely use such examples.

Other Pop Up Boxes

There are three types of pop-up boxes, the *alert*, which we have seen, a *prompt* box and a *confirm* box. The prompt box invites a user to enter some text. Once the user has clicked the OK button, we can use JavaScript to find out what has been typed in.

The confirm box displays a message of our choosing and asks the user to accept the message (confirm it) by clicking *OK* or reject it by clicking the *Cancel* button. JavaScript can determine whether the message was confirmed or rejected.

However, in order to use these other two boxes, we need to know how to 'capture' what a user has typed into a prompt box or which button was selected in a confirm box. That involves the use of *functions*, the subject of the next chapter. We cannot do much more with JavaScript until we know how to use functions.

Jargon

assignment statement: a piece of code which assigns a value on the right of the assignment operator (=) to a *variable* on the left of the operator. $x = x + 1$ Here, x is a variable - we have more to say about variables in the next chapter.

cache memory: part of the computer's memory where some browsers store copies of loaded Web pages (and images) for quick access should that page need to be re-displayed, for example after a page has been re-sized.

event handlers: HTML event attributes, such as *onClick*, have associated JavaScript code as their values. The event handler's code is executed when a user causes an event to happen.

events: things which users may do, such as move a mouse over a hypertext link, click on a button, change text in a text box. See Chapter 7 for more details.

operators: a programming term for the various symbols used within a program. We have seen the following:

- = the *assignment* operator
- > the greater than *comparison* operator
- + the concatenate operator
- + the arithmetic addition operator

Chapter 9 discusses these and others in more detail.

3: <u>Forms & Pop-Up Boxes</u>

What you have learned
1. How to call up an alert box when a user clicks on a button using the *onClick* event.

2. We have seen that there are two basic ways to write JavaScript code:
- by using Form buttons and assigning code to an event handler
- to enclose code within <SCRIPT> tags

3. How to give a user a choice of buttons to select a colour for the background.

4. When to use double quotes and single quotes.

5. Using more than one argument for *document.write()*.

6. How to concatenate quoted strings to form **one** argument. Yes, you should make it clear in your own mind that concatenate is not the same as multiple arguments. It joins all the strings into one argument.

Test: Chap. 3
3.1 Does the *alert()* method belong to the *document* or *window* object?

3.2 In the following, should double or single quotes be used around the message in the alert box?
```
onClick = "alert( the message )"
```

3.3 What is the JavaScript term for the *onClick* attribute?

3.4 What type of value does the *onClick* attribute take?

3.5 When a user clicks on a button, what is this called in JavaScript?

3.6 In OOP languages, what is the formal term for *bgColor* in the following?
```
onClick = " document.bgColor = 'lightblue' "
```

3.7 In the above, would it matter if *bgColor* was typed as bgcolor or BGCOLOR?

3.8 What value will z have after the following code is executed?

```
z = 1;
z = z + 3;
```

3.9 In the above code, is + a concatenate or an arithmetic operator?

3.10 What could happen in Netscape when a window is re-sized?

3.11 Is *onClick* an attribute or an event?

Escape Sequences

The backslash character (\) provides a special purpose in JavaScript strings. It is followed by a character or a number and is called an *escape sequence*. For example, suppose I wish to write out via a *document.write* or *alert* box:

```
Read this play: "Macbeth".
alert("Read this play: "Macbeth".")
```

The second double quotes would be taken as the closing set of the first and would confuse the browser. By using an escape sequence, we bring to the attention of the browser that the second (and third) double quotes are used in a special way.

```
alert("Read this play: \"Macbeth\".")
```

The backslash 'escapes' from the usual interpretation of the character. In the above, it will write out double quotes before and after *Macbeth*.

Sequence	Character
\b	backspace
\n	newline
\r	carriage return
\t	tab
\'	apostrophe
\"	double quote
\\	backslash

\\xnn
AE is ®.
A9 is ©
A5 is ¥.
BD is ½.
E8 is è
	where nn is a hexadecimal number representing a character from the Latin 1 encoding. x indicates a hexadecimal value.
	
	`alert("Hallo. \r I\'m Fred \xAE \t \\`
	`\\my name has been registered.")`

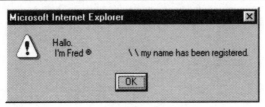

The main strength of JavaScript, as with many other programming languages, lies in its ability to allow programmers to create *functions*. A function is a block of instructions which has been given a name. This will make sense when we come to see how functions are used.

We shall return to a simple exercise shown in the previous Chapter and convert it into a function.

Remember this one from Exercise 4?

```
<FORM>
<INPUT TYPE="button"
       VALUE="Click this button"
       onClick="alert('Hallo, you did
click the button')">
</FORM>
```

When the Form button was clicked, an alert dialogue box popped up. Let us get the event handler to execute a *function* which will do exactly the same. Although it is a simple task, it will illustrate how functions are created. We can do more exciting things later.

Exercise 7: *Creating a function.*

Here is the code, the explanation will follow.

```
<HEAD>
<TITLE>Exercise 7</TITLE>
</HEAD>
```

4: Functions

```
<SCRIPT>
function showalert()
{
    alert("Hallo, the button called a function to
display an alert box!")
}
</SCRIPT>

<BODY>
<H3>Using   a   Function   to   display   an   alert
box</H3>
<FORM>
<INPUT TYPE="button" VALUE="Click this button"
        onClick="showalert()">
</FORM>
<P>
<ADDRESS>Simple-Function-EX7.htm</ADDRESS>
</BODY>
```

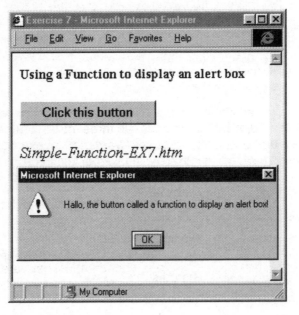

Notes:

1. When the button is clicked, the alert box appears.

2. Why bother to create a function, surely it is simpler to do it the other way, as shown on page 41? Yes, you are right, but we need to start somewhere and this simple example shows how functions are created. The function begins with the word *function* (lowercase) followed by a name (which we invent) followed by opening and closing round brackets. There is nothing in the brackets but they are still required. We shall put something in later. You should never put a space between the function *name* and the round brackets.

3. The entire function is put between a pair of <SCRIPT> tags which, for a change, have been placed between the HEAD and the BODY. They could go inside the HEAD or inside the BODY. They could come after the BODY - but this can be unwise as we shall see. From a practical point of view, and one recommended by serious programmers, all functions should go before the BODY and *within* the <HEAD> tags. Indeed, the new version of HTML (XHTML) is rather strict about this approach.

4. If you had three functions, each one could go within separate <SCRIPT> tags, or all three could be placed within the one pair. In other words, a single pair of <SCRIPT> tags can contain multiple functions.

5. What are the curly brackets { .. } doing? These are required by JavaScript to mark the beginning and the end of the function's code. We have only one statement, but there is no limit to the number of statements within a function. If there is more than one, it is safer to put semicolons after each complete statement. (They are not always used in this text but it is good programming style to do so.)

6. It is important to know that the browser will not execute the statements in a function as the Web page is being loaded. This is not the same as our earlier and more simple scripts, which did not contain functions and, consequently, *were executed* as the page was being loaded and in the order in which they appeared. So when are the instructions in a function executed?

That is the purpose of the *onClick* attribute's event handler. It contains the *name* of the function and the two brackets, but does not include the word *function*.

```
onClick="showalert()"
```

The function will not be executed until a user clicks the Form button. When it is clicked, the browser will look at the value of the *onClick* to see what has to be done. Previously, this was to generate an alert box, but this time it is told to execute the function called `showalert()`.

It will find this function (all functions are stored in a safe place whilst the page is originally being loaded) and then execute the code inside the function's curly brackets. The code in our function asks for an alert box to be displayed along with our message. When the closing curly bracket is encountered, all processing stops.

7. You need to be aware that a function has two parts. The first is called the *declaration* and comprises the *function* keyword, a *name* immediately followed by opening and closing *round brackets* and the actual code enclosed in *curly brackets* also known as *braces*. They are placed within <SCRIPT> tags>

```
<SCRIPT>
function   name()
{ ... JavaScript code ...}
</SCRIPT>
```

It will not be executed until the function is *invoked*. This is the *second part* of the process - a call (an *invocation*) to execute the function. This call consists of just the name of the function and the round brackets. Actually, these round brackets are very important. After a function name they become an *operator* which informs JavaScript that a call has to be made to a function. If you left them out, the process would not work. `onClick="showalert()"`

8. Do be sure that you know when to use round brackets and when to use curly braces.

Exercise 8: *Here is Exercise 5 using functions.*

```
<HEAD> <TITLE> ... <TITLE>
<SCRIPT>
function blue() {
 document.bgColor='lightblue'
} // EoFn

function yellow()
{
 document.bgColor='lightyellow'
} // EoFn
function green() {
 document.bgColor='lightgreen'} // EoFn
</SCRIPT>
</HEAD>

<BODY>
<FORM>
<TABLE WIDTH=100%>
<CAPTION>Click the button for the BGCOLOR you
would like.</CAPTION>
<TR> <TD COLSPAN=3> <HR>
<TR ALIGN=CENTER>
<TD>Blue    <TD>Yellow <TD> Green
<TR ALIGN=CENTER>
<TD><input type="button" onclick="blue()">
<TD><input type="button" onClick="yellow()">
```

```
<TD><input type="button" onclick="green()">
</TR> </TABLE>
</FORM>
<ADDRESS>BGCOLOR-fns-Ex8.htm </ADDRESS></BODY>
```

Notes:

1. We have converted Exercise 5 into one that uses functions. Notice how the one pair of <SCRIPT> tags contains the three functions.

2. It is common practice to put the opening curly bracket on the same line as the function name and to put the closing curly bracket on a separate line as shown for function *blue()*. But as you can see, there are other valid variations depending on the personal style of the programmer. We have shown three different styles in the above. It is good programming practice to be consistent where possible.

3. It will save you a great deal of annoyance if you also go to the trouble of adding a comment (see page 77) after the closing curly bracket of a function to indicate that it is the 'end of the function' - `// EoFn blue()`

Once you begin to write larger scripts, it is easy to forget to type the closing bracket or to mistake it for one that might belong to another programming feature. See Chapter 9.

4. Because `onClick` is part of HTML, case is not significant, hence the use of `onclick` in the example. However, in XHTML, all attributes must be in lowercase. (XHTML is the new version of HTML, the latter will not be developed any further. If you already know HTML, then you already know 90% of XHTML.)

Exercises 9a - 9c: *Using a Prompt dialogue box*
We mentioned in the previous chapter that there are three
types of pop-up dialogue boxes. We will look at the *prompt*
box now. It is used to prompt a user to enter some data.
We shall soon see how we can 'capture' that data so that
we can see what has been typed in. This will introduce us
to the need for *variables* - functions love to use variables.

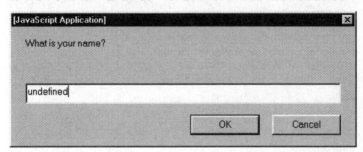

Here is some code which generates the above prompt
dialogue box from within HTML <SCRIPT> tags.

```
<HEAD>
<TITLE> Creating a Prompt box</TITLE>
</HEAD>
<BODY>
<H4> Here is a Prompt</H4>
<SCRIPT>
     prompt("What is your name?")
</SCRIPT>
<ADDRESS>PROMPT-Ex9a.htm </ADDRESS>
</BODY>
```

Notes for Exercise 9a:
1. Note that the syntax for `prompt("message")` is
similar to the *alert()*.

2. The word '*undefined*' means that the user has not yet
typed anything into the prompt box. When he/she does, it

will replace that word. When the user has typed something in and clicked the OK button the dialogue box disappears. Note that the message string (the prompt's argument) is displayed so that the user knows what to do.

3. Seeing the word '*undefined*' is not only ugly but it could terrify your visitors. It is a simple matter to remove it. Unlike *alert()* and *confirm()*, we come to the latter very shortly, *prompt()* can take a second argument.

```
prompt("What is your name?","")
```

It comes after the comma in the above and contains the empty string - `""`. This will replace the word *undefined* with a blank, effectively removing it. You could put something inside the double quotes, in which case, that something would appear in the text box. Try it out for yourself!

Exercise 9b: *Capturing the data from the Prompt box.*

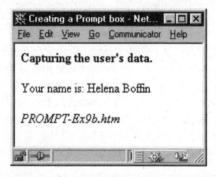

We shall now find out how to capture what the user has typed in. Here is the code using a variable called x.

```
<BODY>
<FONT SIZE=-1>
<B>Capturing the user's data.</B></FONT>
```

```
<SCRIPT>
 x = prompt("What is your name?","");
 document.write("<P>Your name is: " + x);
</SCRIPT>
<P>
<ADDRESS>PROMPT-Ex9b.htm </ADDRESS>
</BODY>
```

Notes for Exercise 9b:

1. We have assigned to a variable 'x' the name which the user has typed into the prompt's text box, here 'Helena Boffin'. A variable is a named storage area inside the computer's memory where its data is kept until it is needed.

2. The next line of code does use the variable via the `document.write` feature:

```
document.write("<P>Your name is: " + x)
```

This is one of the reasons why all programming languages need variables. It is a mechanism for holding data which needs to be used at a later stage in the program. Note how the `document.write` includes not just a text string but also the variable x which does not have quotes around it. If it did, the character 'x' would be written out. Consequently, when something does not have quotes, JavaScript interprets it as a variable. It will then look for this variable to find out what has been stored inside it.

'x' tends to be a very common name for a variable, probably a sign that programmers lack imagination. Certainly, it is one which I use quite frequently! There are rules for creating variable names and these are set out at the end of the chapter.

Exercise 9c: *Using functions and confirm().*
We shall rewrite Exercise 9b using a function and introduce *confirm()*. It is quite a useful box in that you can ask a user to confirm that they really do want some action to take place.

```
<SCRIPT>
function yourname(){
  x = prompt("What is your name?");
  confirm("Did you say your name is "
          + x
          + "?");
} // EoFn
</SCRIPT>
<BODY>
<H4> Here is a Prompt</H4>
<FORM>
<INPUT TYPE="button" VALUE="Tell me your name."
        onClick="yourname()">
</FORM>
<ADDRESS>PROMPT-Ex9c.htm </ADDRESS></BODY>
```

Notes for Exercise 9c:
1. 'x' is a variable which is assigned the value typed in by a user in the prompt dialogue box. It could be any other letter or word and it can be preceded by the keyword `var` (short for 'variable' and rhymes with 'far'), thus:

`var x = prompt("What is your name?")`

That variable can be used in conjunction with the confirm box message. Assuming the name typed in is 'Jasper', we ask the user to confirm the name:

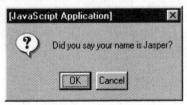

```
confirm("Did you say your name is " + x + "?")
```

2. You can see that `confirm("message")` is similar in syntax to the alert and the prompt boxes. The user can accept (OK) or reject (Cancel) the confirm pop-up box.

(A confirm() *dialogue box is sometimes used to confirm transactions on the Web before allowing a user to part with all their credit card details.)*

3. You need to be aware that the *alert* and *confirm* pop-up boxes can take but **one** argument. So we need to concatenate the three parts of the above message into one by using the concatenate operator (+).

- "Did you say your name is "
- x
- "?"

If we had put commas in, thereby creating multiple arguments, only the first argument would be displayed, the rest would be ignored. Try it out if you do not believe me.

4. Notice that the variable is not enclosed in double quotes. Whatever data it contains (*Jasper* in this case) will be substituted when written out. Indeed, we must *not* use quotes otherwise the letter x would be printed out because it would then become a quoted string.

5. We can now begin to see how JavaScript is able to distinguish between text-strings and variables. Text must be written as quoted strings: "I am a piece of text.", whereas variables are not quoted.

6. Finally, note the presence of a space after the word 'is'. If there was no space then the 'J' of 'Jasper' would come immediately after the 's' of 'is', thus: "Did you say your name isJasper?" When using concatenation, include spaces where necessary.

4: <u>Functions</u>

Built-in Functions or Methods?
You may be wondering whether *write()*, *writeln()*, *alert()*, *confirm()* and *prompt()* are functions. They certainly look like functions. They have a name and a function call operator - (). You would be correct.

They are all examples of *built-in* functions which belong to certain objects and because of this are formally known as *methods* in object oriented languages. These, and many more which we shall come across, form part of the JavaScript language. See the summary at the end of this chapter. *write()* and *writeln()* are methods of the document object; the three pop-up boxes are methods of the window object. (See page 63 for the window object.)

In contrast, the ones created by us are known as *user-defined functions*. In the above examples, blue(), yellow(), green() and yourname() are our own user-defined functions.

Why Bother with Functions?
There are many reasons. One is that if you want to repeat say 10 lines of code in 5 different places in a Web page, rather than type 50 lines of code, you need only type the 10 lines once, and use five invocations to the function. See the rounding() function, Exercise 21, page 140. We shall come across other reasons later in the text.

Jargon
declaration: refers to the instructions inside a function's curly brackets. It declares what must be done when the function is called (invoked) from some other point in the Web page. It is sometimes known as the *definition* since it defines what the function will do. It must include the lowercase keyword *function*, the function *name* followed by *round brackets*.

function: a function is a way of naming a section of JavaScript code which you wish to execute at your leisure. It includes the keyword *function*, a *name* and, so far, empty *round brackets*, plus the *code* to be executed:

```
function somename(){ .. code .. }
```

invoke: a programming term used when we want to execute a function. The function *name* and the *function call* operator must be used:

```
onClick = "myfunction()"
```

variable: a name given to a piece of data so that it can be held in the computer's memory ready to be used when required. It is called a *variable* because the same name can contain different data on different occasions. For example, in Exercise 9c the name 'Jasper' was typed in. However, if the user clicked the form button again he or she could quite easily type in a new name - Susan. The variable 'x' would now store the name Susan. Its content can *vary*.

What you have learned

1. You have learnt how to create a function, using curly brackets (braces) to mark the beginning and end of the function's code.

2. A function must always have a pair of round brackets after its name, even if there is nothing in them. We shall see in the next chapter what can be put in these brackets.

3. We have seen how to use *prompt* and *confirmation* pop-up boxes. But do not use them all the time. It can be quite irritating to your readers.

4. More importantly, we have seen that data entered into a prompt box can be captured for use at a later stage. This is done by storing the data in a *variable*.

5. The distinction was made between built-in and user defined functions.

Rules for creating Variable Names
When creating a name for a variable, case is significant. The first character in the name must be one of the following:

- a lower or upper case letter
- underscore (_   )
- $

Subsequent characters may be any letter or digit, or an underscore or dollar sign. The first character must not be a digit.

Valid	Invalid
i	123
my_var$name	!name
_myvariable	a name
$strg	this-var
X13	1X4

A Point of Interest

Note what appears at the top of the confirm box. The same is seen for the other two pop-up boxes. It says:

[JavaScript Application]

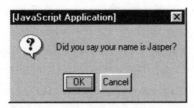

whereas IE displays: *Microsoft Internet Explorer*

The reason for this is to inform the user that the pop-up box was *generated by the browser*.

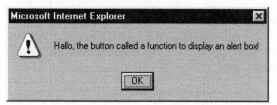

Why? Take a look at this.

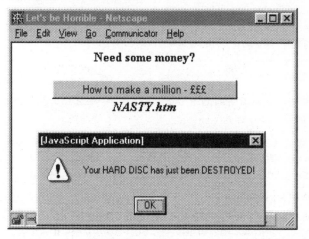

You could write some JavaScript code to generate an alert box with the terrifying message above. Some people have a 'funny' sense of humour.

If *[JavaScript Application]* or the Microsoft equivalent was not included, you might well begin to feel very sick, imagining that it was an operating system message.

(Hmmm! It is tempting though.) ☺

Test: Chap. 4

4.1 In the code for Exercise 9c what forms the *declaration* and what forms the *invocation* of the function `yourname()`?

4.2 How many functions can be placed within a single pair of <SCRIPT> tags?

4.3 How many syntax errors can you find in the following?

```
onclick  "function abc{}'
```

4.4 The prompt dialogue box can take two arguments. What purpose does the second serve?

4.5 What would the following write out?

```
sum = 1.5 + 2;
document.write("The sum is: " + "sum");
```

4.6 When would you want to use an *alert*, a *confirm* and a *prompt* pop-up box?

4.7 You cannot use multiple arguments in the alert() method. What device must you use when you wish to display some text as well as the contents of variables?

4.8 In the following code, in what *order* would the browser would display the Web page on the screen?

```
<HEAD> <TITLE> .. a title .. </TITLE>
<SCRIPT>
function yourname(){
  x = prompt("What is your name?");
  confirm("Did you say your name is " + x +
"?");
} // EoFn
</SCRIPT>
</HEAD>
<BODY>
<H4> Here is a Prompt</H4>
```

```
<FORM>
<INPUT TYPE="button" VALUE="Tell me your name."
       onClick="yourname()">
</FORM>
<ADDRESS>PROMPT-Ex9c.htm </ADDRESS></BODY>
```

4.9 What type of arguments can the *write()* method take?

— — — — — — — — — — — — — — — — — — — .

WARNING:
Many people use Notepad when writing their HTML web pages. I tend to use Word 97 so that when necessary I can use some of the word processing features, for example colouring text functions when trying to find errors. However, if the <FORM> tag is used without a *method* and *action* attribute, Word freezes and I lose all my work. There is no problem when using Notepad.

So, in many of my examples you will see the following:

```
<FORM method="" action=""> .... </FORM>
```

to avoid Word crashing. I would hate for this to happen to you without giving you some warning. There is no need to put anything between the double quotes. Later when we come to using NAME attributes, Word will freeze again unless the NAME attribute follows the method and action:

```
<FORM method="" action="" NAME="somename">
```

4: <u>Functions</u>

Summary of JavaScript so far:

Objects	Methods	Properties
document	write()	bgColor
	writeln()	lastModified
	close()	
window	alert()	
	confirm()	
	prompt()	

Operators	Purpose	Example
=	assignment	x = x + 1
+	arithmetic addition	1+2 (= 3)
+	concatenate	"a"+"b" (= ab)
()	function call	function abc()
{ }	embed function code	
Event Handlers		
onClick	used with form buttons	
Dialogue boxes		
alert	inform user	
confirm	confirm or cancel	
prompt	enter data	

FIVE

Arguments in Functions

We shall now examine the use of arguments in functions. In the previous chapter we saw how useful functions are, but their usefulness can be improved by passing them *arguments*. So, what is an argument? It can be almost any type of data you want. It could be the text typed into a prompt box or the OK or Cancel button clicked in a confirm box. It could be two numbers which indicate a range of numbers the function could work with. We shall look at these and more in the following.

First, we need to introduce the concept of *arguments* via a simple example, finding the square root for any number. Not everyone is madly interested in square roots, but this simple exercise will introduce not only the concept of arguments but also how JavaScript performs calculations. The latter is important, because you may need to calculate the overall cost and tax on some goods (course fees, loan re-payments, etc.) you are offering over the Internet before getting the buyer to agree the amount.

In our square root example, three things need to happen. A user must type in a number, we shall use a prompt box for this; secondly, we need to find out what number has been typed in; and, finally, invoke a function to work out the square root and display the result.

Exercise 10: *A Function using an argument.*
The idea is to write a function which will output the square root of a number entered by a user. We shall see how to

round the result to two decimal places in Exercise 12.
Here is the code.

```
<HEAD>
<TITLE> Calculate the Square Root </TITLE>
<SCRIPT>
function squareroot(sqroot)
{   x = Math.sqrt(sqroot);
    document.write("The square root of "
                    + sqroot + " is: " + x);
}
</SCRIPT>
</HEAD>

<BODY>
<H4>Using Arguments</H4>
<SCRIPT LANGUAGE="Javascript">
  var sqroot = prompt("Enter a number. I will"
            + " give you its squareroot.", "");
  squareroot(sqroot);
</SCRIPT>

<ADDRESS>Arguments-Ex10.htm </ADDRESS>
</BODY>
```

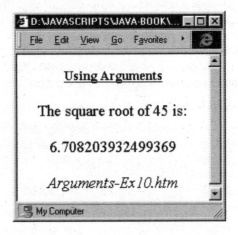

Notes:
1. We have used a prompt box to get the user to type in a number and included a blank string as a second argument to remove the word 'Undefined' from the prompt box.

The value typed in has been assigned to the variable `sqroot`, a name I made up. It is preceded with the keyword `var`. It was not necessary and we have not done so before but it is good practice since it reinforces the fact that we are using a variable and makes the code clearer. (We discuss another reason on page 119.)

2. On the line below, we have a second statement which calls the user defined function: `squareroot(`*`sqroot`*`)`. But note that it contains `sqroot`, the variable assigned to the user's input via the prompt box. Previously, our *function call* operators were empty. When variables are included they are known as *arguments*.

Arguments are the mechanism by which data picked up elsewhere and held in variables can be passed to a function. We need to give the `squareroot()` function the value typed into the prompt box by the user. We do so by passing it over as an argument for use by that function.

3. Our function passes it to a second function - to `Math.sqrt(sqroot)` - which computes and returns the square root which is then assigned to a variable `'x'`.

```
x = Math.sqrt(sqroot);
```

A `document.write` statement is used to write out the original number (`sqroot`) and the computed square root which has been assigned to the variable `'x'`.

Notice the careful use of spacing in the quoted strings of the *write* method and that the variable names are not, indeed must not, be quoted.

```
function squareroot(sqroot)
{
 x = Math.sqrt(sqroot);
 document.write("The square root of "
                    + sqroot + " is: " + x)
}
```

3. But what is this *Math*?

`sqrt()` is one of several special built-in mathematical functions which form part of core JavaScript. It is a method of the *Math* object. Without the reference to the Math object, JavaScript would not recognise the *sqrt()* function as one of its own. But because we have specified the Math object, JavaScript now knows that we are referring to the *sqrt* method of the Math object. We can use this function to work out the square root rather than do all the hard work ourselves.

Summary:

- we have invited the user to enter a value and we are using JavaScript as a pocket calculator to work out the square root
- this value is assigned to a variable `sqroot`
- it is passed as an argument to our calculator function: `squareroot(sqroot)`
- our function passes it to JavaScript's built-in function `sqrt(sqroot)`
- since `sqrt()` is a method of the Math object, we had to mention the Math object

Functions can have as many arguments as required and the same function can be used time and again. Thus, in our exercise, the user could enter a different value each time the prompt box appears. Each time the function is invoked, the argument will contain a different value.

Objects - Methods - Properties

Let us digress for a moment to explain what *object* and *method* mean in more detail. It is probably about time.

We have met several *objects* so far. One being *document*, and now *Math*. We have been using a third one but may not have actually realised it, namely, *window*. (Note that Math has a capital M, whereas the other two begin with lowercase. Yes! it all helps to make sure that we type the wrong thing in and spend time wondering why nothing works.)

Strictly speaking, when we used the three pop-up boxes, we should have typed:

```
window.alert("... some message ...")
window.prompt("... some message ...")
window.confirm("... some message ...")
```

These three are built-in functions (methods) of the window object. If we leave the 'window.' part off, as we have done earlier, JavaScript assumes that we meant to include it. Why could it not assume the same if we left off the Math object? If we did, it would assume that sqrt() was a user defined client-side function and begin looking for it. But by associating it with the Math object, JavaScript will know that it is one of its core functions.

JavaScript is an object based language. This means that our JavaScript code works with *objects* and many of them have *methods* associated with them. When we need to 'do something' to an object, for example, to write something to the current document, we have to use the appropriate method of that object:

```
document.write(" .. something ..")
```

So far, we have used two methods of the *document* object: *write()* and *writeln()*. Each method does something to its object. The three pop-up boxes are methods belonging to the *window* object. *sqrt()* is one of the many methods in the *Math* object's repertoire. Others can be seen in Chapter 10.

So why is the *Math* object different to the other two by starting with a capital letter? There are two[1] parts to JavaScript. There is the basic *core language* which makes JavaScript a stand-alone language, just like Java, C, Fortran, Basic, etc. Then there are the additions, the *client-side* additions, which allow programmers to work with Web browser objects, something which the other languages cannot do.

The *Math* object is part of the JavaScript core language. There are seven other core objects, some of which we shall meet later, such as *Date* and *String* - both of which also begin with a capital letter. Math, Date and String were defined with capital letters in the core JavaScript.

On the other hand, *document* and *window* are some of the additional objects which permit a programmer to work with Web browsers. These were defined with lowercase letters and form part of client-side JavaScript.

Do you remember `document.bgColor` in Exercise 8? *bgColor* is a *property* of the document object. So, we have these three terms.

> *Objects* - the basic 'things' we work with
> Objects have *methods* (functions)
> Objects also have *properties*

---

[1]   In fact, there is a third part to JavaScript, namely those features which allow programmers to interact with a server. These are known as server-side JavaScript as opposed to what we are studying, namely, the client-side (browser) aspects of JavaScript. See page 4 for an explanation of client-side and server-side.

This analogy may help. A car is an *object*. It has a colour *property* - say, maroon. It has *methods* which allow it to move forward or backwards, faster or slower. It is important to try to understand these three terms since they are in use all the time. It took me some time to begin to understand them. However, the more you use JavaScript, the more they begin to make sense. Programming in object orientated languages is all about playing around with objects and with the various properties and methods associated with those objects.

That is enough for now. See Chapter 16 for more details.

Exercise 11: *Using NAMEs in <FORM>.*
We shall now ask a user to enter a calculation and make JavaScript return the answer. (This will help us to understand a much more sophisticated program in Chapter 10 which works out monthly payments for a loan at whatever interest the user desires. You can use this to determine whether the monthly payments on the purchase of your car are indeed accurate and to ensure that you are not being fleeced.) Here is the code:

```
<HEAD> <TITLE> ... </TITLE>
<SCRIPT>
function cal(){
document.formcal.answer.value =
        eval(document.formcal.calculator.value);
} // EoFn
</SCRIPT>
</HEAD>

<BODY>
<FONT SIZE=2>
If you enter a calculation, you will be given
the answer when you click the
<I><B> Calculate </B></I> button.
</FONT>
```

```
<FORM method="" action="" NAME="formcal">
<INPUT TYPE="text" SIZE="12" NAME="calculator">
<INPUT TYPE="button" VALUE="Calculate"
       onClick="cal()">
<INPUT TYPE="reset" VALUE="Reset">
<BR>
Answer:  
<INPUT TYPE="text" SIZE="12" NAME="answer">
</FORM>

<ADDRESS>NAME-Ex11.htm </ADDRESS> </BODY>
```

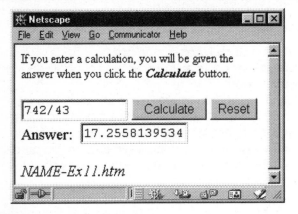

Notes:

In the next Chapter, we shall see how to round down the result to two decimal places. First, we need to discuss the basics.

1. The user is invited to enter a calculation and then to click the *Calculate* button. Note that this button has a NAME attribute and we shall soon see the reason for this. The cal() function performs the calculation and displays the answer in the *answer* text box, see the illustration above. But how is it done? Here is the code which does it all and is a perfect example of how object orientated languages work.

```
document.formcal.answer.value =
     eval(document.formcal.calculator.value);
```

We need to examine the above very carefully. It looks rather like a simple assignment statement: `x = y` and, indeed, that is exactly what it is.

eval()

On the right-hand side of the assignment operator there is a special function `eval()` which forms part of the core JavaScript language. Why does it not begin with a capital letter then, like *Math* and *Date*? It does not and must not begin with a capital letter. Those are the rules! (You are not going to win. Consistency is not one of JavaScript's strong points.)

Its purpose here is to convert its argument from a text string into a mathematical format - a calculation. Our user had to type the calculation into a *text* box: `"742/43"`

Since there is no 'TYPE=number' for the <INPUT> tag, we had to use:

```
<INPUT TYPE="text" SIZE="12" NAME="calculator">
```

Text cannot be calculated, so we need a function which will try to make sense of the text which is typed in and convert it into an arithmetic expression and evaluate the expression. If words had been typed in, rather than what looks like an proper arithmetic expression, then the *eval()* function would not be able to convert and evaluate it. But it does recognise numbers and arithmetic operators.

Now, this is an important bit. The following JavaScript code looks like an assignment statement: x = y.

```
document.formcal.answer.value =
     eval(document.formcal.calculator.value);
```

5: <u>Arguments</u>

That is precisely what it is. Whatever is on the right-hand side is assigned to whatever is on the left-hand side of the assignment operator. So, we now need to examine what is on the right side.

```
= eval(document.formcal.calculator.value)
```

The argument of the *eval* function is better read from right to left, as follows:

Evaluate: (the *value* of *calculator* which is a property of *formcal* which is a Form property of the current *document*).

There are *four* boxes in the Form *formcal*: two are text-boxes, one is a button which can be clicked, and one is a reset button. Each has a value of its own. So we have to tell the *eval* function which one of the four we are referring to. That is the purpose of the NAME attribute. We want to refer to the value which belongs to the text box NAMEd 'calculator'.

```
<INPUT TYPE="text" SIZE="12" NAME="calculator">
```

By giving names to the various INPUT elements we are able to refer to any one of them. Since we do not need to refer to the input and reset buttons, we have not bothered to give them names.

These elements are contained within FORM tags. But in which Form is the named element *calculator*? I know we only have one FORM tag, but we could have several forms in our document or we may wish to add others later. However, even if we have only one FORM, we still need to NAME the form so that we can refer to it. So, we give it a name:

```
<FORM NAME="formcal">
```

Finally, because the FORM is a property of an object, we need to specify its object, namely, the current *document*.

Hopefully, this is beginning to make sense because this is what programming in an object orientated language is all about. We wanted to evaluate the *value* of a specific INPUT element, *calculator,* contained in the Form *formcal which is a property* of the current document object.

(I hope the following will not confuse matters, but since properties belong to objects and only objects can have properties formcal, *in the above code, has to become an object in its own right so that it can have its own property, namely,* calculator.

Likewise, calculator *becomes an object with a property value. This is really just a technical nicety. Properties cannot contain properties, so the original property has to become an object so that it can take a property. In other words, some properties can also become objects in their own right.)*

We should now be in a position to read the left-hand side of the assignment operator with ease.

```
document.formcal.answer.value =
        eval(document.formcal.calculator.value);
```

Very simply, we are assigning the evaluated result of the *eval() function* to the *value* of:

"*answer* (a named text box) which is a property of *formcal* (a form element) which is a property of the current document."

```
<FORM NAME="formcal">
<INPUT TYPE="text" SIZE="12" NAME="calculator">
<INPUT TYPE="button" VALUE="Calculate"
               onClick="cal()">
<INPUT TYPE="reset" VALUE="Reset">
<BR>
Answer:  
<INPUT TYPE="text" SIZE="12" NAME="answer">
</FORM>
```

I think we need a rest! In the next Chapter, we shall see how to round the answer to two decimal places.

Jargon

arguments: values which are passed to a function so that it can process (do something with) them.

method: a term used in object orientated languages to mean a function. Most objects have methods associated with them as well as properties.

object: in object orientated languages, programmers work with basic *objects*. These objects are manipulated by using their methods and properties. For example, the document object can have its background colour property changed by giving a colour value to the *bgColor* property:

```
document.bgColor = 'lightblue'
```

property: most objects have properties which can change their object in some way.

variable: a programming term which refers to where a computer has stored a piece of data in its memory. The data is retrieved by using the *name* of the variable. Variables can be passed as arguments to functions.

What you have learned

We have covered a great deal in this chapter and seen what object oriented programming is all about. It is worth studying carefully and may need several visits. When you feel comfortable with the material in this Chapter, you will be well on the way to understanding how to program with objects in JavaScript.

1. How to pass a *variable* as an argument to a function.

2. How to use the *sqrt* method of the *Math* object.

3. That the Math object is part of core JavaScript whereas objects such as *window* and *document* are client-side JavaScript which allow a programmer to work with a Web browser.

4. The distinction between objects and their methods and properties.

5. Why we need NAMEs for forms and INPUT buttons and text boxes.

6. How to use the *eval()* function.

7. How to assign values to text boxes.

Test: Chap. 5

5.1 How can you find out what a user has typed into a prompt box?

5.2 Why are arguments useful?

5.3 To what object does the `sqrt()` method belong?

5.4 Is the Math object part of core or client-side JavaScript?

5.5 Give one reason for giving an INPUT element a name attribute.

5.6 If you only have one Form and wish to refer to it via JavaScript code, does it still need to be given a name attribute?

5.7 Why must an invoked function include the function call operator - `()` - rather than just the function name?

5: <u>Arguments</u>

Is JavaScript a real programming language?
Yes! But it does not behave like many other languages.

JavaScript is not as strict as some programming languages to the extent that some programmers do not regard JavaScript as being a proper language. For example:

- sometimes an object can be 'assumed' but not on other occasions. Compare alert() and Math.sqrt(). Here, the *window* object does not need to be mentioned

- variables do not have to be initiated before being used

- the same variable can store different types of data

- a calling function (invocation) can pass a different number of arguments to the number in the declaration.

The latter two 'features' horrify traditional programmers.

SIX

Arithmetic in JavaScript

In this chapter, we shall look at some of the basic arithmetic features of programming with special reference to JavaScript.

Exercise 12: *Rounding to two decimal places*

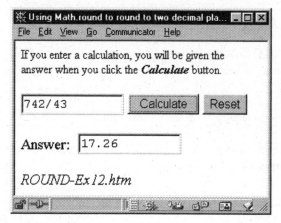

Here is the code:

```
<HEAD> <TITLE> ... </TITLE>
<SCRIPT>
function rounding(x)
{ document.example.answer.value =
                        Math.round(x*100)/100;
}  // EoFN
</SCRIPT>
</HEAD>
```

```
<BODY>
<FONT SIZE=2>If you enter a calculation, you
will be given the answer when you click the
<I><B>Calculate</B></I> button. </FONT>
<FORM NAME="example">
<INPUT TYPE="text" SIZE="12" NAME="calculator">
<INPUT TYPE="button" VALUE="Calculate"
       onClick="cal()">
<INPUT TYPE="reset" VALUE="Reset">

<BR>
Answer:  
<INPUT TYPE="text" SIZE="12" NAME="answer">
</FORM>
<SCRIPT>
// A BAD PLACE to put this code. See Note 4.
function cal()
{
  data=eval(document.example.calculator.value);
  rounding(data);
} //EoFn
</SCRIPT>
<ADDRESS>ROUND-Ex12.htm </ADDRESS> </BODY>
```

Notes:

1. The function *cal()* has changed slightly from its use in Exercise 11 in Chapter 5.

```
data = eval(document.example.calculator.value);
rounding(data);
```

We are now assigning the user's input (typed into the text element `calculator`) to the variable `data` rather than assigning it to the value of another text box. On the following line, we call another function `rounding(data)` and pass the input stored in `data` as an *argument*.

```
function rounding(x){
  document.example.answer.value =
          Math.round(x*100)/100;} // EoFn
```

But wait a moment, why is the rounding() function's argument in the *declaration* now named x rather than data? In all our previous examples, we have used the *same* name as the one in the *invocation*.

Dummy Arguments

We could use data here, instead of x, but it is a common practice amongst seasoned programmers to give the argument in the declaration a different name. It is sometimes referred to as a *dummy argument*. Although this may appear strange, the reasoning behind it is very practical. During the *execution* of the *rounding* function, the dummy argument will take on the value of the argument passed to it by the *calling* statement. In other words, 'x' will become 'data'.

Why is this so dramatic? Frequently, the same function may be called from several places, each time with different data variables to work on. (See Exercise 21 in Chapter 10.)

```
<SCRIPT>
function workhorse(x){
  y = x*10;
  return y; } //EoFn workhorse
... code ...
... workhorse(data1)
... workhorse(data2)
... workhorse(data3)
... code ...
</SCRIPT>
```

Each time workhorse(*argument*) is invoked, the dummy argument 'x' in the declaration is replaced by the argument of the invocation - data1, data2, data3. In other words, you do not need three separate function declarations each with its argument *data1*, *data2*, *data3*.

(Pages 143 and 180 discuss the return *statement.)*

6: __Arithmetic__

These dummy arguments prove useful in yet other ways:

- you may discover someone else's function, such as my *rounding()* function, and wish to use it in one of your own web pages
- or, you may wish to copy and paste one of your own functions into another Web page you are creating rather than having to type it out all over again

After you have copied and pasted the function into your own Web page, all you would need to do would be to create a function call and pass it whatever argument you want, with your own names. You would not have to change the argument names in the original function declaration.

2. Let us look at the main piece of code in the `rounding` function of Exercise 12.

```
document.example.answer.value =
                    Math.round(x*100)/100;
```

With our growing understanding of object orientated programming, we can see that we are using the *round* method of the *Math* object. This method rounds its argument to the nearest integer, thus `2.54` becomes `3` and `-2.54` becomes `-2`. However, that is no good because we want to round to two decimal places, if and when they exist. We can do so by multiplying `x` by 100, rounding and then dividing the result by 100.

This result is then assigned to the value of the INPUT object named `answer` which is a property of the `form` (now an object!) named `example` which is a property of the *document* object. Is this beginning to make some sense?

3. Look at the following line in Exercise 12.

```
// A BAD PLACE to put this code. See Note 4.
```

The two forward slashes are treated as a comment symbol wherever they appear within <SCRIPT> tags. Whatever follows it, *up to the end of the line,* is ignored by JavaScript. In this way programmers can add comments to their code. But what if you want more than one line for a comment? You then have to use /* the comment */

```
/*   first line of the comment
     and another comment line
     and yet a third comment line. */
```

4. But why is it not a good place to put the code? Remember that the browser reads a Web page from top to bottom. If it got as far as displaying the text buttons and then had to go off to download a large image, an over enthusiastic reader might start entering values and clicking on the *Calculate* button before the remainder of the page was fully loaded. Because the *cal()* function has been placed at the end of the page, the browser may not have had time to load that function and would be at a loss to know what to do when the *Calculate* button was clicked. The whole process would fail. (See also, Chapter 18, error 16.)

So the moral is, to keep all your functions **before** the <BODY>. In that way, you can be sure that all functions have been loaded by the browser before the user has a chance to start clicking on any button displayed via the BODY tags. The new XHTML which is to replace HTML requires us to place all functions within the <HEAD> tags.

Arithmetic & Computers
What answer would you give to the following: 3+2*4 = ?

Computers can only pick up two values at any one time and it does not matter how much you pay for your computer. Computers have always been designed to work in that way. In the above, the computer has been given three numbers. It can choose only two to begin with. The two it selects is based on the *rules of arithmetic* which state that + & - have a lower ranking than * or /. So a computer would look at what is *between* the numbers and would select 2 * 4 because that has a higher ranking order than 3+2.

It would work out that $2*4 = 8$. The computer remembers that there are more numbers in the original statement, so it would next add 3 to the 8 to give 11.

If you were using a pocket calculator and typed in the above formula, you would get 20 as the answer. The reason for this is that the first two numbers input would be 3+2 and when you pressed the multiplication symbol, the calculator's computer would evaluate those two numbers (giving 5) *before* continuing to obey your next key strokes. Thus, $5*4$ would become 20.

In programming, in order to force a computer to evaluate numbers in some other order, you can surround any part of a calculation in brackets (often called *parentheses*). Any expression in brackets is always evaluated before anything else. Those are the rules of *arithmetic*.

Thus: $(3+2)*4 = 20$. $4*(3+2)$ would also equal 20.

You need to be in control of the order in which you want your numbers calculated. After all, it is your formula and if you wanted the answer to become 20, why not?

Priority Levels	Arithmetic operators
1 - Highest	( ) parentheses
2	^ exponentiation 3^4
3	* /
4 - Lowest	+ -

The *eval()* method

1. In the previous chapter, we said that the *eval* method tries to make sense of any numbers and arithmetic symbols it comes across as its argument and 'converts' them into arithmetic expressions. What the *eval()* function actually evaluates are JavaScript statements:

```
data=eval(document.example.calculator.value);
```

The above argument is a JavaScript statement, so, too, is the following: `eval(x + "+ 100")`

```
<SCRIPT>
x = 22;
y = eval(x + "+ 100");
alert("answer is: " + y);
</SCRIPT>
```

2. If *eval()* is a method, like *round()*, where is the object to which it belongs? The *eval* method belongs to **all** objects, that is why it is a *special* method, unlike most other methods which belong to one particular object. Thus, *writeln()* can only belong to the *document* object, *alert()* only to the *window* object.

It is a *global* method of core JavaScript which evaluates a string containing JavaScript code. If the string is an arithmetic expression, it will evaluate the expression and return its value. If the string is a JavaScript statement (or statements), *eval()* will execute the statement(s) and return the value, if any.

round is associated only with the Math object which is why Math must be included: `x = Math.round(data)`

Hmm! So that is why it takes so long to become really familiar with JavaScript, or any language. Each one has its own quirks and seems to change the goalposts at almost

6: Arithmetic

every turn. All beginners have to go through this learning curve. You are not the only one to have suffered.

Exercise 13: *Distance Learning*

Here is a simple *distance learning* example. We shall ask the user to type in the calculations shown. When the user clicks the *Calculate* button, the answer will be given. We trust that the user will work it out manually first and then check his/her results with the computer's answer.

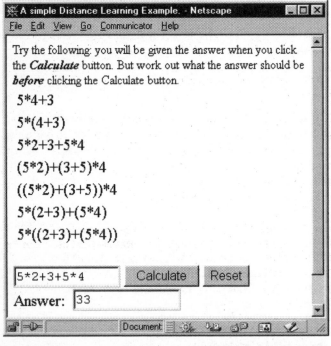

We could also make sure that the user types in an answer before showing the computer's result. We could even print out a score at the end. However, we would need to understand some of JavaScript's programming features (Chapters 9 and 15.) before being able to program those facilities.

Here is the code:

```
<HEAD> <TITLE> ... </TITLE>
<SCRIPT>
function calculate(){
document.example.answer.value=
  eval(document.example.calculator.value);
}  // EoFn
</SCRIPT>
</HEAD>
<BODY>
<FONT SIZE=2> Try the following: you will be
given the answer when you click the
<I><B>Calculate</B></I> button. But work out
what the answer should be <I> <B> before </B>
</I> clicking the Calculate button. </FONT>
<TABLE>
<TR> <TD> 5*4+3
<TR> <TD> 5*(4+3)
<TR> <TD> 5*2+3+5*4
<TR> <TD> (5*2)+(3+5)*4
<TR> <TD> ((5*2)+(3+5))*4
<TR> <TD> 5*(2+3)+(5*4)
<TR> <TD> 5*((2+3)+(5*4))
</TABLE>
<FORM method="" action="" NAME="example">
<INPUT TYPE="text" SIZE="12" NAME="calculator">
<INPUT TYPE="button" VALUE="Calculate"
       onClick="calculate()">
<INPUT TYPE="reset" VALUE="Reset">
<BR>
Answer:  
<INPUT TYPE="text" SIZE="12"
       NAME="answer">
</FORM>
<ADDRESS>Arith-Ex13.htm </ADDRESS>
</BODY>
```

6: **Arithmetic**

Notes:

If you have been following the previous scripts, the code should be quite easy to follow.

The user is invited to type in one of the calculations. When the *Calculate* button is clicked, the event handler invokes the *calculate()* function. This function evaluates the user's entry and assigns it to the value of the text box NAMEd `answer`.

If the user mis-typed a calculation, say a missing bracket, Netscape will pinpoint the error if `javascript:` is typed into the location box (do not forget the colon). Internet Explorer, on the other hand, will display a less meaningful error message.

Jargon

distance learning: in this context, it means presenting teaching material to users who are not sitting in a classroom but who access the WWW in order to learn. JavaScript can be used to interact with such users.

dummy arguments: an argument which is used within a function but which has no identity until the function is invoked by a function call. That call will have a *real* argument which is passed over to the function and used in place of the dummy argument.

parentheses: brackets surrounding part of a calculation which you want to be computed before any other part.

What you have learned

1. Seasoned programmers tend to use *dummy arguments*. They can copy and paste functions from other programs without having to alter the original function code.

2. It is wise to place all functions before the <BODY> part of an HTML page. In that way, you are sure that they have

been loaded before a user can begin clicking buttons which may have associated event handlers.

3. Computers are designed to calculate only two numbers at a time. When presented with more than two, computers follow the rules of arithmetic when determining which two numbers to calculate first.

4. Before entering a calculation, a programmer needs to work out in advance the order in which the numbers are to be calculated.

5. Entering calculations into a program is not the same as entering numbers into a pocket calculator. One has to make a mental adjustment when using arithmetic with computer programs.

What is next:
In the next section we shall change an image on an existing Web page when a user clicks a button. We shall then look at some JavaScript programming features because until we know some of the basic features we really cannot do very much. We shall learn how to use the IF-ELSE statement to make choices based on what a user has typed.

Test: Chap. 6

6.1 What is a dummy argument and why is it useful?

6.2 For the following : 5 + 4 * 2 + 3

a) What result would be given by a *computer*?
b) What result would be given by a *pocket calculator*?

6.3 Why are *comments* used by programmers?

6.4 How do you create a *single* line comment?

6.5 How are *multiple* line comments created in JavaScript?

6: Arithmetic

6.6 How many errors can you find in the following script?

```
function dothis(sqroot)
 x = Maths,sqrt(squroot);
 document.write("The square root of: "
                + squroot + " is: " + x)
}
```

Why do we use the following symbols instead of the more usual arithmetic symbols?

Arithmetic operators
( ) parentheses
^ exponentiation 3^4
*   /
+   -

Back in time, during the 1940's, when computers were first being designed, the character set used was very restricted.

26 letters of the alphabet	uppercase only!
10 digits	0 - 9
13 special symbols	+ - * / ' ( ) , = $. : space

The nearest symbol that 'looked like' multiplication was the asterisk. The forward slash was used for division as in 1/2.

The circumflex symbol (^), now used by many programming languages to mean exponentiation (raising to a power), is a comparative newcomer. The Fortran programming language still uses two asterisks for exponentiation.

SEVEN

Using JavaScript with Images

Exercise 14: *Change an Image*

This is a simple example of how to change one image for another when a user clicks on a button. It will be extended in Exercise 15, so that when a user moves the mouse over an image it changes to another image and when the user moves the mouse out of the replacement image, the original is re-displayed. Using a mouse has the advantage of being able to return to the original image without the user having to click another button. Here is the code for the simple button click change of image.

- 85 -

```
<HEAD>
<TITLE>IMG example</TITLE>
<SCRIPT LANGUAGE = Javascript>
function ChangeImage(){
 document.img1.src = "images/winter-tree.gif";
 document.form1.tree.value
                   = "Can't wait for Summer.";
} // EoFn
</SCRIPT>
</HEAD>
<BODY>
<CENTER><FONT SIZE=-1>
<B>The<I> Ash Tree </I>in Summer &amp; Winter
</FONT>
<P><IMG NAME="img1"
       SRC="images/summer-tree.gif" >
<FORM  method=" " action=" " NAME="form1">
<FONT SIZE=-2>
<INPUT TYPE=button NAME="tree"
       VALUE="The Winter Look"
       onClick = "ChangeImage()">
</FONT>
<BR>
</FORM>
<ADDRESS>Image-Ex14.htm</ADDRESS>
</CENTER>
</BODY>
```

Notes:

1. Both images were re-sized in PhotoShop and saved in a sub-folder called "*images*". When the page is loaded `Summer-tree.gif` is displayed.

```
<IMG NAME="img1" SRC="images/summer-tree.gif" >
```

2. Although there is one Form on this page, it has been given a NAME so that it can be referenced as a property of the document object in the *ChangeImage()* function.

```
<FORM method="" action="" NAME="form1">
<INPUT TYPE=button VALUE="The Winter Look"
       onClick = "ChangeImage()">
</FORM>
```

Likewise, the <IMG> tag has a name so that it too can be identified as a property of the document object. It has its own property src.

```
function ChangeImage(){
  document.img1.src = "images/winter-tree.gif";
  document.form1.tree.value
                = " Can't wait for Summer.";
} // EoFn
```

3. When a user clicks on the button, the ChangeImage() function is invoked and the image is replaced by the new one.

```
document.img1.src = "images/winter-tree.gif"
```

> "the `src` of the image tag named *img1* (which is a property of the current document) is assigned the value *winter-tree.gif* which is in a sub-folder called *images* ."

This is how an image can be changed when a user clicks a button and provides an example of why people use JavaScript. It allows a web page to be changed so that it is no longer a static page, like a page in a book.

Note too that the *value* of the `tree` button is changed - from "The Winter Look" to "Can't wait for Summer." This is what is meant by *dynamic* HTML. Via JavaScript pages can be changed.

4. Both images should be the *same* size otherwise distortion will occur in Netscape. The size of the new image will be forced into the same space as the original. (See Exercise 15.) However, Internet Explorer allows a new image to retain its own size. This illustrates, yet again, the need to test your JavaScript code with *both* main browsers to see whether there are any idiosyncrasies between the two.

Exercise 15: *Swapping between images*
In this exercise, we shall see how to change one image for another and then how to return to the original. This is done with two other event handlers - *onMouseOver* and *onMouseOut*. These two events, however, cannot be used with a form button. They have to be used with the <A> tag.

JavaScript refers to this tag as a *link* rather than an *anchor* tag which is what it is known as in HTML. The reason for this, is that the two event handlers can also be used with the <AREA> tag when creating *hot-spots* for image maps. The AREA tag is also a link to some other reference. Consequently, JavaScript uses the word *link* to include both the <A> and the <AREA> tags.

"See My Photograph" is in fact an image.

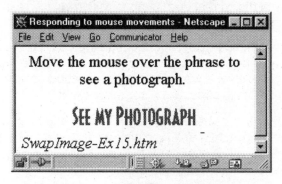

```
<HEAD> <TITLE> ..</TITLE>
<SCRIPT LANGUAGE= "JavaScript">
  function ImgOver() {
  document.img1.src = 'images/mari.gif';
 } //EoFn
  function ImgOut() {
  document.img1.src = 'images/photo1.gif';
 } //EoFn
</SCRIPT>
</HEAD>
<BODY> <CENTER>
<FORM method="" action="" NAME = "form1">
<B>Move the mouse over the phrase to
   see a photograph.</B><BR>
<A NAME="stayput"> </A> <!-- See page 96 -->
<A HREF="#stayput" onMouseOver = "ImgOver()"
                   onMouseOut  = "ImgOut()" >
<IMG NAME="img1" BORDER=0
     SRC = "images/photo1.gif">
</A></CENTER>
<ADDRESS>SwapImage-Ex15.htm</ADDRESS> </BODY>
```

When the mouse is moved over the image, the following is
shown. Note how it becomes distorted in Netscape (the
second illustration) but not in Internet Explorer version.

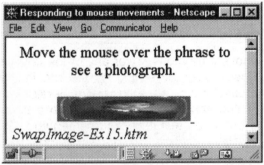

When the user moves the mouse out of the picture, it returns to the original state. You may be thinking of many situations in which this could be useful for your own Web pages.

Exercise 16: *Changing colours on Mouse Over & Out*
The *onMouseOver/Out* event handlers are especially
useful for lists (contents, index, etc.). In the following Web
page, each item in the list is an image containing a small
blue cube plus some text and saved as a transparent GIF
file. A second set was created but with a red cube and the
same text. (If you have used any image processing
package, you will know that it takes just a few minutes to
create all six - three blues and three reds.)

As a user moves the mouse over any of the items in the
list, it changes colour by calling up the red image file.
When the mouse moves out of the image, it returns to the
blue image. You cannot see the changes in a black and
white page, but if you test it on your screen you will. The
Where we are is in a different 'colour' to the other two.

```
<HEAD> <TITLE> ... </TITLE>
<SCRIPT LANGUAGE= "JavaScript">
function ImgOver1() {
  document.img1.src="images/who2.gif"; } // EoFn
```

```
function ImgOut1()  {
  document.img1.src="images/who1.gif"
} // EoFn
function ImgOver2() {
  document.img2.src = "images/what2.gif"
} // EoFn
function ImgOut2()  {
  document.img2.src = "images/what1.gif"
} // EoFn
function ImgOver3() {
  document.img3.src = "images/where2.gif"
} // EoFn
function ImgOut3()  {
  document.img3.src = "images/where1.gif"
} // EoFn
</SCRIPT>
</HEAD>

<BODY>
<CENTER>
<H3>A Home Page</H3>
<a name="stayput1"> </a>   <!-- see page 96-->
<A HREF="#stayput1"
           onMouseOver = "ImgOver1()"
           onMouseOut  = "ImgOut1()">
<IMG NAME="img1" BORDER=0
     SRC="images/who1.gif">
</A>
<BR> <!-- HREF has an empty value. See page 96. -->
<A HREF="" onMouseOver = "ImgOver2()"
           onMouseOut  = "ImgOut2()">
<IMG NAME="img2" BORDER=0
     SRC="images/what1.gif">
</A>
<BR> <a name="stayput3"> </a>
<A HREF="#stayput3"
           onMouseOver = "ImgOver3()"
           onMouseOut  = "ImgOut3()">
<IMG NAME="img3" BORDER=0
     SRC="images/where1.gif">
```

```
</A>
<BR>
</CENTER>
<ADDRESS>OVER-Ex16.htm</ADDRESS>
</BODY>
```

Notes:

1. Notice that we have NAMEd the three images so that the relevant function can refer to each one.

2. Since the *onMouseOver* and *onMouseOut* events are used, we need <A> tags.

3. Although it seems that a great deal of typing was necessary, most of it can be done with a quick copy and paste followed by changing just a few words.

4. See page 96 for a discussion about:
    <a name="stayput1"> </a>

Jargon

dynamic HTML: those features of HTML version 4 which allow the content of a Web page to be changed. In this text we use JavaScript to alter a page's content. This is in contrast to static Web pages containing conventional HTML where the content cannot be altered.

link: JavaScript refers to both the <A> tag and the <AREA> tag as links, since both can be used to load other web documents. Both tags can use the *onMouseOver/Out* handlers.

transparent GIF: a GIF image (*Graphical Image Format*) is one of two main image formats which web browsers can recognise and display. (Browsers cannot display *tiff*, *psd*, *pcx* images, for example.) Many image processing packages allow an image in one format to be saved as either GIF or JPEG files. JPEG is the other main browser image format (*Joint Photographic Experts Group*).

A GIF image can be made transparent so that the background shows through any irregular border rather than being boxed into a rectangular frame.

What you have learnt

1. How to use the *onMouseOver* and *onMouseOut* events. These are used with the <A> tag, not with the usual INPUT elements such as buttons.

2. These two events are trapped whenever a mouse moves over or out of the hypertext or image within the <A> tags.

3. When swapping one image for another, the Netscape browser forces the second image into the same size border frame as the first one. So, both images must be the same size to avoid distortion. IE is more tolerant and will resize the remainder of the page to accommodate the size of the new image.

4. Using the *onMouseOver* and *onMouseOut* events avoids asking users to click buttons in order to achieve some desired effect. When using event handlers, we now

need to think about whether we want a user to click a button or to move over an image.

5. If an *onMouseOver* event is used, an appropriate *onMouseOut* event is frequently required to take into account what should happen when the user moves the mouse out of the image.

Test: Chap. 7

7.1 Can the HTML <IMG> tag be a property of the document object?

7.2 How can one image be replaced by another image in JavaScript?

7.3 What happens in Netscape if the image which replaces another is of a different size to the one it replaces? Will the same thing happen in Internet Explorer?

7.4 Can the onMouseOver event handler be used with a text box INPUT element?

7.5 With which HTML tags are the *onMouseOver* and *onMouseOut* event handlers usually associated with?

7.6 What user event will the *onMouseOut* event handler trap?

Three things you should know

1. We have used the onMouseOver/Out to swap one image for another. To achieve this we have used the <A> tag. We do not need the HREF attribute, therefore, leave it out:

```
<A  onMouseOver = "ImgOver1()"
    onMouseOut  = "ImgOut1()">
```

It works a treat in IE5 but, unhappily, not in Netscape. The images will not be swapped. Thus, we need to include the

HREF attribute if we want our pages to work with both main browsers.

But what value do we give to the HREF attribute? We could put nothing in:

```
<A   HREF   onMouseOver = "ImgOver1()"
            onMouseOut  = "ImgOut1()">
```

This now works with both IE5 and Netscape. But there is another little problem. Should a reader decide to click on the image, Netscape will display a directory listing of the contents of the folder in which the web page is stored. (IE5 will not!)

However, if an empty value is given to the HREF attribute:

```
<A HREF=""   ... etc ... >
```

then both main browsers display a directory listing.

To make sure that nothing happens for both IE5 and Netscape, should your reader inadvertently click an image, use the HREF value to move to another part of the page. This is done via a section marker - the hash # symbol.

```
<a NAME="stayput1"> </a>
<A HREF="#stayput1"
        onMouseOver = "ImgOver1()"
        onMouseOut  = "ImgOut1()">
```

This forces the browser to redisplay the page at the point where there is a corresponding <A> tag with a NAME attribute whose value is the same as the HREF value (but without the # symbol). If this is placed nearby, the page will effectively remain at the same spot. Of course, if you do want a new page to be displayed when the image is clicked, then you would put in the appropriate URL.

2. We can include an onClick event as well as an HREF URL:

```
<A HREF="test.htm"
   onMouseOver = "ImgOver1()"
   onMouseOut  = "ImgOut1()"
   onClick = "alert('Tell me a story')" >
<IMG NAME="img1" BORDER=0
     SRC="images/who1.gif">
</A>
```

Here, an alert box will pop up when the image is clicked. Once the box is closed by the user, the browser will display the `test.htm` web page.

3. Finally, did you notice the little lines after the images on pages 89 and 90 in the Netscape version? Here is Exercise 16 in Netscape. Compare it with the Internet Explorer version on page 91 which does not have the little lines. Since the text is part of the actual image the lines follow after the text.

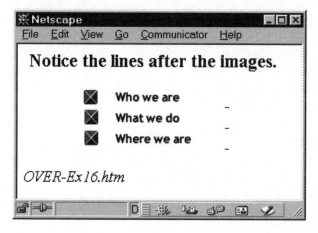

7: Images

It is simple to remove the little lines from Netscape:

```
<IMG NAME="img1" BORDER=0
     SRC="images/who1.gif"></A>
```

You need to ensure that there is no space between the image tag and the closing anchor tag.

It is also important *not to place* the closing anchor tag on the next line since the Enter key will be treated as a space by Netscape and will again make the line appear.

```
<IMG NAME="img1" BORDER=0
     SRC="images/who1.gif">
</A>
```

EIGHT

Creating Dynamic Web Pages

If event handlers can be used to display one image for another, why not get them to display a separate window when, for example, a button is clicked or the mouse is moved over a phrase? One such use could be for a contents list or index of short phrases. When a user moves the mouse over one, another window pops up with more explanation. We could use an alert box, but they tend to become irritating and we have little control over the formatting of the text (see page 40).

Exercise 17: *Changing to a new Window*
In this exercise, we shall open a new window when a button is clicked and load an existing web page into it. To open a new window simply use the following:

```
window.open("new_webpage.htm")
```

```
<HEAD>
<TITLE> Opening a second window. </TITLE>
<SCRIPT LANGUAGE = JavaScript>
  function openWindow()
  {
    window.open("BGCOLOR-Ex5.htm")
  } // EoFn
</SCRIPT>
</HEAD>

<BODY><CENTER>
<H3>Opening a new window.</H3>
<FORM method="" action="">
<BR>
```

```
<INPUT TYPE = "button"
       VALUE = "Click to Open a new window"
       onClick = "openWindow()">
</FORM>
<ADDRESS>OpenWin-Ex17.htm</ADDRESS>
</CENTER>
</BODY>
```

Notes:

1. When the button is clicked, the event handler will open a new window and load the associated web page into it. In our case, the *openWindow()* function will load one of our earlier web pages, the one that offers a choice of background colours.

2. The new window, containing BGCOLOR-Ex5.htm, is the one which can have its own background colours changed, but will not change the window which opened it.

3. Why not simply use an <A> tag?:

```
<A HREF="BGCOLOR-Ex5.htm"> click me </A>
```

Well, what we shall see in the next exercise is that rather than having to make an extra trip over the Internet to retrieve the web page we can use a function to write

HTML code into the new window. This will speed up the whole process since the web page will be 'created' by the client's own computer, otherwise, we would have preferred to use a simple <A> tag.

Exercise 18: *Creating a new window on the fly*
When a button is clicked, we shall create a new window and write an HTML document into it, complete with its own background colour. Here is the code:

```
<HEAD>
<SCRIPT>
function multselections(){
var win = window.open("",null,
 "height=400,width=500,status=yes,resizable=1");
win.document.write("<BODY BGCOLOR='D5EAFF'>"
+ "<H4>How to Select Messages.</H4>"
+ "<P>To select <I>one </I> message, click it."
+ "<P>To select a group of <I>consecutive </I>"
+ "messages, click the first and whilst holding"
+ "down the Shift key, click the last one."
+ "<P>To select messages <I>out of sequence,"
+ "</I>"
+ " click the first and for subsequent messages"
+ " hold down the Control key and click."
+ "<P><IMG SRC='images/happyx.gif'>"
+ " For the really smart ones, you can combine"
+ " Shift & Control to select groups of"
+ " consecutive messages which are out of"
+ " sequence.<P> <CENTER><FONT COLOR='FF0000'>"
+ "<I>Close this window once you have read the"
+ " content.</I> </FONT></CENTER>"
+ "<FORM> <INPUT TYPE=button VALUE='Close Me!' "
+ "onClick='self.close()'> </FORM>");
} // EoFn
</SCRIPT>
</HEAD>
```

```
<BODY BGCOLOR="cccc99"> <CENTER>
<H3>Selecting Messages</H3>
You can select multiple messages (using
<I>Shift</I> and/or <I>Control</I>, click button
below for details) ... <I>continue with
paragraph</I>  ...
<FORM method = "" action = "">
<INPUT TYPE = button
       VALUE = "Making multiple selections."
       onClick = "multselections()">
</FORM><ADDRESS>NEW-WIN-EX18 </ADDRESS>
</CENTER>   </BODY>
```

Once the button '*Making multiple selections*' is clicked, see
below, a new window will appear. We shall now examine
the code which produces this new window.

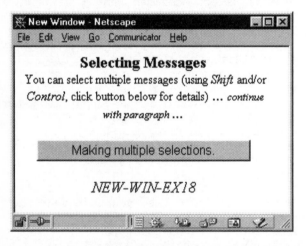

We need to look at the arguments of *window.open* before
examining the rest of the code in detail.

window.open()
It contains four arguments, we have used three.
```
window.open(url, name, [features, [replace]])
```

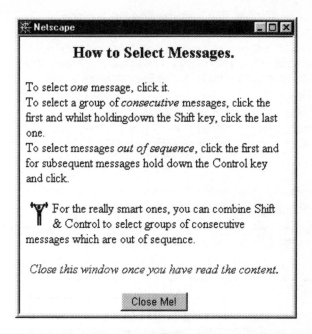

url: is a string value containing the web address of the document to be fetched and opened by the window object. That was the only argument we used in the earlier example. It can be a complete or partial web address.

```
window.open("BGCOLOR-Ex5.htm")
```

It fetches the web page referenced. If the argument is empty (``""``), the new window will contain a blank document.

name: this argument can be used as the window name to use in the TARGET attribute of a <FORM> or <A> tag. (If you are into frames, this could be useful.) If none exists put in ``null`` or an empty argument - ``""``.

features: specifies what browser features you want in the new window.

(Notice that both the features *and the* replace *arguments are in square brackets.*

`[features, [replace]].` *In many reference texts, the square brackets signify that those arguments are optional.* prompt(arg1, [arg2]) *is another example.)*

toolbar:	Back and Forward buttons, etc.
location:	the URL location field
directories:	What's New, What's Cool, etc.
status:	the browser's status line
menubar:	the menu at the top of the window
scrollbars:	enables scrollbars when necessary
resizable:	allows the window to be resized
width - height:	the windows dimension in pixels

(When using the features *argument, it is most important to separate each feature with a comma and* **not** *to use spaces between each one. If you do include spaces, Netscape will not display the new window as you intend.)*

When the *features* string argument is absent, the new browser window has all the standard features. When it is specified, the window includes *only those features specified*. Features may be specified by *yes* or *no* or with digit *1* (yes) or *zero* (no).

```
window.open("", null,"height=400,width=500,
status=yes,resizable=1");
```

replace: an optional Boolean value (*true* or *false*) which allows new entries to be made to the Browser's *history*. It does not make much sense to use this argument for newly created windows. It is intended for use when changing the contents of an existing window. We shall ignore this feature. (See Chapter 9, page 117 for Boolean values.)

Now let us examine our own code.

Notes for Exercise 18:

1. First of all, there is:

```
var win = window.open("",null,
  "height=400,width=500,status=yes,resizable=1");
win.document.write("<BODY BGCOLOR='D5EAFF'>"
  + "<H4>How to Select Messages.</H4>" ... etc ...
```

This code creates an instance of the *open* method of the *window* object and assigns it to a variable `win`. In other words, it creates a new window called `win`. We have to assign the new window to a variable because we need to use the *document.write()* method to write our HTML code. But because there are now two windows, the original window and this new window, we must specify which window to write into. We refer to the new window via the variable `win`.

A new window object is assigned to `win`. It has an empty *url*, in which case, a new window will be opened with a blank document. It is not destined to become the value of a frame or form *target* attribute, so the second argument is set to `null`. We wish to specify the following *features*:

- width and height of 400 x 500 pixels
- we allow the user to *resize* the window if he/she desires
- finally, we have included the status bar

All other features which are not specifically mentioned will not be included.

3. What is in the next piece of code?

```
win.document.write("<BODY BGCOLOR='D5EAFF'>"
+ "<H4>How to Select Messages.</H4>"
+ "<P>To select <I>one </I> message, click it."
+ "<P>To select a group of <I>consecutive </I>"
+ "messages, click the first and whilst holding"
+ "down the Shift key, click the last one."
```

```
+ "<P>To select messages <I>out of sequence,
+ "</I>"
+ " click the first and for subsequent messages"
+ " hold down the Control key and click."
+ "<P><IMG SRC='images/happyx.gif'>"
+ " For the really smart ones, you can combine"
+ " Shift & Control to select groups of"
+ " consecutive messages which are out of"
+ " sequence.<P> <CENTER><FONT COLOR='FF0000'>"
+ "<I>Close this window once you have read the"
+ " content.</I> </FONT></CENTER>"
+ "<FORM> <INPUT TYPE=button VALUE='Close Me!' "
+ "onClick='self.close()'> </FORM>" );
} // EoFn
```

It is the *write()* method of the `win` document object and it contains all the HTML code we wish to display. (Remember `win` is the name of the variable we assigned to the new window).

What is so wonderful about this? Well, instead of getting a user to click on a `<A HREF="url">` hypertext, thereby forcing the browser to use the Internet to retrieve a copy, our page will be created on the fly by the browser at the client-side.

4. It is important to remind your readers to close this new window before moving back to the original. If it is not closed, it remains open and can cause problems. For this reason, we have added a button which the user can click in order to close the new window. Here is the code:

```
+ "<FORM> <INPUT TYPE=button VALUE='Close Me!' "
+ "onClick='self.close()'> </FORM> </CENTER>"
```

Do note the correct use of double and single quotes!

`close()` is a method of the *window* object. It takes no arguments. Its purpose is to close a window. *self* and *window* are synonyms for 'the current window'. So, either `self.close()` or `window.close()` could be used.

Since *close()* is also a method of the document object, we had to specify that it was a *window* that had to be closed.

Exercise 19: *Using onMouseOver & onMouseOut*

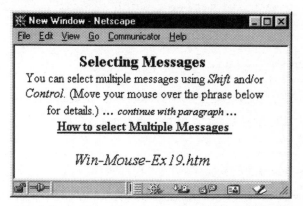

We shall repeat the previous exercise but use mouse event handlers. They are sometimes more effective.

```
<SCRIPT>
function removewindow(){
 win.close() // make sure win is typed, not window
 } //EoFn

function multselections(){
 win = window.open("","","height=400,width=500,
status=yes,resizable=1");
 win.document.write("<BODY BGCOLOR='D5EAFF'>"
+ "<CENTER><H4>How to Select Messages.</H4>"
+ "</CENTER>"
+ "<FONT SIZE=-1><P>To select <I>one </I>"
+ "message, click it."
+ "<BR>To select a group of <I>consecutive </I>"
...... as before .....
```

```
...... as before .....
} //EoFn
</SCRIPT>

<BODY BGCOLOR="D5EAFF">
<CENTER>
<B>Selecting Messages</B>
<BR>
You can select multiple messages using
<I>Shift</I> and/or <I>Control</I>.
(Move your mouse over the phrase below for
details.)
<I>continue with paragraph</I>
<BR>
<A HREF="" onMouseOver="multselections()"
          onMouseOut = "removewindow()">
<B>How to select Multiple Messages </B>
</A>
<P>
<ADDRESS>Win-Mouse-Ex19.htm </ADDRESS>
</CENTER>
</BODY>
```

Notes:

1. Since *onMouseOver* and *onMouseOut* are events of the <A> tag, the user will have to move the mouse over and out of some hypertext words in order to generate these events, or you could use an image, of course.

2. When the user moves over the hypertext words, the *onMouseOver* event handler will create the new window. When the user moves out of the phrase, the *onMouseOut* event handler will close the window. So we can dispense with the *Close Me* button in the new window and replace it with the removewindow() function which is invoked by the *onMouseOut* handler when the user moves the mouse away from the hypertext.

3. If you try the above, you may experience problems with IE. The new window may keep flashing on and off, depending on whether the mouse is moved out of the hypertext. For this reason, I preferred to dispense with the `onMouseOut` altogether and include a *close me* button in the new window.

```
<SCRIPT>
function multselections(){
win = window.open("",null,
"height=400,width=500,status=no,toolbar=1,resiz
able=1,location=1,scrollbars=yes");
win.document.write ( "<BODY BGCOLOR='D5EAFF'>"
+ " <CENTER><B>How to Select Messages."
+ "</B> </CENTER>"
+ "<FONT SIZE=-1><P>To select <I>one </I>"
+ " message, click it."
+ "<BR>To select a group of <I>consecutive"
+ "</I> messages, click the first and whilst"
+ "holding down the Shift key, click the last"
+ "one.<BR>To select messages <I>out of"
+ "sequence</I>, click the first and for"
+ "subsequent messages"
+ " hold down the Control key and click."
+ "<P><IMG SRC='images/happyx.gif' ALIGN=left>"
+ " For the really smart ones, you can combine"
+ " Shift & Control to select groups of"
+ " consecutive messages which are out of"
+ " sequence.<P> <CENTER><FONT COLOR='FF0000'>"
+ "<I>Close this window once you have read the"
+ " content.</I> </FONT> <FORM> "
+ "<INPUT TYPE=button VALUE='Close Me!' "
+ "onClick='self.close()'> </FORM> </CENTER>");
} // EoFn
</SCRIPT>
</HEAD>

<BODY BGCOLOR="D5EAff">
<CENTER>
<B>Selecting Messages</B>
```

```
<BR>
<FONT SIZE=-1>You can select multiple messages
using <I>Shift</I> and/or <I>Control</I>. (Move
your mouse over the phrase below for
details.)</FONT>
   ... <FONT SIZE=-2>
<I>continue with paragraph</I> </FONT> ...
<BR> <a name="stayput"> </a>
<A HREF="#stayput"
   onMouseOver="multselections()">
<FONT SIZE=-1><B>How to select Multiple
Messages </B></FONT></A>
<P>
<ADDRESS>Win-Mouse-Ex19.htm - Revised
</ADDRESS>
</CENTER> </BODY>
```

4. Because we are using the <A> tags, we no longer needed to use a FORM tag with an input button. If, like me, you think the buttons look a bit ugly, you could create an image for the mouse to move over:

```
<BR> <A NAME="stayput"> </A>
<A HREF="#stayput"
   onMouseOver="multselections()">
<IMG SRC="images/pretty.gif" BORDER="0">
</A>
```

5. Finally, Cascading Style Sheets[1] - CSS - allow the author to remove the underline from hypertext and to format the hypertext. An example of a style sheet is given on page 297 following.

What you have learnt

1. You can create new windows (as opposed to pop-up boxes - confirm, alert and prompt) with whatever text and

---

[1] See "XHTML and CSS explained" by John Shelley in this Babani series.

HTML tags you wish. Pop-up boxes allow just plain text entry which cannot be formatted with HTML.

2. By creating your own windows, the browser does not have to connect to the Internet in order to display a copy of the page. It saves time!

If you think about it, you may find this sort of feature useful in many distance learning environments. If someone is not sure about a term being used, rather than spell it out to all those who already know it thus wasting their time in having to scroll past it, invite your readers to click on a button or move their mouse over the term to reveal further details.

3. When using *onMouseOver*, it is often necessary to include a complementary *onMouseOut* handler to describe what to do when the mouse is moved out of the phrase or image contained within the <A> tags.

4. We have seen the relative merits of using *onClick* and *onMouse* handlers to create new windows.

5. The *onMouse* handlers may be used with either text or images provided they are encased within <A> tags. (*IE5 does allow onMouseOver/Out events within the <IMG> tag, but Netscape 4 does not.*)

6. By using *window.close()* or *self.close()* we are able to close a window which has been opened.

What is next:

In previous chapters, we have examined some of the things we can do with JavaScript, such as:

- write out messages
- use pop up boxes
- create event handlers to execute functions
- pass relevant data as arguments to functions

- perform calculations
- replace images
- create our own windows

Now we need to extend our knowledge of the JavaScript programming language so that we can do more. In Chapter 9, then, we shall examine the programming features of JavaScript so that we can begin to do such things as:

- validate Form input
- create order forms and calculate customer invoices
- animate images
- work with dates and time
- create cookies

Test: Chap. 8

8.1 How many arguments does the *window.open()* method take?

8.2 You want to use only the first and the third arguments of the window.open() method. Is it still necessary to include the second argument?

8.3 In the following code, why is `null` not in quotes?

```
var win = window.open("",null,
  "height=400 width=500 status=1
  resizable=yes status=0");
```

8.4 Why was it necessary to assign the new window object to the variable `win` in Exercise 18 &19, but not in Exercise 17?

8.5 What do you think would happen if you were to use *window* rather than *win* in the *removewindow* function for Exercise 19?

```
function removewindow()
{
  window.close(); }   // EoFn
```

It has not been discussed fully in this Chapter, but see if you can work it out before looking at the answer. You will need to do this kind of investigative work when writing your own programs.

8.6 Can we use onMouseOver and onMouseOut with an <IMG> tag?

8: <u>Dynamic Pages</u>

Summary of JavaScript so far:

Object:	its Methods	its Properties
window *client-side*	alert() confirm() prompt() open() close()	
document *client-side*	write() writeln() close()	bgColor lastModified and many HTML tags, e.g. forms, images, anchor
Maths *core*	sqrt() round()	
All objects	eval()	

Operators	Purpose	Example
=	assignment	x = x + 1
+	arithmetic addition	1+2
+	concatenate	"a" + "b"
()	function call	function abc ()
{}	embed function code	

Event Handlers		
onClick	used with FORM's text box & button	
onMouseOver onMouseOut	used with <A> and <AREA> tags	

Keywords	Meaning
null	special value indicating 'no value'
undefined	special value indicating 'does not exist'
var	defines a variable name

NINE

Programming with JavaScript

In this chapter we shall begin to examine some of the programming features of JavaScript and to understand the jargon. Some more features are discussed in Chapter 15.

Our natural languages have different character sets: English has 26 letters; Italian has 20 characters similar to our own; Greek and Cyrillic languages have characters which look different to our own.

Likewise, each programming language has its own 'feel' and rules, although all have features which are similar. JavaScript is similar to C and Java, but is different to some other languages such as Fortran, Pascal or COBOL. However, *all* programming languages comprise the following basic features:

- creating, storing and moving data
- input and output of data
- making decisions
- repeating instructions

In practice, there is not a great deal to the basics of programming. The four features above summarise the whole of programming. They can all be learnt in a few hours. But what does take time and effort is *practice* and from practice we gain experience.

So what follows is not difficult - perhaps a new way of thinking for those who have not programmed before - but it will need time to put into practice.

(This is why many firms advertising for programmers want someone with a minimum of six to twelve months experience. First, if you have not been 'let go' by your company before six months, you must have programming potential. Secondly, after about a year's practice, you will have gained sufficient experience to be useful to your new employer.)

Each programming language has a set of rules (the *syntax*) whereby each can recognise and differentiate between such things as numbers and text. There are specific rules for:

- how decisions are made
- how to repeat a series of instructions
- how to create variable names
- indeed, how to write numbers

For example, we have already seen that when using variable names *case* is significant, thus a variable *ABC* is not the same as a variable *abc* or *aBc*. Likewise, the object document is correct but not DOCUMENT.

When using numbers, 123 signifies a *decimal* number, whereas 0123 would indicate an *octal* number and 0x123 would signify a *hexadecimal* number. We shall not discuss octal and hexadecimal numbers in this text since their usage is rather specialised.

Programming features of JavaScript

1. Data

1.1 Data types
Data may be numbers, text, or Boolean values (*true* and *false* - 'yes' or 'no'). The latter are mainly used with decision and repetition features.

Numbers
123 is called an *integer* (a *whole* number) because it has no decimal places whereas 123.45 is a *real* number

(sometimes called a *floating point*) because it does have a decimal point and digits after it.

There are also *octal* and *hexadecimal* numbers which are used in certain circumstances. Octal (base 8) and hexadecimal (base 16) need to be specified in a special way so that they can be distinguished from decimal (normal) numbers.

octal: 0123 would be recognised as an octal number because of the leading zero. This implies that normal *decimal* numbers must not be preceded by zeros.

hexadecimal: These numbers need to be preceded by `0x` (zero x) and the digits used are `0-9 A B C D E F`. Thus: `0xE` = decimal 14. Case is not significant, therefore, `0XE` is the same as `0xe`.

Text

In programming, any piece of text is usually called a *string* (a string of characters). They are enclosed in double quotes or single quotes and are sometimes referred to as 'quoted strings'. Thus:

`"The cat sat on the mat"` is a string. Likewise, `"123"` is a text string because it is enclosed in quotes.

Boolean Values

With some features, such as '*if.. else*', it may be necessary to test whether something is *true* or *false* (see Exercise 20). These are known as Boolean elements (after George Boole who first used them in conjunction with *Boolean algebra*). They take one of two values, *true* or *false*. Quotes are not allowed, otherwise it would become a text string.

```
x = true;    result = false;
```

1.2 Variables - Storing Data

We have already seen examples of how variables are used. They contain values: numerical, text or Boolean. However, in JavaScript case is significant.

`var ABC = 12` is not the same as `var abc = 12`.

Rules for Naming Variables

Variables are also known as *identifiers*. When creating variable names you must abide by the following rules:

A variable name **must** begin with a letter, a $ or an underscore (_). The latter two are sometimes used by programmers when they wish to draw attention to a particular use of a variable, otherwise, most variables begin with a letter. The subsequent characters in the variable name may consist of digits and other letters but spaces are never permitted.

Variable names must not be the same as *reserved* words which have a particular significance to JavaScript and form part of the syntax of the language. We have met many, such as *return, function, close, open, Math, document, window,* etc. These cannot be used as identifiers.

Case

Because JavaScript is case sensitive, AbC, abc, ABC would be seen as three totally different identifiers. Here are some valid examples: `Number1`, `number2`, `number_3`, `_number4`, `$number`. It is conventional for seasoned programmers to keep all variable names in lowercase, unless they wish to draw attention to a particular variable.

Certain reserved words have their own special case identity which, if not strictly adhered to, JavaScript will not recognise. We have already seen that *eval()* and *alert()*

have a different case to *Math*. *Date* is another one which we shall meet in Chapter 11.

Intercapping

JavaScript and HTML allow for ***interCapping***. This is when some characters in the middle of a word are in uppercase. We have already met several: *onClick*, *onMouseOut*, and so on. Since these are attributes of HTML tags, their case is not significant. However, it is customary to type them as shown. On the other hand, some words must be correctly interCapped, such as *bgColor* and *indexOf* when they form part of the JavaScript language.

Variables are automatically created when assigning a value to them: abc = 12;

Here abc is *declared* and also *initialised* by having the decimal value 12 assigned to it. Whereas: var abc; is declared but not yet initialised - it would be *undefined*.

ABC = "Hallo there!" The variable ABC is created and assigned the string value "Hallo there!"

Scope of variables

If you precede a variable name with the keyword var ***and*** it is used within a given function, then it becomes *local* to that function. In other words, if the same variable name is used in another function, it will not be the same one. However, if the keyword var is left off, then the variable will be recognised in other functions within the same Web page. It would then be known as a *global* variable.

Generally speaking, if you use a variable within a function which you do not intend to use anywhere else in your Web page, you should make it *local* to that function. That allows you to use the same name, either by design or inadvertently, in other functions within the same Web page and there will be no clash of identity.

Scope, then, refers to whether a variable is local or global. When a variable is created in a function using the keyword var, it becomes local to that function. If the var keyword is omitted, it becomes global and will be recognised by every other function within the same page. Note that any variable created within <SCRIPT> tags, but not within a function, has global scope, with or without the var keyword.

Should you wish to test the use of var, try this from Chapter 8, Exercise 19. Simply add the reserved word var to the win in the multselections() function.

```
function removewindow(){
 win.close() // make sure win is typed, not window
 } //EoFn

function multselections(){
 var win = window.open("","",
"height=400,width=500,status=yes,resizable=1");
 win.document.write("<BODY BGCOLOR='D5EAFF'>"
 .... etc.
```

We have made win in multselections() local because of the var keyword. It will no longer be recognised in the removewindow() function. Your browser would tell you that it is *undefined*.

1.3 Operators: - Working with Data
These are symbols which have some meaning. For example 1+2, means 'add 1 to 2'. The + sign is called an *arithmetic operator*. Incidentally, if you wrote the following expression: 1+2; JavaScript would calculate the result (3) but since it has not been assigned to a variable nothing else would occur.

In the following table we show many of the common operators used when working with data, such as assigning data to a variable, comparing one value with another, incrementing a variable by 1.

Operator	Type of operator	Operation performed
+ - * /	arithmetical	basic arithmetical functions
+	string	concatenate (*not addition*) used in *write() & alert()*
&& || !	logical	AND, OR, NOT
=	assignment	assignment (*not equals*)
The next six are the comparison operators		
==	equality	tests for equality
!=	inequality	tests for inequality
<	less than	
<=	less than or equal to	num <= 99
>	greater than,	
>=	greater than or equal to	
Special operators		
++	increment	add 1
--	decrement	subtract 1

There are others which we shall come across later.

1.4 Expressions
An expression contains any mixture of numbers, variables, text strings, operators and logical values which JavaScript supports. They are often assigned to variables and are found on the right-hand side of the assignment operator. Here are some examples:

Assign	Right-hand Expression
x =	3+4
x =	"one string" + "a second string"
number =	73.9

Assign	Right-hand Expression
x =	number + 23 / 56
test =	false

1.5 Literals

Since *literal* looks a rather odd term, it is mentioned here more out of completeness than need. It refers to any data value that appears within a program. For example:

12	12.34
'a piece of text'	"another piece of text"
false	true
null	undefined

Frequently, they are operated on by operators. Thus, in the following, two numerical literals are added together and the result assigned to a variable:

```
x = 23 + 45.7;
```

2. Input & Output of Data

As with all programming languages, JavaScript typically works on data (*data literals* to be pedantic). Before it can do so it needs to obtain some data. This can be done in several ways. Either by assigning data to a variable:

```
data1 = 23;
```

or, by getting a user to enter some data via a prompt dialogue box or a FORM text box. This is what is meant by inputting data. Once we have the data, it can be processed and results output via a document.write() method or via a FORM's *value* property. All of these have been discussed in detail in the preceding chapters.

```
document.form1.address1.value
                = "Please enter your address.";
var x = 123;
document.writeln("Print out value: " + x);
```

JavaScript can also evaluate users' actions (events) such as: clicking a button or moving the mouse over an image or hypertext in <A> tags and <AREA> hot-spots. In one sense, we can class these events as 'data' since they can be trapped and some action taken by our program.

3. Making Decisions

This is something we all do many times each day. In programming, it is sometimes necessary to make a decision based on some input. The input could come from a prompt box or some result generated by a function.

Here is a very simple example, yet it illustrates all the syntax for this feature. Suppose, we need to find out whether someone is over 18 years old. If so we can let them into our Shopping Mall, otherwise we have to refuse them entry. This is one of the basic features used for validating user input in FORMs.

> **WARNING:** to make the following pages more readable, *if* and else have sometimes been put in uppercase. They must always be written in lowercase in your JavaScript code!

Exercise 20: *if .. else* statement

```
<BODY>
<B>if-else Exercise</B>
<SCRIPT LANGUAGE="Javascript">
var x =
    window.confirm("Are you over 18 years old?");
if (x == true) {
 document.write("Welcome to My Shopping Mall.");
 }
else
 {document.write("Sorry, you are too young.");
 } // EofIF-ELSE
</SCRIPT>
<ADDRESS> if-else-Ex20.htm </ADDRESS></BODY>
```

 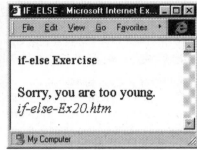

Notes:

1. We first set up a Confirmation box inviting the user to be honest and tell us whether he/she is over 18. If OK is clicked, JavaScript assigns *true* to my variable x. If Cancel is chosen, variable x is assigned the value *false*. This provides an example of the use of a *Boolean* value.

2. The next step is to test which of the two values has been stored in the variable x. It is the IF.. ELSE statement which makes this easy. (*Statement* is a term used to refer to such programming features; *command* may also be used in place of *statement*.)

Notice how the variable is put into round brackets:
`(x == true)` and that the *equality* operator is being used - a double equals. If it is true, we want to welcome the person into our Shopping Mall, otherwise we have to refuse them entry.

Here is the general syntax for this statement:

```
if ( condition to be evaluated )
   { do whatever is necessary if TRUE }
else
   { do whatever is necessary if FALSE}

... carry on here when either the IF or the
    ELSE block has been executed ......
```

The *condition* (in our case, 'does x equal true') is tested automatically by JavaScript when it meets the IF statement. If the result is *true*, whatever follows the IF's opening curly bracket will be executed until it meets the corresponding closing curly bracket. It will then continue with whatever statements *follow* the ELSE's closing *curly bracket*. In other words, the ELSE part is ignored.

If the result is *false,* the IF block is ignored and whatever follows the ELSE's opening curly bracket will be executed until it meets the corresponding closing curly bracket. Then it will continue with whatever instructions follow.

All this is done automatically by JavaScript since this behaviour has been built into the IF.. ELSE statement.

3. Notice that there is a set of curly brackets for the IF and another for the ELSE. They help to mark the beginning and end of each block. We call the statement(s) after the IF and after the ELSE a *block*. In our example we have only one instruction, but there can be as many instructions as needed. Although optional, it is highly recommended that each instruction should end with a semi-colon.

4. The instruction *following* the IF .. ELSE statement will always be executed regardless of whatever action was taken inside the feature. As programmers, you must be aware of this and ensure that it is the correct thing to do in either situation.

5. The positioning of the curly brackets is the same as for functions.

Further points about the IF .. ELSE

1. You do not need to have an ELSE. Thus the following is valid provided nothing needs to be done when x is false.

```
if ( x )
  { window.alert("Welcome to My Shopping Mall")
  } // end of IF block
... next instruction whether x is true or false
```

In the above, *next instruction* will be executed when either the *alert* box has been cancelled or when x is false. In the latter case, the alert box will not appear.

2. Why do we simply have (x) rather than (x == true)? This looks strange, until we realise that x is a Boolean variable which can take the value of either *true* or *false*. When JavaScript tests this variable, the result is one of the two possibilities. Therefore, we only need to type in the Boolean variable name. The longer version makes the code easier to read, but is not necessary.

3. Strictly speaking the IF and the ELSE and many other commands process *single* statements. Hence there is no real need for the curly brackets. Therefore, this is valid:

```
if (x)
 alert("x is true")
else
 alert("x is false")
 ... carry on here whether x is true or false...
```

There are no curly brackets, but it is more difficult to follow and prone to errors. To see an example of how easy it is to make programming errors, look at the Test question 9.10. *A must!*

More often than not, you *do want* to execute more than
one instruction in which case you have to use a *compound*
statement. A compound statement is a group of
instructions enclosed within curly brackets. The
instructions within the curly brackets effectively become a
'single' statement.

```
if (condition)
  { instruction 1;
    instruction 2;  instruction 3;
  }
else
  {instruction 1;instruction 2;
   instruction 3;
   instruction 4;
  }
... carry on here ...
```

Note how useful the curly brackets are when trying to read
the above. They clearly mark the start and end of a block
of code. As a matter of style, I would include them even if
there is only a single instruction. You never know when
you might wish to add an extra instruction or two and then
forget to use curly brackets to indicate a *compound
statement*.

Notice that each instruction ends with a semi-colon. When
more than one instruction is put on the same line, you
must include semi-colons. But it is recommended practice
to always include them, even when there is only one
instruction per line.

4. The condition can be any JavaScript expression that
evaluates to true or false, even functions. Thus:

```
if (xyz == 10)
  { document.write("The number is 10"); }
else
  { document.write("The number is not 10");}
```

```
// another example
if (username == "Fred")
  { document.write("Your name is Fred"); }
else
  { document.write("Your name is not Fred");}
// another example
if (userentry <= 69)
{ document.write("Your entry is less than 70");
}
else
{ document.write("Your entry is more than 69");
}
```

Note the presence of the double equal sign (==) operator, meaning *is equal to* and (<=) meaning *less than or equal to*. There must be no space between the two symbols. These are called *comparison* operators. See page 121.

(Beginners frequently confuse the *assignment* operator (=) with the *equality* operator (==). But they are different. In an IF statement, the condition in round brackets must be evaluated via an equality operator to see whether it is equal to *true* or *false*. Depending on the outcome, either the IF block or the ELSE block of instructions will be executed. In an *assignment statement* the single equal symbol is an *assignment* operator. If the assignment operator is used instead of the equality operator, the assignment will take place and if greater than zero, the 'condition' is treated as true. If it is zero, it is treated as false. See Test question 9.13.)

5. The condition tested by the IF statement can be a function. This makes it a very powerful feature. See page 180 for a discussion about the *return* statement.

```
if ( my_function() ) {
   .. do this when function returns true .. }
```

> **WARNING:** to make these pages more readable, `for` has sometimes been put in uppercase. It must always be written in lowercase in your JavaScript code!

4. Repetition

We now turn our attention to a feature which allows for *repetition*. A FOR loop repeats a set of instructions enclosed in curly brackets until a specified condition is met. It then proceeds with the rest of the script.

The `FOR` loop consists of three parts within round brackets:

```
for (initialise; condition; increment)
   { instructions to repeat ... } // EofFor
      ... next instruction once the above
         has stopped being repeated ...
```

In order to repeat a series of instructions, you have to start at some value (*initialise*); then test it to see whether the loop needs to be repeated again (*condition*); and, finally, increment the value (*increment*) if the condition has not been met.

Here is a simple example. Suppose we wish to sum the first ten numbers and print out the result. Not very exciting, but it does illustrate how this feature works. This will involve repeating some instructions and stopping once a condition has been met. Here is the code:

```
<SCRIPT>
sum = 0;
for ( i = 1; i <= 10; i=i+1)
   { sum = sum + i;   } // EofFor
document.write("numbers 1-10 = " + sum)
</SCRIPT>
```

When JavaScript first meets this FOR loop, *i* will be set to 1 - the *initialisation* step. (It will not repeat this part again.)

It is usually a simple assignment statement. Note the semi-colons after the initialise and condition statements.

It will then test whether the condition - i <= 10; - has been met. Note how comparison operators are used for this part. First time around, *i* is not less than or equal to 10, so JavaScript will execute the code between the curly brackets. *(If the condition were not true the first time, the* for *loop's instructions would not be executed.)*

When the FOR block has been executed, the variable *i* will be incremented according to the *increment* statement - here *i* is incremented by one: (i=i+1) *i* is now = 2; (but it could be incremented by more than 1 or by a negative value if a descending order were required! or, even, by a *real* number, e.g. 0.5).

It then returns to the *condition*, to determine whether to repeat the code again. The value 2 does not meet the condition, so it then repeats the instructions in the loop for a second time. After which, *i* is incremented again - now equal to 3, the condition is tested to see whether *i* exceeds 10 ... and so on.

Eventually, *i* will exceed 10, in which case the code will no longer be executed. JavaScript will then move to whatever instruction follows the FOR loop. See Chapter 14, page 224, for another example of the FOR loop.

The Increment Operator
One of the unusual features of the C programming language, and also part of JavaScript, is the use of the increment operators: ++x & x++. C was devised by programmers for programmers. The most common arithmetic statement in any program is: x=x+1. Those who devised the C language created a shortcut to this statement. Thus: x++ is equivalent to x=x+1.

The increment operator increments its variable by 1 and only by 1. This operator will not increment by any other value. It is ideal for incrementing the loop variable within a FOR loop. Thus, we frequently see the following :

`for (i = 1;  i > 10; i++)` which is the same as:
`for (i = 1; i > 10; i=i+1)`

Another odd thing about this feature is that you can add 1 to the variable, `i` in our example, *before* (`++i`) the loop is executed each time or add 1 *after* each execution (`i++`).

`i++` is called the *postfix operator*, 1 (and only 1) is added to the variable `i` *after* doing something;

`++i` is called the *prefix operator*; 1 is added to `i` *before* doing anything else. Sometimes one is better than another. You will know instinctively which to use if and when the occasion arises.

Decrement Operator
This works in exactly the same way as the increment operator except that it *subtracts* 1 from its variable. We do not have an example in this book, but bear this feature in mind should it ever prove useful (`--k` and `k--`). (Some programmers use them for traversing *arrays* from the bottom up. See page 220 for use of arrays.)

Jargon
block: refers to a group of instructions, for example those repeated by a *for* loop or when an *if* condition proves true. They are also sometimes referred to as a *clause*. (Sorry about this, but you may come across these terms in other texts and wonder what on earth they are talking about.)

compound statement: Many features execute single statements. But when more than one statement needs to be executed, the 'single' statement has to be converted into a *compound* statement by enclosing all the statements in curly brackets. The *many* effectively become *one*.

identifier: another term meaning a variable.

interCapping: the use of Capital letters within a word.

reserved words: those words which have special meaning in JavaScript. Many have a fixed case and if the case is not preserved, they will not be recognised by JavaScript. Examples are: `if, else, for, alert()` (all lowercase); `Math` with `M` in uppercase; `bgColor` (interCapping). Such words should *never* be used as variable names (identifiers).

scope: refers to where a variable is recognised. *Local* variables are recognised only within the function in which they were created. *Global* variables can be recognised by any other function within the same Web page.

What you have learnt
1. We saw that all programming languages have four basic features:
- creating, storing and moving data
- input and output of data
- making decisions
- repeating instructions

and looked at the JavaScript syntax for these features.

2. There are several types of data: numbers, text and Boolean. Typically, data is assigned to variables.

3. The rules for creating variable names and the scope of variables.

4. How to use the various types of operators with data.

5. How to get users to input data.

6. How to make decisions and how to repeat instructions.

7. The special *increment* and *decrement* operators so beloved by C programmers. Once you begin to use them, you too will get to love them! (I did not believe I would when I first came across them.)

8. We have looked at the *core* features of the JavaScript language. Previously, most of what we have discussed has belonged to the *client-side* JavaScript.

Test: Chap. 9

9.1 What are the four basic features of any programming language?

9.2 What is an *integer* number and what is a *real* number?

9.3 How can you capture, for subsequent processing, what a user has typed into a text box or a prompt box?

9.4 Give one example of where case is not significant and one where it is?

9.5 What is happening in the following code?
```
var x = 1;
```

9.6 What is happening in the following code?
```
if (x == 1) { ... }
```

9.7 According to its syntax, an `if` statement can execute only a *single* instruction. How do you make it execute more than one instruction?

9.8 What do the following do?

a) `++i`   b) `k--`

9.9 What will be written out by the `document.write()` method for the following?

```
<SCRIPT>
var aBc = 12
var abc
document.write("Variable abc is: " + abc
        + "<BR>Variable aBc is:  " + aBc)
</SCRIPT>
```

9.10 Look carefully at the following code and work out what will be written out after the code has been executed.

(a) i = j = 12; is another shortcut, beloved by C programmers and now part of JavaScript, which assigns a value to more than one variable in one statement.

(b) IF statements can be nested as we see in the following.

```
i = j = 1;  // both i and j assigned value of 1
k = 2;
if (i == j) // i does equal 1 therefore true
  if (j==k)
    document.write("i equals j");
else
  document.write("i does not equal j");
                                    // Oops!
```

9.11 Why cannot a variable name begin with a digit?

9.12 What will happen in each of the following?
The first one is correct.

```
a) <SCRIPT>
sum = 0;
for ( i = 1; i <= 10; i++)
  { sum = sum + i;  }
document.write("numbers 1-10 = " + sum);
</SCRIPT>
```

```
b) <SCRIPT>
sum = 0;
for ( i = 2; i <= 10; i++)
```

```
   { sum = sum + i; }
document.write("numbers 1-10 = " + sum);
</SCRIPT>
```

```
c) <SCRIPT>
for ( i = 1; i <= 10; i++)
   { sum = sum + i;   }
document.write("numbers 1-10 = " + sum);
</SCRIPT>
```

```
d) <SCRIPT>
var sum;
for ( i = 1; i <= 10; i++)
   { sum = sum + i;   }
document.write("numbers 1-10 = " + sum);
</SCRIPT>
```

```
e) <SCRIPT>
var sum = 0;
for ( i = 1; i = 10; i++)
   { sum = sum + i;   }
document.write("numbers 1-10 = " + sum);
</SCRIPT>
```

9.13 Test the following:

```
<script>
x = 5;
 if (x=6)   // assignment not equality used in error!
   { alert("do IF TRUE") }
 else
   { alert("do IF FALSE") }
document.write("X = " + x)
 </script>
```

a) Which alert box will be displayed and what will be the value printed out for x?
b) Then assign zero to x rather than 6 and run the script again. Which alert and what value will x now have?

9: <u>Programming</u>

Why were computers used?

The main reason for using computers is their ability to make decisions and to repeat instructions at high speed without getting tired.

Decisions are necessary when any data, read in by a program, is unknown and one of several actions needs to be taken depending on the value of the data. The decision-making ability of the `if` ... `else` feature is fundamental to programming.

Repetition is also crucial. Give a human being a task which involves repeating some actions many times, and boredom and loss of concentration will overpower the human. Mistakes will then be made. However, a computer will quite happily repeat the same old task, hundreds, thousands, even millions of times and never fall foul of our human condition.

Incidentally, it was precisely this feature which led the mathematician Charles Babbage to invent 'computers' back in 1819. His were mechanical unlike our electronic versions. The computation of logarithms made him aware of the inaccuracy of human calculation. He wrote in *"C Babbage, Passages from the life of a philosopher (London, 1864)"*:

> *"I was sitting in the rooms of the Analytical Society, at Cambridge, my head leaning forward on the table in a kind of dreamy mood, with a table of logarithms lying open before me. Another member, coming into the room, and seeing me half asleep, called out, 'Well, Babbage, what are you dreaming about?' to which I replied 'I am thinking that all these tables (pointing to the logarithms) might be calculated by machinery.' "*

For an excellent article about Babbage, try the search engine AskJeeves (`http://www.askjeeves.com`) and enter "Who was Charles Babbage?". From the many choices offered, I chose: "Where can I learn about the mathematician - Babbage."

TEN

Calculator Example

So far, all our exercises have been relatively short, although practical. In this Chapter, we shall see what a large JavaScript program looks like. It is not a difficult exercise but it is worth studying carefully. It uses many of the features we have already covered and a few of the functions associated with the Math object which we have not yet covered. These are explained in the notes which follow. It will also explain how to use JavaScript code to compute loan payments. You will be able to think of many more uses for your own Web pages.

Exercise 21: *Computing a loan payment*
We invite someone to enter the following information and get JavaScript to calculate the payments. See page 140.

- how much to borrow
- over how many years
- at what interest

(We could use the following to see whether our car repayments computed by our 'friendly, local' second-hand car dealer are indeed accurate.)

```
<HEAD><TITLE> Want a Loan?</TITLE>
<SCRIPT LANGUAGE="JavaScript">
function calculate(){
/* - get user's input from FORM
   - convert the annual rate to a monthly rate
   - convert interest from a % to a decimal
```

```
   - convert payment period from years to months
   - compute the monthly payments */
var principal =
         document.loan.principal.value;
var interest  =
         document.loan.interest.value / 100 /12;
var payment  =
          document.loan.years.value * 12;
var x  = Math.pow(1 + interest,payment);
var months = (principal*x*interest)/(x-1);
/* Check that the result is a finite number.
   If so display the results */
if ( !isNaN(months)
    && (months != Number.POSITIVE_INFINITY)
    && (months != Number.NEGATIVE_INFINITY) )
 {document.loan.payment.value =
         rounding(months);
  document.loan.total.value =
         rounding(months*payment);

  document.loan.totalinterest.value =
         rounding((months*payment) - principal);
 }    // EofIF
// user's input invalid so display nothing.
else
 {document.loan.payment.value="";
  document.loan.total.value="";
  document.loan.totalinterest.value="";
 }      // EofElse
} // EoFn Calculate
// round to 2 decimal places function
function rounding(x) {
 return Math.round(x*100)/100;
} // EoFn rounding
</SCRIPT></HEAD>

<BODY>
<FORM method="" action="" NAME="loan">
<TABLE>
<TR><TD COLSPAN=2><B>Loan Information:</B>
```

```
<TR><TD> Annual &#37; rate of interest:
<TD> <INPUT TYPE=text NAME=interest SIZE=12
          onChange="calculate()">
<TR><TD> Repayment period (in years)
<TD> <INPUT TYPE=text NAME=years SIZE=12
          onChange="calculate()">
<TR><TD>Amount of loan (any currency)
<TD> <INPUT TYPE=text NAME=principal SIZE=12
          onChange="calculate()">
<TR><TD COLSPAN=2 ALIGN=right>
    <INPUT TYPE=button VALUE="Calculate Loan"
          onClick="calculate()">
<TR>
<TD COLSPAN=2>
<B> Payment Information: </B>
<TR>
<TD> Your Monthly payment:
<TD> <INPUT TYPE=text NAME=payment SIZE=12>
<TR>
<TD>Your total payment:
<TD> <INPUT TYPE=text NAME=total SIZE=12>
<TR>
<TD> Your total interest payments:
<TD> <INPUT TYPE=text NAME=totalinterest
          SIZE=12>
</TABLE>
</FORM>
<ADDRESS>Loan-Ex21.htm</ADDRESS></BODY>
```

Notes:

1. Most of the code should be familiar by now, apart from some of the *Math* methods which are examined below. It is worth spending some time studying this Exercise since it will bring together many of the features of JavaScript which have been discussed in the preceding chapters.

% is the HTML character entity for the percentage symbol %.

2. Before we tackle the mathematical bit, note how `var x` in *Calculate()* is local to that function. Function *rounding()* also uses a variable `x`, but there will be no confusion with the value of the dummy argument `x` in *Calculate()*.

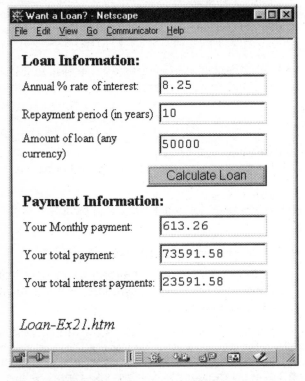

3. The *rounding()* function was discussed in Chapter 6, page 76. We have one *rounding()* function which is invoked from three places, yet each time with a *different* argument. The point was made in Chapter 6, page 75, how one function can be used to work on different data via arguments. Now we can see a working example.

The purpose the *return* statement used in the *rounding()* function is discussed below and in more detail on page 180 of Chapter 12.

4. I hope you agree that the use of indentation, especially for the *if .. else* statements, makes the code easier to read. Note also, the use of comments before the functions and at the end of functions and *if .. else* blocks. More typing is involved, but it can save hours of debugging time.

5. When any change is made to one of the three input text boxes (and the user has clicked outside or into another text box) the *Calculate()* function is invoked again via the *onChange* event. In other words, the user does not have to click the *Calculate Loan* button each time a change is made, although that is probably more intuitive. See page 169 for more details on how the *onChange* event works.

Math.pow(x,y)

`pow()` is a function of the Math object. It raises `x` to the power of `y` - x^y . Thus:

`j= Math.pow(7,2)` results in `j` being assigned 49 (7^2)

You will have to consult a mathematician as to why this helps to compute the monthly repayments. But the main point is its use in (a) below.

We need to ensure that the user does not enter values such as 0% interest, a 0 repayment period, text or some ridiculously huge or small value. JavaScript has various means by which it can trap such errors. Here are some.

(a) `pow()` returns *NaN* (not a number) should a user inadvertently enter text.

(b) POSITIVE_INFINITY and NEGATIVE_INFINITY are special numeric values which are returned when an arithmetic operation generates a value which is greater than the largest number which JavaScript can represent. They are both properties of the Number object. (Note the case used.) This traps any ridiculously large or small number entered by a user.

(c) *isNaN()* is a function which determines whether its argument is 'NaN' (not a number). It is a built-in JavaScript function and part of the core language. It is not a method and is not associated with any object.

So, to check that the numbers generated by the following two statements are 'sensible':

```
var x  = Math.pow(1 + interest,payment);
var months = (principal*x*interest)/(x-1);
```

the code includes the following if statement:

```
if ( !isNaN(months)
    && (months != Number.POSITIVE_INFINITY)
    && (months != Number.NEGATIVE_INFINITY) )
```

> "*if* months *is not (!) 'not a number' (therefore it is a number) AND* months *is not equal to (!=) positive infinity AND* months *is not equal to negative infinity*"

then display the results of the calculations. Otherwise, the *else* clause is invoked to blank out the text boxes which would have shown the results.

The Math object is also part of core JavaScript. It contains functions and constants (for example, PI and LN2). Strictly speaking, functions such as pow() and round() are called functions and not methods. They are functions of the core Math object. Note the case of the constants such as Math.PI, Math.LN2, respectively, the value of π (3.141592653589793) and the natural logarithm of 2 (0.6931471805599453).

The return statement

We came across the return statement in Chapter 6, but did not discuss it. We were not ready for it then. The one thing we need to know about functions is that they always return a single value when they have finished. So far, we have not needed to be aware of this, but now we do.

Our `rounding(x)` function rounds its argument to two decimal places. That is what it returns: x rounded to two places via the `Math.round()` function. It is called as follows:

```
document.loan.payment.value =
                    rounding(months*payment);
```

The contents of the three text boxes, `payment`, `total` and `totalinterest` have their values rounded down. The single value returned by the *rounding()* function is assigned as their values. In the above, this is assigned to the value of the `payment` text box. See page 180 for a full discussion about the *return* statement.

Summary of Exercise 21:

(1) The user is invited to enter information into three boxes:

> Annual % rate
> Repayment in years
> Amount of loan

then click the *Calculate Loan* button.

Under *Payment Information*, the program displays:

> Monthly payment
> Total payment
> Total interest payment

(2) All entries are picked up and calculated when the button is clicked. These are stored in variables: `principal`, `interest` and `payment`.

(3) If any of the boxes are changed, the *onChange* event will invoke the `calculate()` function and all values will be re-calculated and re-displayed.

(4) Note that the *rounding()* function is used three times, each time with a different argument. The dummy argument will take on these different values at each invocation.

```
rounding(months)
rounding(months*payment)
rounding(months*payment)-principal
```

`months` is calculated and passed as the real argument to the dummy argument `x` in the *rounding* function's declaration - `rounding(x)`. (The same for the other two.)

(5) The *rounding* function invokes the *Math.round* function and passes it the value of the dummy argument (now, of course, `months` for the first invocation).

(6) This result, (rounded to an integer) is returned to the point of the original invocation.

(7) It is multiplied by 100 and that result divided by 100.

_____

ELEVEN

Working with Date & Time

JavaScript has a built-in object that allows us to manipulate the date and time. However, before we can use the Date object, it is necessary to get JavaScript to *activate* it. Why?

The Date object is part of the programming language (the core) rather than part of client-side JavaScript. In order to allow a browser to manipulate dates, it is necessary to create what is called a *new instance* of the Date object. Although a little simplistic, it is rather like making a 'copy' of the real thing specifically for the browser. The browser, using client-side JavaScript, can then manipulate dates and times using the copy or the *instance* as it is formally called. Fortunately, this can be done easily by assigning the date to a new date object, using the *new* operator:

```
var mydate = new Date()
```

Date() is the Date object; new creates a 'copy' of it which has been assigned to a user defined object mydate. This new object can now be used in various ways by the browser via the variable name mydate. Table 11.1 shows some of the methods of the Date object which we can use.

How to use the Date object
Suppose we want to write out today's date in our Web page. We first create a new instance of the Date object and assign it to a new Date object via the *new* operator.

```
var today_date = new Date();
```

You could name it anything you want. After creating an instance of the Date object, that instance can use all the methods shown in the Table 11.1.

Method	Returns	Comment
getDay()	the day of the week	its values are numbers: 0 (Sun) - 6 (Sat)
getDate()	the day of the month	values are between 1 - 31
getMonth()	the month	0 (Jan) -11 (Dec)
getYear()	the year	last two digits (*see Notes*)
getHours()	the hour	0 (midnight) - 23 (11p.m.)
getMinutes()	the minutes	0 - 59
getSeconds()	the seconds	0 - 59
getTime()	the date (*in a really peculiar format*)	the date as a number of milliseconds since 1/1/1970

Table 11.1: Some methods for the Date object

Here are some of the more important methods:

```
var mytoday=today_date.getDate()
```

means: "get the numerical day of the month". These are returned in the range 1-31.

```
var mymonth=today_date.getMonth()+1
```

means: "get the month". Since JavaScript counts months starting from '0', not '1', (is there no consistency?), we have to add '1' to the month.

```
var myyear=today_date.getYear()
```

means: "get the year and put it in a variable `myyear`."

Having stored Date values in variables, these can be written out using the *document.write()* or *document.writeln()* methods:

```
document.write("Today's date (UK) is: ")
document.write( mytoday + "/"
```

```
        + mymonth + "/"
        + myyear)
```

Assuming the computer's date is 29th Sept, 2003, the output from the above would be:

```
Today's date (UK) is: 29/9/2003
```

View the same Web page tomorrow, and the date shown would be: `Today's date is: 30/9/2003.`

Years in the 20th century are truncated to the last two digits: Thus: `29/9/99`.

Exercise 22: *Displaying all the methods of Date()*
Here is some code using many of the methods of the Date object.

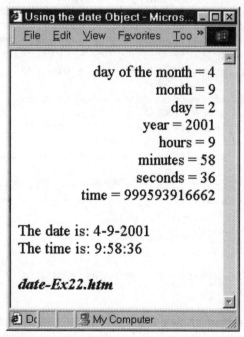

```
<HEAD> <TITLE> Using the Date Object  </TITLE>
<SCRIPT>
// create an instance of Date()
var mydate   = new Date()
// now use this instance below
var monthday = mydate.getDate()
var month    = mydate.getMonth() + 1
var day      = mydate.getDay()
var year     = mydate.getYear()
var hours    = mydate.getHours()
var minutes  = mydate.getMinutes()
var seconds  = mydate.getSeconds()
var time     = mydate.getTime()
document.write("<DIV ALIGN='right'>"
             + "day of the month =  "
             + monthday   + "<BR>")
document.write("month =  " + month + "<BR>")
document.write("day = "    + day   + "<BR>")
document.write("year = "   + year  + "<BR>")
document.write("hours = "  + hours + "<BR>")
document.write("minutes =  " + minutes
             + "<BR>")
document.write("seconds =  " + seconds
             + "<BR>")
document.write("time =  "    + time
             + "</DIV> <P>")
document.write("The date is: " + monthday + "-"
             + month + "-"     + year )
document.write("<BR>" + "The time is: "
       + hours + ":" + minutes + ":" + seconds)
</SCRIPT>
</HEAD>
<BODY>
<P>
<ADDRESS><B>date-Ex22.htm</B> </ADDRESS> </BODY>
```

Notes:

*(Netscape shows the year as 101, see page 162,
and page 163 on how to overcome the 'problem'.)*

1. Since we cannot use the Date object directly, JavaScript requires that we create a client-side instance of the object. This is done with the `new` operator. Usually, operators are *symbols* such as increment (`++`) or logical AND (`&&`). However a few are in fact words. (`this` is another which we shall meet later on pages 193 and 207.)

We have called our instance `mydate` via the following code: `var mydate = new Date()`

2. Assuming the computer's date is Saturday, 7th October, 2000:

the day of the month = 7 - `getDate()` *(the days are numbered 1 - 31)*

the month = 9 (0 -11) - `getMonth()` *(9 = October, we had to add 1 to this to make it 10 when displayed)*

`var month = mydate.getMonth() + 1`

the day of the week = 6 - `getDay()` *(6 is a Saturday, (0 being Sunday, 6 being Saturday).* We do not display it in our example

hours, minutes and *seconds:* The last two are numbered from 0 - 59 and the hours numbered 0 - 23, a 24-hour clock. *(In Exercise 23, we shall convert to a 12-hour clock.)*

`getHours(), getMinutes(), getSeconds()`

time is the number of milliseconds since the 1st Jan, 1970. Seems somewhat weird but it works! *(We shall use this in some later examples.)* - `getTime()`

3. The full date and time have been printed out via the last two `document.write()` lines of code.

4. We shall see how to print out the actual day of the week, for example, 'Monday', in Exercise 25 and how to create a continuous clock in Chapter 18, page 295.

5. Notice the `<DIV ALIGN='right'> ... </DIV>` in the *document.write* code to make the dates and times right justified, with whatever follows being left justified.

With the above knowledge and previously having learnt how to write out HTML code via JavaScript, you can now display the current date and time on any of your Web pages.

You could even display a different image depending upon whether it is *before* or *after* noon.

Exercise 23: *Choosing an Image depending on whether it is a.m. or p.m.*

```
<HEAD>
<TITLE>Choose an Image depending on whether it
is a.m. or p.m.</TITLE>
<SCRIPT LANGUAGE="Javascript">
var current_date = new Date();
var hours        = current_date.getHours();
var minutes      = current_date.getMinutes();
var seconds      = current_date.getSeconds();
```

```
var ampm           = "a.m."
if (hours>=12)
 { // {}s required for the compound statement
    ampm="p.m.";
    hours=hours-12;
 }
if (hours==0)
    hours=12;
if (minutes<=9)
   minutes="0"+ minutes;   /* we want to see 07
                              rather than just 7 */
if (seconds<=9)
   seconds="0"+ seconds;
document.write("<CENTER>" + hours + ":"
                + minutes + ":" + seconds
                + " " + ampm + "<BR>");
// choose image depending on whether AM or PM
 if (hours<=12)
   document.write("<IMG SRC='images/am.gif'>");
else
   document.write("<IMG SRC='images/pm.gif'>");
// notice correct use of double & single quotes
</SCRIPT>
</HEAD>

<BODY>
<ADDRESS>am-pm-Ex23.htm </ADDRESS>
</CENTER> </BODY>
```

Notes: Handling the Hours

1. We want a 12-hour clock. The current hour has been stored in a variable `hours` and will be a numeric value in the range of 0 - 23. If the hours exceed 12, we can simply subtract 12 from the value to convert it into a 12-hour clock. This is done by the following code:

```
var ampm = "a.m."
if (hours>=12)  {
    hours=hours-12;
    ampm="p.m."; }
```

Because the IF statement is supposed to take only a single statement and we have more than one, we need to enclose the statements within curly brackets so that they become a *compound* statement. We have also taken the opportunity to set the variable ampm to the text string 'p.m.' since we would like to add this to our time when it is the afternoon.

2. If the value of hours is within 0 - 12, then it is before noon and the above code will not be executed when the condition is tested in the IF statement. In fact we do nothing at all. However, we would like to add the text string 'a.m.' to the time. Note the neat trick of setting the variable ampm to 'a.m.' before testing the hours. This ensures that ampm will contain 'a.m.'. It is set to 'p.m.' *only when we have discovered* that the hours equal or exceed 12.

3. But what if the time is 12? As this code is written, the hour would become zero. So, we test hours separately and *after* the code in Note 1. If it equals 0, we set it to 12.

```
if (hours==0)
    hours=12;
```

(Because this is a single statement, we did not use curly brackets, although it would be good programming practice to do so. In my own scripts, I would usually put in the brackets, but have omitted them here to illustrate the point.)

Note too that because the previous code has already detected that hours was equal to 12, the ampm has been set to 'p.m.'.

Handling the Minutes & Seconds
4. We wish to include a leading zero when the minutes and seconds are in the range: 0-9, (00, 01 .. 09). This is

achieved through a simple test using the IF statement. When the minute is less than or equal to 9, the variable `minutes` is assigned a leading zero and the actual minute is concatenated using the *concatenate* operator (+), as follows:

```
if (minutes<=9)
    minutes="0" + minutes;
if (seconds<=9)
    seconds="0" + seconds;
```

5. A `document.write()` follows which prints out the time, separated by colons (:), together with 'a.m.' or 'p.m.' as appropriate in `hh:mm:ss a.m` format..

```
document.write("<CENTER>" + hours + ":"
                + minutes + ":"
                + seconds + " "
                + ampm + "<BR>");
```

6. Finally, notice how everything is centred. There is an opening `<CENTER>` tag in the first `document.write` but the closing `</CENTER>` tag is in the BODY. It seems to work, but I could not claim it would work on all browsers.

Exercise 24:
How long have you been connected to your ISP?

Let us allow people to see how long they have been connected to their ISP.

Notes:
1. Study the code below. Essentially, as the page is loaded, the current date and time (in milliseconds) is placed in a variable `start_time`. When a user clicks on the *Connect time* button, the function `connect()` is invoked. This function creates a new and second instance of the current date (`mydate2`) and assigns this new time to a variable called `end_time`. In turn, this is assigned as

the value of the Form's text box NAMEd *nowtime* in milliseconds.

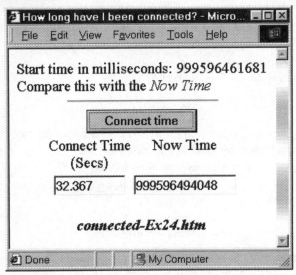

2. The two variables are subtracted, (remember that getTime() returns the date and time in milliseconds), and the result is stored in variable connect_time.

3. Divide this by 1000 (to convert milliseconds to seconds) and assign it as the value of the text box answer.

```
<HEAD>
<TITLE>How long have I been connected?</TITLE>
<SCRIPT LANGUAGE="Javascript">
  mydate     = new Date()
  start_time = mydate.getTime()
document.write("Start time in milliseconds: "
     + start_time + "<BR>"
     + "Compare this with the <I>Now Time </I>")
```

```
function connect(){
      mydate2 = new Date();
      end_time = mydate2.getTime();
 document.howlong.nowtime.value = end_time;     ◄─┐

 connect_time = end_time - start_time;            │
 document.howlong.answer.value      ◄──────────┐  │
                = (connect_time/1000);         │  │
}  //EoFn connect()                            │  │
</SCRIPT>                                       │  │
</HEAD>                                         │  │
                                               │  │
<BODY>                                         │  │
<HR WIDTH=60%> <CENTER>                         │  │
<TABLE>                                         │  │
<TR>                                            │  │
<FORM method="" action="" NAME="howlong">       │  │
<TD COLSPAN=2 ALIGN=center>                      │  │
<INPUT TYPE="button" VALUE="Connect time"        │  │
       NAME="timeconnected"                      │  │
       onClick="connect()">                      │  │
<TR>                                             │  │
<TD ALIGN=center>Connect Time<BR>(Secs)          │  │
<TD ALIGN=center VALIGN=top>Now Time             │  │
<TR>                                             │  │
<TD ALIGN=center>                                │  │
<INPUT TYPE=text SIZE=10 NAME="answer">     ◄────┘  │
<TD ALIGN=center>                                   │
<INPUT TYPE=text SIZE=15 NAME="nowtime">    ◄───────┘
</TABLE>
</FORM>
<P>
<ADDRESS><B>connected-Ex24.htm</B> </ADDRESS>
</CENTER> </BODY>
```

Exercise 25: *What day of the week were you born on?*

We shall print out the day of the week as a word.

Do you know what day of the week you were born on, or the day of the week of the last millennium (01/01/1900)?

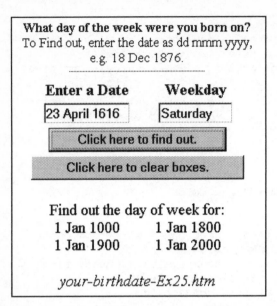

What day of the week were you born on?
To Find out, enter the date as dd mmm yyyy,
e.g. 18 Dec 1876.

Enter a Date   **Weekday**

| 23 April 1616 | | Saturday |

Click here to find out.

Click here to clear boxes.

Find out the day of week for:
1 Jan 1000   1 Jan 1800
1 Jan 1900   1 Jan 2000

your-birthdate-Ex25.htm

Using this program, we can see that William Shakespeare
died on a Saturday, 23rd April, 1616.

Here is how we can do it.

> ***Warning:*** *This works for versions 4 of both Netscape
> and Internet Explorer. Earlier versions may not work
> with some early dates.*

However, we need to know about two more Date
methods: `Date.parse()` and `setTime()` which are
explained in the Notes below. First, here is the code:

```
<HEAD>
<TITLE> Work out day of the Week </TITLE>
<SCRIPT>
function getdayofweek(){
   // create an instance of the date
 var mydate = new Date();
   // store the user's entry in userdate
```

```
  userdate=document.weekday.thedate.value;
    // convert to milliseconds via Date.parse
  parseit = Date.parse(userdate);
    // set this new date to mydate
  mydate.setTime(parseit);
    // use mydate methods as normal
  var day = mydate.getDay();

    // work out which day of the week it is
if (day==0)
      dayofweek = "Sunday";
if (day==1)
      dayofweek = "Monday";
if (day==2)
      dayofweek = "Tuesday";
if (day==3)
      dayofweek = "Wednesday";
if (day==4)
      dayofweek = "Thursday";
if (day==5)
      dayofweek = "Friday";
if (day==6)
      dayofweek = "Saturday";
document.weekday.answer.value = dayofweek;
} //EoFn getdayofweek()

function clearit() {
  // blank out the text boxes
   document.weekday.thedate.value= "";
   document.weekday.answer.value = "";
} // EoFn clearit()
</SCRIPT>
</HEAD>
<BODY>
<FONT SIZE=3><B>What day of the week were you
                 born on?</B>
<P>To Find out, enter the date as dd mmm yyyy,
<BR> e.g. 18 Dec 1876.
<CENTER>
```

```
<HR WIDTH=50%>
<TABLE>
<TR>
<FORM NAME="weekday">  <!-- No method or action -->
<TD ALIGN=center>
<B>Enter a Date</B>
<TD ALIGN=center>
<B>Weekday</B>
<TR>
<TD ALIGN=center>
<INPUT TYPE=text SIZE=12 NAME="thedate">
<TD ALIGN=center>
<INPUT TYPE=text SIZE=10 NAME="answer">
<TR>
<TD COLSPAN=2 ALIGN=center>
<INPUT TYPE=button
       VALUE="Click here to find out."
       onClick="getdayofweek();">
<TR>
<TD COLSPAN=2>
<INPUT TYPE=button
       VALUE="Click here to clear boxes."
       onClick="clearit()">
</FORM>
</TABLE>
Find out the day of week for:<BR>
1 Jan 1000        
1 Jan 1800<BR>
1 Jan 1900        
1 Jan 2000<P>
<ADDRESS><B>your-birthdate-Ex25.htm</B>
</ADDRESS>
</CENTER>
</BODY>
```

Notes: `setTime()`

1. So far we have been able to pick up the computer's *current* date and time by using the *new* operator and creating a new instance of the date. That is fine, but

- 158 -

suppose we need to use some other date, such as a birthday? There is a Date method (`setTime()`) which will allow us to set the date and time to some other date:

```
mydate.setTime(date-in-milliseconds).
```

That is the good news! The bad news is that this method will accept dates only in *milliseconds*.

Date.parse()

Well, I for one could not work out my date of birth in milliseconds, could you? However, to the rescue comes yet another method. `parse()` is a method of the Date object. This allows you to enter a date as a string (in normal text) and it will convert the string into milliseconds. It works like this: `Date.parse("string")`.

We can now use the *Date.parse()* method to convert a string date into milliseconds so that it can be used with the *setTime()* method. Here is how they are used together:

```
parseit = Date.parse("15 Feb 1999")
var mydate  = new Date()
mydate.setTime(parseit)
```

The first line of code uses the `Date.parse` method. However, it is a little different to the other methods we have seen. (It would be, would it not?) It is called a *static* method, but let us not get too depressed by that. What it means is that we **cannot** use it with a user-made instance of the Date() object, such as: ***mydate**.parse("string")*, we have to use the *Date.parse* method and assign it to a variable and then use the variable:

```
parseit = Date.parse("string").
```

In our code, we have assigned it to `parseit` which now contains our date in milliseconds. This variable can be used with the *setTime* method which requires its argument to be in milliseconds. However, before we can use the *setTime* method, we must create a new instance of the Date object (`mydate`). This is our second line of code:

```
var mydate  = new Date()
```

This new instance, `mydate`, will contain the *current* date in milliseconds. So our third line of code changes the current date to the date we entered in the first line.

```
mydate.setTime(parseit)
```

At long last, `mydate` contains our chosen date in milliseconds. From here on, we can use `mydate` as we have done in the preceding examples, except that we have changed its date to a date of our own choosing. We chose the date when Shakespeare died: 23rd April, 1616.

2. Note that we did not need to assign the third line to a variable. We simply used the *setTime* method to give the `mydate` object our chosen date.

3. Now we can set about finding the day of the week for the given date which was the original purpose of this exercise. Using `mydate` as the object, we make use of its `getDay()` method: `var day = mydate.getDay()`and store the result in the variable `day`.

This, of course, is a number from 0 - 6. So the next block of code, via IF statements, tests to see which number `day` contains and assigns the appropriate weekday as text to the variable `dayofweek`. One of the IF statements will prove true, all the others will be ignored.

4. In turn, `dayofweek` is assigned as the *value* of the text box NAMEd `answer`, which is an element of the FORM NAMEd `weekday` which is in the current document. Or more simply:

```
document.weekday.answer.value = dayofweek
```

5. Finally, we have included another button which will clear out the contents of the two text boxes. When clicked, it will invoke function `clearit()`. This simply assigns nothing (`""`) as the value of the text boxes - `thedate` and `answer`.

> ***Did you notice*** *that we have not used method/action in the Form tag. I usually do so to prevent Word 97 crashing when opening an HTML file when they are not included. We have also seen that if the NAME attribute is present, Word 97 will crash if the name attribute comes before method/action. However, if a Form is included in a Table, Word does not crash when method/action are absent. (Now do not ask me why!)*

A Much Simpler Way to Set a New Date

There is a much simpler way to create a new date without using the above two methods. Sorry about that, but I wanted to introduce the `setTime` and `Date.parse` methods since they may prove useful to you one day.

The `Date()` object can take any one of the following four forms:

1. `mydate = new Date()`
   when blank, it becomes the current date and time

2. `mydate = new Date("18 Dec 1978")`
   type in your own string (this is what we could have used instead of *setTime*)

3. `mydate = new Date(year, month, day-of-month, [hours, minutes, seconds])`

   for example: 14th Sept 1987 13:45: would be typed in without quotes as:

   `mydate = new Date(1987,8,14,13,45)`

If the hours, minutes and seconds are not included, they are optional, they become zero. (Remember the purpose of [] ? They signify optional arguments.)

4. `mydate = new Date(milliseconds),`
    e.g. `new Date(946684799000)`

(The milliseconds given above represent 31st Dec 1999, 23:59:59. Do you remember that time?)

A Final Word
One reference book lists some 42 methods for the Date object. The ones we have covered should be enough for most practical uses. However, should you need to delve deeply into date and time manipulation, you will need to refer to one of the references listed in the Bibliography.

Using the Date object in earlier browsers (prior to versions 4) caused problems. Dates prior to 1970 were not allowed. There is still a problem with some date years. For example, in Netscape 4, retrieving the year from a date prior to 1900 or after 2000 gives negative numbers for years before 1900, and positive numbers for years after 2000. Internet Explorer will provide the actual year itself as shown in the following table:

Year: 12 Oct yyyy	Netscape 4.5	I.E 4
1345	-555	1345
1666	-234	1666
1890	-10	1890
1900	0	0
1967	67	67
2000	100	2000
2010	110	2010
2345	445	2345

In other words, Netscape subtracts 1900 from whatever date you supply, providing positive or negative results. That is why, it would give 101 as the year in Exercise 22 on page 148. Internet Explorer also subtracts 1900 but only for dates 1900 - 1999. All other dates are shown as a full year. So you will have to take this into account when manipulating years. Or, make use of yet another method which will provide the full year in *both* of the main browsers: `getFullYear()`

```
var year = mydate.getFullYear()
document.form_weekday.year_answer.value = year
```

Another odd thing is that the display of the date is implementation dependent. Thus the following code in version 4 browsers:

```
mydate = new Date()
document.write(mydate)
```

produces for 16th Oct 2001:
`Tue Oct 16 15:04:17 UTC+0100 2001` (in IE)
but: `Tue Oct 16 15:04:28 GMT+0100 (GMT Daylight Time) 2001` (in Netscape)

What you have learnt
In this long chapter, you have learnt how to manipulate the date and time using the *Date* object and some of its various methods.

We have learnt how to use the standard methods for getting the day, month and year as well as hours, minutes and seconds. We have also seen how to use `Date.parse()` and `setTime()`, two other potentially useful methods.

You have been warned about the different results when using `getYear()` with Netscape and Internet Explorer. Consequently, you may wish to use `getFullYear()`. In this chapter, the results have come from versions 4.5 of Netscape and version 5.0 of Internet Explorer. You should find out what happens on your own browsers.

11: <u>Date & Time</u>

We came across the *new* operator which allowed us to create a new instance of the *Date* object and by using this instance we could use the *Date* object's methods, with the exception of `Date.parse()` which is different.

We are now able to:

- write out the current date and time
- write out any other date we choose
- display one of several images depending on the time of day
- work out how long we have been connected to our ISP
- extract any part of the date and time, for example to find out which weekday it is
- write out a date in American or UK format

Jargon
ISP = Internet Service Provider
UTC = Universal Coordinated Time

Test: Chap 11
11.1 Try writing some JavaScript which will tell a user how long it has taken to load a page.

> **Hint:** you will need two <SCRIPTS> one positioned in the HEAD of the document and one just before or after the closing </BODY> tag.

11.2 Write another piece of code to work out how many days are left to Christmas Day.

For this you will need to use the *setMonth()* and *setDate()* methods of a new instance of the *Date()* object.

```
var xmas = new Date()
xmas.setMonth(11)
xmas.setDate(25)
```

will effectively change the current date's month and day to December 25th. The year will still be the current year.

Because we do not want parts of days, we could use the *Math.floor()* function. This simply returns the greatest integer less than or equal to its argument. Thus:

`Math.floor(45.95)` returns 45
and `Math.floor(-45.95)` returns -46.

11.3 Convert Exercise 24 to show how many *minutes* someone has been connected to their ISP.

11.4 Try the following in both Netscape and IE.

```
<HEAD>
<TITLE> Using the date Object  </TITLE>
<SCRIPT>
// Enter your own date
mydate = new Date("18 Dec 1686")

var monthday = mydate.getDate()
var month    = mydate.getMonth() + 1
var day      = mydate.getDay()
var year     = mydate.getYear()
var fullyear = mydate.getFullYear()

document.write("<h3>Full Year Test </h3>")
document.write("Full year is: " + fullyear)
document.write("<DIV ALIGN= right>"
            + "day of the month =  "
            + monthday + "<BR>")
document.write("month =  " + month + "<BR>")
document.write("day =  "    + day + "<BR>")
document.write("year =  "   + year + "<BR>")
document.write("The date is: " + monthday
            + "/" + month + "/" + year )
// Get current date
var today     = new Date()
var monthdayx = today.getDate()
var monthx    = today.getMonth() + 1
var dayx      = today.getDay()
var yearx     = today.getYear()
```

```
document.write("<BR>Today's date is: "
              + monthdayx + "/"
              + monthx + "/" + yearx )
</SCRIPT>
</HEAD>
<BODY>
<ADDRESS><B>fulldate.htm</B> </ADDRESS>
</BODY>
```

What do you observe for the year 1686 when using Netscape?

TWELVE:

Form Validation

JavaScript is particularly useful for checking the entries made by users when they fill in forms. Usually, form data has to be validated by a *web server*. A program at the server end will check the form's entries and, if there are any errors, the program has to send back an error message to the user. This process takes time. Information has to be passed from the user (called the *client-side*) back to the server (the *server-side*), processed and returned to the user.

When validation takes place at the client-side, there is no need for the server to be involved until the data entered into the form is correct. (As a security measure, any self-respecting server site would re-check the data, to make sure it is valid. See page 290 on security.)

In this book, all our examples are about client-side JavaScript. Creating JavaScript programs for a server relies on a knowledge of how the server is set up and what sort of operating system is being used as well as some experience with the Java language. That is why few JavaScript books exist which go into detail about server-side JavaScript. It is frequently too site-dependent.

Form Validation
Let us take a simple example of a form which requires the user to enter his/her name. If the text box has not been filled in, the form will not be submitted to the server. We therefore need to check that the box has been filled in.

12: **Form Validation**

What is really being tested is whether the box is empty or not. This exercise will demonstrate many of the basic features of form validation. Once we have looked at these basic features, we can discuss a few more useful techniques. *(Exercises 26 and 27 are not very practical and are more for illustration purposes.)*

Exercise 26: *A simple validation of a single text box.*

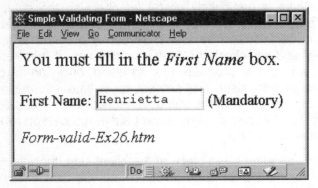

```
<HEAD><TITLE> Simple Validating Form  </TITLE>
<!-- If user deletes data in text box, display
an Alert box. -->
<SCRIPT>
function checkdata(){
   firstname = document.userform1.first.value;

   if (firstname==""){
      alert("Please fill in the name box.");
   } //EoIF
}  // EoFn
</SCRIPT>
</HEAD>
<BODY>
<FONT SIZE=4>You must fill in the First Name
box.</FONT>
<P><FORM method="" action="" NAME="userform1">
First Name:
```

```
<INPUT TYPE=text SIZE=12 NAME="first"
       onChange="checkdata()"> (Mandatory)
</FORM>
<P><ADDRESS>Form-valid-Ex26.htm</ADDRESS>
</BODY>
```

Notes:

1. We have no submit button as yet, we shall add one later. In the BODY we set up a text box named 'first'.

```
<INPUT TYPE=text SIZE=20 NAME="first"
       onChange="checkdata()"> (Mandatory)<BR>
```

2. The *text element* has an onChange event handler associated with it. (Not all elements support this event, and, at the end of this chapter, we have a list of which FORM elements take which events. The *button* element, for example, does not support the onChange event.)

3. An onChange event is activated once a user has entered text in a text box and then clicks outside the box, for example, into a second box or some other part of the window. This is called *losing focus*, see below.

This event was convenient for the *Calculator* example in Chapter 10 where a user could repeatedly change the interest rate, amount of loan and/or the repayment period. Each time a box was changed, the calculate() function was re-invoked.

4. The checkdata() function, assigns the value typed in by the user to a variable 'firstname':

```
firstname = document.userform1.first.value
```

This is tested by an if statement to see whether it is empty (""):

```
            if (firstname == "")
```

If the box is empty, then an alert box appears:

```
alert("Please fill in the name box.");
```

Make sure you do not put in a space between the two double quotes, otherwise you will be testing for a space rather than an empty box!

5. This is not a practical example, yet, since the user would have to type something into the text box, click outside and then delete the text and, again, click outside.

6. Let us now discuss the `focus()` method.

```
document.userform1.first.focus();}
```

focus means putting the cursor into a text box, effectively inviting the user to enter something. Without this line of code, the user would have to click into the box before being able to type in anything. Why did we not put the *focus* onto this text box when the page was first loaded? That is what we shall do in this piece of code.

```
<SCRIPT>
function focusonfirst(){
    // set box to blank, i.e. empty, then set focus.
 document.userform1.first.value = "";
 document.userform1.first.focus();} // EoFn
</SCRIPT>
</HEAD>
<BODY onLoad="focusonfirst()">
<FONT SIZE=4>You must fill in the mandatory
boxes.</FONT>
... etc ...
</BODY>
```

Notes:

1. The `focusonfirst()` function performs two actions. The first action sets the *value* of the `first` element to blank. `first` is a NAMEd property of the form object called `userform1` in the current document..

```
document.userform1.first.value = "";
```

Secondly, it puts the focus onto the text box NAMEd `first`, in other words, the cursor will be sitting in the text box, ready for the user to begin typing. `focus()` is a method of an input text element, here NAMEd `first`.

```
document.userform1.first.focus();
```

2. But how is `focusonfirst()` invoked? Note that the BODY tag has the following code in it:

```
<BODY onLoad="focusonfirst()">
```

The BODY tag can take an `onLoad` attribute which effectively is an event and as such can take a handler, such as a function. Once the web page has *fully* loaded (the event), the event handler is automatically invoked, `focusonfirst()`. This can be quite useful for doing any initialisation before allowing the user to do anything.

Exercise 27: Further Form Validation
In this exercise, we shall use the above knowledge to validate a form which requires a user to enter his/her *first* and *last* names as well as an *e-mail address*.

All three boxes must be filled in. There is a comment text box, which is optional.

However, before we dash off our code we need to think a little. "What is the neatest way of constructing the code?" This is all part of learning how to write programs in JavaScript or in any other programming language. This Chapter and the next will look at some aspects of programming style.

Give the same task to three programmers and they will produce three different programs. Each one will successfully complete the task, but one might be 'better' than another. We shall understand what is meant by *better* after we have examined the various approaches.

12: **Form Validation**

Exercise 26 employed the onChange event. However, this may not always be the best one to use as Exercise 27 demonstrates. Not much thought has been given to how the onChange event works. When a user fills in the first box and then clicks into a second box, an alert box will pop up telling the user to fill in the second box. When this alert box is closed, another alert will tell the user to fill in the third box. This would infuriate any user. Here is the code which would 'work' but would not be user-friendly.

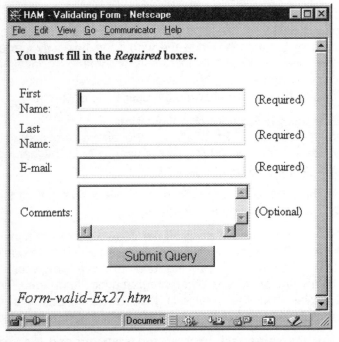

```
<SCRIPT> // A Ham Fisted approach, with no thought given to it.
function checkdata(){
  firstname = document.userform1.first.value;
  lastname  = document.userform1.last.value;
  emailadd  = document.userform1.email.value;
```

```
  if (firstname==""){
    alert("Please fill in first name box.");
    document.userform1.first.focus();
    }
  if (lastname==""){
    alert("Please fill in last name box.");
    document.userform1.last.focus();
    }
  if (emailadd==""){
    alert("Please fill in e-mail box.");
    document.userform1.email.focus();
    }
} // EoFn checkdata
</SCRIPT>
<BODY>
<TABLE>
<TR> <TD WIDTH=30%>
<FORM method="" action="" NAME="userform1">
First Name:
<TD><INPUT TYPE=text SIZE=20 NAME="first"
     onChange="checkdata()">
<TD>(Required)
<TR> <TD WIDTH=30%>Last Name:
<TD><INPUT TYPE=text SIZE=20 NAME="last"
     onChange="checkdata()">
<TD>(Required)<BR>
<TR> <TD WIDTH=30%>E-mail:
<TD><INPUT TYPE="text" NAME="email"
     onChange="checkdata()">
<TD>(Required)
<TR> <TD WIDTH=30%>Comments:
<TD><TEXTAREA ROWS=2 COLS=20> </TEXTAREA>
<TD>(Optional)
<TR>
<TD COLSPAN=3 ALIGN=center> <INPUT TYPE=submit>
</FORM>
</TABLE>
<ADDRESS>Form-valid-Ex27.htm</ADDRESS>
</BODY>
```

Note also that if the *submit* button were clicked before the user fills in the boxes, the form would be sent off with all the boxes empty. So how can we improve it? We shall examine two classic approaches below.

Both methods let the user fill in the boxes (or maybe only some of them) but when the *submit* button is clicked, all the entries are checked at one go. If all of the entries are filled in, the FORM is submitted. If they are not, an alert box pops up requesting the user to try again.

Example 28 - *Approach 1: Using the submit() method*
Since we just want to see how the basic mechanics work, we shall restrict our test to just one text box.

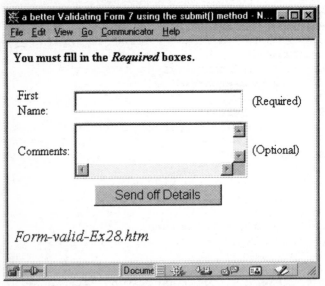

```
<HEAD><TITLE>a better Validating Form  </TITLE>
<!--If user does not enter data in the text box,
pop up an alert box. Otherwise submit the FORM.
-->
```

```
<SCRIPT>
function checkdata(){
  firstname = document.userform1.first.value
  if (firstname==""){
    alert("Please fill in all the Required"
        + " boxes.");
    document.userform1.first.focus();
    }
    else {
    document.userform1.submit();
    } // EofIF
} // EoFn checkdata
</SCRIPT>
</HEAD>
<BODY>
<H3>You must fill in the <I>Required</I>
    boxes </H3>
<P>
<TABLE>
<TR>
<TD WIDTH=30%>
<FORM ACTION="mailto:j.shelley@ic.ac.uk"
      METHOD="post" NAME="userform1" >
 First Name:
<TD><INPUT TYPE=text SIZE=20 NAME="first">
<TD>(Required)
<TR>
<TD WIDTH=30%>Comments:
<TD><TEXTAREA ROWS=2 COLS=20 NAME="comments">
    </TEXTAREA>
<TD>(Optional)
<TR>
<TD COLSPAN=3 ALIGN=center>
<INPUT TYPE=button VALUE="Send off Details"
       onClick="checkdata()">
</FORM>
</TABLE>
<ADDRESS>Form-valid-Ex28.htm</ADDRESS>
</BODY>
```

12: Form Validation

Notes:

1. An `onClick` has been substituted for the `onChange` event and is attached to an input-button element, not to a submit button. If fact, we do not use a submit button at all.

```
<INPUT TYPE=button VALUE="Send off Details"
    onClick="checkdata()">
```

When this button is clicked, the `checkdata()` function tests the user's entry to see whether anything has been typed in. If nothing has, an alert box is produced requesting that all those boxes marked *Required* be filled in. When the user closes the alert box, the function stops and the user is returned to the web page. We have also set the focus back onto the offending text box.

However, when the *firstname* box has been filled in, then the program submits the form via the following:

```
document.userform1.submit();
```

2. Remember that many HTML tags are properties of the document object. But they can also be objects in their own right and, as such, can have their own properties. The FORM object is a property of the document object but it can also become an object if one of its methods is specified. One of FORM's methods is *submit()*. This method submits the specified form and performs the same operation as though a *submit* button had been clicked. That is why the submit button is not required.

3. For once we have included proper values for the ACTION and the METHOD attributes in the FORM tag. We have sent the form via e-mail using `mailto`.

Tip: send yourself an e-mail when you need to test that a form has been submitted. See page 181 if using Netscape.

4. Summary: when the "Send off Details" button is clicked, *checkdata()* is invoked. This function performs a test. If the test detects an empty text box, the function calls an alert box. When the user closes the alert box, focus is set back to the text box and the function ends. If the test does not detect an empty text box, it calls the *submit()* method to submit the associated form.

```
function checkdata(){
  firstname = document.userform1.first.value;
  if (firstname==""){
    alert("Please fill in all the Required"
        + "boxes.");
    document.userform1.first.focus(); }
  else {
    document.userform1.submit();
  } // End of IF-ELSE
}  // End of function
```

Example 29: *Approach 2: Using the onSubmit event handler*

This second approach makes use of the *onSubmit event handler* to perform the same task as the above.

```
<HEAD>
<TITLE>Validating Form using the onSubmit event
handler  </TITLE>
<!--If user does not enter data in the text box, pop up an alert
box. Otherwise submit the FORM. -->
<SCRIPT>
function checkdata(){
  firstname = document.userform1.first.value;
  if (firstname==""){
    alert("Please fill in all the Required"
        + " boxes.");
    document.userform1.first.focus();
    return false;    }
  else { document.userform1.submit1.value
                                ='SENT OFF'
```

12: Form Validation

```
        return true;      } // End of If-Else
} // EoFn checkdata()
</SCRIPT>
</HEAD>

<BODY> <CENTER>
<B>You must fill in the <I>Required</I>
boxes.</B>
<P>
<TABLE>
<TR>
<TD WIDTH=30%>
<FORM onSubmit="return checkdata()"
      ACTION="mailto:j.shelley@ic.ac.uk"
      METHOD="post" NAME="userform1">
First Name:
<TD><INPUT TYPE=text SIZE=20 NAME="first">
<TD> (Required)
<TR>
<TD WIDTH=30%>Comments:
<TD><TEXTAREA ROWS=2 COLS=20 NAME=comments>
</TEXTAREA>
<TD>(Optional)
<TR>
<TD COLSPAN=3 ALIGN=center>
<INPUT TYPE=submit NAME="submit1"
      VALUE="Send off Details"
      onClick="alert('Details being checked')">
</FORM>
</TABLE>
<ADDRESS>form-valid-Ex29.htm</ADDRESS>
</CENTER>
</BODY>
```

Notes:
1. The *onSubmit* event must be placed in the opening
FORM tag. You must also include a *submit* button within
an INPUT element. The reason being is that when the
submit button is clicked, it will cause the *onSubmit* event
to be triggered.

- 178 -

2. We use a *submit* button (sometimes called the *submit object* or *submit element*) within the form:

```
<INPUT TYPE=submit NAME="submit1"
    VALUE="Send off Details"
    onClick="alert('Details being checked.')">
```

When the submit button is clicked, its *onClick* event handler is invoked and processed. In my code, this simply displays an alert box. (It could equally be a call to a function whereby many statements could be processed.)

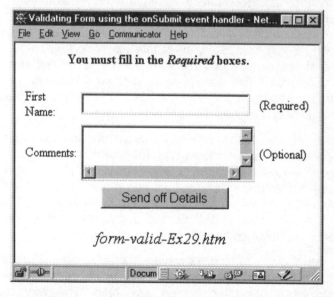

form-valid-Ex29.htm

3. This is the important bit. Once the submit button's *onClick* event handler has performed its task, the *onSubmit event handler* in the FORM tag is automatically activated and `checkdata()` invoked.

```
<FORM onSubmit="return checkdata()"
    ACTION="mailto:j.shelley@ic.ac.uk"
    METHOD="post" NAME="userform1">
```

Thus, we see that the process involves two steps. The first step is to process the event handler's code (optional) when the *submit button* is clicked. When this task has been completed, the second step follows, namely, the form's *onSubmit* code is executed.

4. What is the *return*? It is time we had a look at this in detail because it is an important part of functions.

The *return* statement
Functions *always* return a value. If a *return* statement is not included, the function executes all the statements in the function body and returns the *undefined* value to the calling invocation. So what is this *undefined* value? It is one of several special JavaScript values. When a variable is used which has not yet been defined (*declared*), or a variable has been declared but has not yet been assigned a value, it is assigned the *undefined* value.

Now, in the case of a function which has no *return* statement, it is the calling statement which takes on the *undefined* value once the function has completed its work. In all our examples so far, this has not been a problem. We simply wanted a function to do its work and stop. The fact that its calling statement, the invocation, may have become *undefined*, was of no concern to us.

In the above situation, however, it *has* become a matter for our concern. We want the form to be submitted but only when the user entries are valid. The way the *onSubmit event handler* works is that if a *return* statement is *false*, the form is prevented from being submitted. Any other returned value (such as *true* or even *undefined*) will cause the form to be submitted. If the return true statement were omitted, the form would still be submitted, because the value returned would not be *false* but *undefined*. Those are the rules of this game.

Therefore, there is no real need for us to include the `return true` statement. However, it is highly recommended to do so since it makes the logic of the program clearer to the human reader.

If there are several *return* statements in a function, the first one encountered will stop the entire function and return to the invocation statement.

What is the difference between *submit()* and *onSubmit*?
The *submit()* method can be called from any function, without the need for a submit button to be displayed on the Web page. When encountered, it is identical to what happens when a user clicks a submit button.

The *onSubmit* event handler, on the other hand, *does* require a submit button. Without a submit button to click, the *onSubmit* event handler could not be called and the form would never be submitted.

Warning: *Do not use the submit() method to send FORMs via mailto:, news: or snews: via Netscape 4. It is set up to ignore such protocols for security reasons. If you wish to use those protocol, you will have to use the onSubmit event handler or just a simple submit button. Internet Explorer 5 seems to ignore this proviso.*

We have covered a great deal of ground in this chapter. We need a rest and a chance to assimilate and to practise what we have learnt. We have a more to say about Form Validation in the next chapter because there are a few neat features which we can employ.

The example which follows summarises the material covered in this chapter. It is worth studying in detail at your leisure.

12: Form Validation

Example 30 - *The full code for validating our Form.*

```
<HEAD><TITLE>Final Validating Form using the
onSubmit event handler  </TITLE>
<SCRIPT>
function focusonfirst(){
  // set box to empty and set focus.
 document.userform1.first.value="";
 document.userform1.first.focus();
} // EoFn focusonfirst
function checkdata(){
  firstname = document.userform1.first.value;
  lastname  = document.userform1.last.value;
  emailadd = document.userform1.email.value;
 flag = 0;
 if (firstname==""){
   alert("Please fill in all the Required"
        + " boxes.");
   document.userform1.first.focus();
   flag = 1;
   return false;    }
if (lastname==""){
    alert("Please fill in all the Required"
         + " boxes.");
    document.userform1.last.focus();
    flag = 1;
    return false;
   }
if (emailadd==""){
    alert("Please fill in all the Required"
        + "  boxes.");
    document.userform1.email.focus();
    flag = 1;
    return false;
   }
if (flag == 0){
 document.userform1.send.value="Details Sent.";
 return true;     }
} // EoFn checkdata
```

```
function when(){
  alert("Your data is about to be checked.");
} // EoFn when
</SCRIPT> </HEAD>

<BODY onLoad="focusonfirst()">
<FONT SIZE=4>You must fill in the
<I>Required</I> boxes.</FONT>
<P><TABLE>
<TR><TD WIDTH=30%>
<FORM onSubmit="return checkdata()"
      ACTION="mailto:j.shelley@ic.ac.uk"
      METHOD="post" NAME="userform1" >
  First Name:
<TD><INPUT TYPE=text SIZE=20 NAME="first">
<TD>(Required)
<TR><TD WIDTH=30%>Last Name:
<TD><INPUT TYPE=text SIZE=20 NAME="last">
<TD>(Required)
<TR><TD WIDTH=30%>E-mail:
<TD><INPUT TYPE=text SIZE=20 NAME="email">
<TD>(Required)
<TR><TD WIDTH=30%>Comments:
<TD><TEXTAREA ROWS=4 COLS=20 NAME="comments">
    </TEXTAREA>
<TD>(Optional)
<TR><TD COLSPAN=3 ALIGN=center>
<INPUT TYPE=submit NAME="send"
       onClick="when()">
</FORM>
</TABLE>
<ADDRESS>Form-valid-Ex30.htm</ADDRESS>
</BODY>
```

Notes:

1. In the above, we have chosen to use the *onSubmit event handler* in the FORM tag rather than the *submit()* method.

12: Form Validation

```
<FORM onSubmit="return checkdata()"
ACTION="mailto:j.shelley@ic.ac.uk"
      METHOD="post" NAME="userform1" >
```

2. When the user clicks on the submit object (the submit button), two things happen. First, it calls the *when()* function which alerts the user to the fact that the details are going to be checked. (Good style!)

```
<INPUT TYPE=submit NAME=submit1
      onClick="when()">
```

The second thing to happen is that when the user closes the alert box, generated by the *when()* function, the *onSubmit* handler in the FORM tag is automatically invoked. This is a call to the `checkdata()` function which checks the user's data. Without a *submit* type button, the *onSubmit* could not be executed.

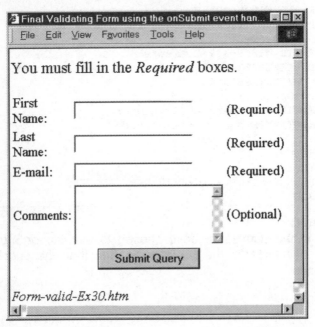

3. The `checkdata()` function has a series of IF statements, each one checking one of the text boxes. If one is empty, it alerts the user and requests that *all* boxes must be filled in. It then sets the focus on to the offending box and assigns the numeric value '1' to variable `flag`.

```
if (lastname==""){
    alert("Please fill in all the Required"
        + " boxes.");
    document.userform1.last.focus();
    flag = 1;
    return false;}
```

Finally, the *return* value is set to *false* to prevent the form from being submitted. Any of the *return* statements will stop the function.

4. If there are any errors, the user corrects them and then clicks the submit button once more. Once all boxes have been found to be non-empty, that is, all the IF statements fail, there is one final IF statement. This tests to see whether `flag` equals zero. (*Note that this flag has been assigned zero at the start of the function.*)

```
flag = 0;
 ... etc ...
if (flag == 0){
 document.userform1.send.value="Details Sent.";
 return true;     }
```

If `flag` does equal zero then it cannot have been set to 1 by any of the IF statements and, therefore, we know that the form can be safely sent off to the server. The *value* of submit button, `send`, is changed to "Details Sent" and `return` is set to *true*. Since this return value is 'not false', JavaScript will now automatically submit the form.

5. We have included proper values for the *action* and the *method* attributes in the FORM tag. We have sent the form

via e-mail using `mailto`. Both Netscape and IE will submit the form because we have used the OnSubmit handler.

```
<FORM onSubmit="return checkdata()"
      ACTION="mailto:j.shelley@ic.ac.uk"
      METHOD="post" NAME="userform1">
```

In practice, you will have an existing program on your server to handle the data. This would typically be accessed via an `http://..url` in the *action* attribute. Since we consider *client-side* JavaScript in this text, it is assumed that our task is simply to submit the form's data to whatever program we have been told to use. In other words, someone else will have written the server-side program and supplied us with the correct 'url'.

If you want to use *mailto*: for both main browsers, you cannot use the *submit()* method. It fails without warning in Netscape, if the FORM's *action* is mailto:, news: or snews:. This is for security reasons. You will have to use the standard *submit* button or the *onSubmit* event handler which triggers the submit button to work.

6. As a matter of style, it is always useful to add a JavaScript comment marking the end of a function:

```
function xyz() {
    ... function code ...}  // end of function
```

What we have learnt
We have seen how to validate user data entered into forms at the client-side before a form is submitted to a server. Client-side validation helps to reduce the server's workload as well as reducing the amount of traffic over the Internet.

To validate user data, we introduced the *onChange* event which called a function to perform the necessary validation. Later we used the *onClick* event in conjunction with the *submit()* method of the FORM element.

We looked at another approach using the *onSubmit* event handler which is triggered when the submit button is clicked. This method allows the use of the `mailto:`, `news:` and `snews:` protocols for both of the main browsers.

The *onLoad* event handler can be used to initialise the page immediately after the page has loaded. We shall see this again when we animate images in Chapter 14.

The *focus()* method was used to place the cursor inside a text box so that the user could begin typing without having to physically click inside the text box.

We also discussed the *undefined* value and its use with the *return* statement. The latter has to be used with the *onSubmit* event handler and must return a value of *false* when we need to prevent the submission of a form.

We considered some aspects of programming style and made use of a variable to flag whether we should submit a form or not.

Jargon

client-side: when a user wishes to obtain a web page, the browser becomes the client of the request.

flag: in programming, a common technique to discover whether something has happened or not (such as some data being invalid) is to give a value to a variable. This variable, often called a *flag variable*, can be tested to see which state it is in and react accordingly. Many programmers use the numeric values 1 and zero, but you could also use the Boolean values *true* or *false*.

12: <u>Form Validation</u>

focus(): a method which causes a text box or textarea box to be given focus. It is equivalent to a user physically clicking into the text or textarea box.

onLoad: an event handler contained within the BODY tag. When the page has completed loading, the event handler is automatically invoked and its JavaScript code executed. The following is not to be recommended. It can become very irritating to your users.

```
<BODY onLoad="alert('Welcome to my Web page.')"
```

onSubmit: an event handler within a FORM tag. Once the submit button is clicked, the JavaScript code associated with the handler is executed. Typically, it is used to validate form data. A *return* statement which evaluates to *false* must be used to prevent the form from being submitted. Any other value will cause the form to be submitted, even an *undefined* value.

return: all functions return a value when they have completed their work. It takes the Boolean value *true* or *false* or the *undefined* value. It is also possible for other values to be returned, in fact, any value. For example, the following function returns the square of its argument:

```
function square(x) {
  y = x*x;
  return y;             } // end of function
```

or more succinctly

```
function square(x) {
  return x*x;} // end of function
```

server-side: the server which holds the web pages and any validating programs requested by a user's browser.

submit(): a method which submits a form. It requires the name of the form as its object. For security reasons, it fails without warning if *mailto: news:* or *snews:* is used in a form's *action* attribute.

*undefine*d: a special value which is given to any variable or object or function call which has not been explicitly defined and assigned some other value.

Events & Methods - summary so far

Event	Associated with	Comment
onLoad	BODY and IMG	page (image) must be completely loaded before the handler is invoked
onSubmit	FORM	automatically invoked when the submit button is clicked
onChange	text or textarea element	activated when a user enters text and clicks outside of the text box
onClick	button, checkbox, radio, reset & submit buttons and also used with links	links refer to the <AREA> & <A> tags
onMouseOver	used within links	reacts when user moves mouse over a link
onMouseOut	used within links	reacts when user moves mouse out of a link

Methods	Where used	Comments
submit() *associated with a FORM*	used within a function	performs the same action as though the submit button was pressed
focus() *associated with a text box*	used within a function	performs the same action as though a user had clicked into a text box or a textarea box

12: Form Validation

Test Chap 12:

12.1 Which INPUT elements are allowed to take the *onChange* event handler?

12.2 How is the onChange event handler triggered?

12.3 *What do you see when the following is run?*

```
<head> <title> ... </title>
<script>
function abc() {x = 2;} // EoFn
</script>
</head>
<body>
<script>
  alert("Are you ready?");
  y = abc();
  alert("Y = " + y) // What value has variable y?
</script>
</body>
```

12.4 A form may be submitted in any of three ways. What are they?

12.5 To which object does the *submit()* method belong?

12.6 What function does the *submit()* method perform?

12.7 *onSubmit* is an event handler of which HTML tag?

12.8 What purpose does the *onSubmit* handler perform?

12.9 When does the *onSubmit* event handler send the form to a server?

What is next

We shall look at some more features and tricks associated with form validation. Some of these will reduce the amount of typing and others will extend our knowledge of what other tests can be carried out when validating forms.

THIRTEEN

Further Form Validation Techniques

In this chapter, we shall look at some other validation techniques using:

- the *indexOf()* method
- the *length* property
- and the *this* operator

We begin with the this operator, but we need to set the background for its use by first looking at Exercise 31.

Exercise 31: *The old approach:*

Suppose we need to validate a job application form for a mountaineering post where applicants must be healthy young things between 18 and 35. In previous exercises, when we referred to, say, the value of an INPUT element we had to type the following:

```
firstname = document.userform1.first.value;
```

13: **Further Form Validation**

There is a shorter and more elegant way, using the JavaScript operator this which we shall use in Exercise 32. For the moment, here is the code using the old approach: document.formname.elementname...etc.

```
<SCRIPT>
function focusonage(){
// set box age to blank, i.e. empty & focus.
 document.ageform.age.value="";
 document.ageform.age.focus();
}   // EoFn
function checkage(){
 userage = document.ageform.age.value;
 if ((userage < 18) || (userage > 35))
   {alert("Sorry you are either past it or too"
          + " young!");
    document.ageform.submitage.value
                       = "Must be 18-35.";
    document.ageform.age.value="";
    return false; }
 else
   {alert("You will be notified");
    document.ageform.submitage.value
                       = "Details Sent.";
    return true;}
} // end of function
</SCRIPT> </HEAD>

<BODY onLoad="focusonage()">
You must fill in the <I>Age</I> box.
<P>
<FORM onSubmit="return checkage()"
      ACTION="mailto:j.shelley@ic.ac.uk"
      METHOD="post" NAME="ageform" >
<TABLE>
<TR>
<TD WIDTH=30%>Type in your age:
<TD> <INPUT TYPE=text NAME=age >
<TR>
```

```
<TD COLSPAN=2>
<INPUT TYPE=submit NAME=submitage>
</FORM>
</TABLE>
<ADDRESS>Valid-Age-Ex31.htm</ADDRESS>  </BODY>
```

1. After the document has been loaded, the *onLoad* event handler of the BODY tag calls function *focusonage()* which blanks out the text box age and sets the focus on to the text box.

2. When the *submit* button is clicked, the Form's *onSubmit* handler invokes the *checkage()* function where there are four references to: document.ageform. In the next exercise we shall use the this operator instead.

3. If the age is outside the limits, checkage() will return false to prevent the form from being submitted. Notice that we have included a return true when the age is found to be within the correct age limits. This was not actually necessary, since all functions always return something, whether the return statement is used or not. Consequently, our function *checkage()* would have returned something other than *false*, which would have forced the form to be submitted. However, the return true statement is recommended to indicate that we are serious about what needs to be returned.

Exercise 32: *Using the* this *operator*
This is identical to Exercise 31 except that we shall use the this operator.

Notes:
1. In the FORM tag, the *onSubmit* event handler has added the keyword this as an argument. We have also passed the age limits as arguments - 18 to 35. this is a shorthand way of referring to the current object which, in

this instance, is the *form* named `ageform` which is a property of the current document: `document.ageform`.

```
<FORM NAME=ageform
      onSubmit="return checkage(this,18,35)"
```

```
<HEAD>
<TITLE>Validating Applicants' Age using "THIS"
</TITLE>
<SCRIPT>
function focusonage(){
 document.ageform.age.value = "";
 document.ageform.age.focus();
 document.ageform.submitage.value =
                          "Send Details. "
} //EoFN
function checkage(obj,lowage,highage){
 userage = obj.age.value
 if ((userage < lowage) || (userage > highage))
   {alert("Sorry you are either past it or too
young!");
    obj.submitage.value=" Must be 18-35.";
    obj.age.value="";
    return false; }
 else
  { alert("You will be notified");
    obj.submitage.value="Details Sent.";  }
} // EoFn
</SCRIPT>
<BODY onLoad="focusonage();">
You must fill in the <I>Age</I> box.<P>

<FORM onSubmit="return checkage(this,18,35)"
      ACTION="mailto:j.shelley@ic.ac.uk"
      METHOD="post" NAME="ageform" >
<TABLE>
<TR>
<TD WIDTH=30%>Type in your age:
<TD> <INPUT TYPE=text NAME="age" >
<TR><TD COLSPAN=2>
```

```
<INPUT TYPE=submit NAME="submitage"
      VALUE="Send Details.">
</FORM>
</TABLE>
<ADDRESS>Valid-Age-Ex32.htm</ADDRESS></BODY>
```

this is passed to the dummy argument `obj` in function `checkage()` where it will now take on the value of `this` namely `document.ageform`.

```
function checkage(obj,lowage,highage){
 userage = obj.age.value  .. etc. ...}
```

2. In the function `focusonage()`, we also refer to `document.ageform`. However, we could not use `this` as an argument in the `focusonage()` function which is loaded by the BODY tag because it would then become a reference to the BODY and not to the form NAMEd `ageform`.

Wherever `this` is used, it takes on the appearence of its local context. We have only one form, but suppose we had three forms - one for children (5-17), another for adults (18-64) and a third for OAPs (65+), each one making use of the `checkage()` function:

```
onSubmit="checkage(this,5,17)"
```

Whichever one of the three submit buttons was clicked, the `this` operator would assume the mantle of the local form.

3. Numeric values typed in by users can be checked using the *comparison* operators. This is quite simple.

```
if ((userage < lowage)||(userage > highage))
```

But note that each tested expression must be surrounded by brackets when logical operators (`&&` `||`) are used:

```
if ( (expression_one) || (expression_two) )
```

13: <u>Further Form Validation</u>

In our example, the value entered by the user is checked against low and high boundary values - 18 and 35 - which are passed as arguments via the *onSubmit* handler's invocation to the *checkage()* function.

Some more Tests which can be applied
Sometimes it is not convenient to allow leading spaces to be entered by users. For instance, we may intend to store the applicants' names in a data base and perform an alphabetical sort at a later time. Sorting is based on the first character. If some names have a leading space and some do not, the sort will not be correct. To trap leading spaces, we can use the *indexOf()* method.

`indexOf()` **method**
This is a method of the *String* object. It returns the index, that is the position, of the first occurrence of its argument in a specified string.

```
a_string = new String("The Owl and the
Pussycat went to sea.")
```

Note how its construction is similar to that of the *Date* object (see page 145).

A new instance of the String object can be created by a simple assignment statement. The following behaves identically to the above:

```
a_string =
      "The Owl and the Pussycat went to sea."
```

The following finds the first occurrence of the character 'w' in the above string: `a_string.indexOf("w")`

and would return 5, as its position (index) in the associated string, `a_string`.

Why 5? Because the first character is numbered zero. Hence, the sixth character is index 5. The first character

("T" in our example) would be index 0. Note that spaces are always included in the count since a space represents a physical character.

"What's the big deal?", you cry. Well, it can help to find out if someone has put in a leading space or whether a particular character, a word or a phrase has been included. The main point about the indexOf() method is that if the character is *not* found, it returns -1 as its value. This can be tested (using an if statement) and if the returned value is -1, you know that the character, word or phrase has not been entered by the user.

```
<BODY>
<CENTER>
<B>The Owl and the Pussycat went to sea.</B>
<SCRIPT>
a_string="The Owl and the Pussycat went to sea."
charpos = a_string.indexOf("w") + 1
document.write("<P>Lowercase <I>w</I>"
        + " occurs at index "
        + a_string.indexOf("w") // interesting!
        + " as the "
        + charpos
        + "th character in the given string.")
</SCRIPT>
<P>
<ADDRESS>indexof-1.htm</ADDRESS>
</CENTER></BODY> XXX
```

In the following code, we test for a leading space. Here is the code where obj is the same as in Exercise 32, namely: document.ageform. We assume there is a textbox NAMEd surname.

```
if (obj.surname.value.indexOf(" ") == 0) {
    alert("Please remove leading spaces!");
    obj.surname.focus(); }
```

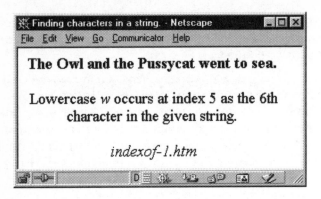

indexOf() always begins its search at the start of the string unless you add a second argument. Therefore, if the index equals zero, there is a leading space as the first character. Note, too, that we have put a space between the double quotes (" ") because that is the character we are searching for. Thirdly, we have set the *focus* back on to the text box.

Here is the full syntax for *indexOf()* where the second argument is a numeric value from which to begin the search. It rarely has any viable purpose, unless you want to find the second or third, etc., index of a given character. (See page 201 for an example.) The second argument can be any expression or statement which returns a numeric value. When omitted, the search begins at the first position.

```
a_string="The Owl and the Pussycat went to sea"
a_string.indexOf("Pussycat", 7)
```

The search for *Pussycat* in the above would start at the 8th character and 16 would be returned as the index (the 17th character). Case is significant in this method. Thus, if 'pussycat' were searched for, the returned index would be -1 as shown. If I searched for 'went to sea', index 25 would be returned, but if I typed in 'went sea', -1 would be returned. It is always the starting position of a word or phrase which is returned.

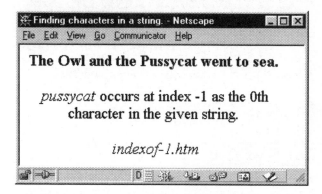

Testing that *two* words have been entered

If you have just one text box in which you invite users to enter their full name, it may be necessary to check that two words have been entered. One way would be to search for a space, since words have a space between them, and test for -1 to be returned. If it is, then there are no spaces and you can assume a one word entry.

```
if (obj.value.indexOf(" ") == -1) {
  alert("Please re-enter your first name and
         surname");
  obj.focus(); }
```

Exercise 33: *Using the* length *property*

In this exercise, we are going to check that a user has entered a fixed number of characters. In some instances, users may be required to enter data as a fixed number of characters, perhaps it is a postcode which can be between 6 and 9 characters or a date in a fixed format of dd/mm/yy with leading zeros for digits 1-9. You can force

13: **Further Form Validation**

your users to enter an exact number of characters by making use of the *length* property.

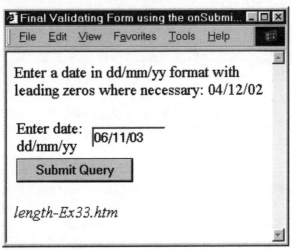

length-Ex33.htm

```
<SCRIPT>
function checkdate(obj2){
  if (obj2.date.value.length == 8)
    { obj2.submit1.value
              = obj2.submit1.value.toUpperCase();
      return true;}
  else { alert(obj2.date.value
              + " is not valid.");
         return false; } // EofIF
  } // EoFn
</SCRIPT>
<BODY>
<FONT SIZE=3>Enter a date in dd/mm/yy format
with leading zeros where necessary:
04/12/02</FONT>
<P>
<TABLE>
<TR><TD WIDTH=30%>
```

```
<FORM onSubmit="return checkdate(this)"
      ACTION="mailto:j.shelley@ic.ac.uk"
      METHOD="post" NAME="dateform" >
Enter date: dd/mm/yy
<TD><INPUT TYPE=text SIZE=10 NAME="date">
<TR>
<TD COLSPAN=2>
<INPUT TYPE=submit NAME="submit1">
 </FORM>
</TABLE>
<ADDRESS>length-Ex33.htm</ADDRESS>
</BODY>
```

Notes:

1. `length` can be a property of a 'string value' entered by a user into an INPUT text box. Let us suppose that we need to be strict about how dates are entered, say, with leading zeros and a two digit year, `01/10/02`. This format requires 8 characters. We can check the length of an entry thereby forcing a user to meet our demands.

```
if ( obj2.date.value.length == 8 )
```

2. As the program stands, there is nothing to stop a user typing in: '12345678' or even 'abcdefgh'. It meets the requirements. Thus, the canny programmer would also need to check that *forward slashes* have been included at specific places by using the *indexOf()* method below.

```
if ( (obj2.date.value.length == 8) &&
     (obj2.date.value.indexOf("/") == 2 ) &&
     (obj2.date.value.indexOf("/", 4) == 5) )
  { obj2.submit1.value =
           obj2.submit1.value.toUpperCase();
    return true;
  } // EofIF
```

The above is an example of when it may be necessary to force users to enter data in a strict format in order to ensure that a valid date format has been entered and not just a jumble of characters.

So, the *indexOf()* method and the *length* property can prove useful for form validation.

3. In the above, we have also used the *toUpperCase()* method. This converts the value of the *submit1* element to upper case. We could simply have set the value to an upper case string:

```
obj2.submit1.value = "SUBMIT QUERY"
```

However, you need to be aware of this method as well as its opposite, `toLowerCase()`.

4. Why do we have to add the *second* argument here?

```
if (obj2.date.value.indexOf("/", 4) == 5)
```

In order to start searching for the *second* forward slash, we need to begin the search after index 3, otherwise, it would start at the beginning and meet the first again.

5. An alert box is shown when the user enters an invalid date:

Exercise 34: *A Little Help*

The last thing we shall do is to put in a little help box. If it is checked, a window pops up explaining how to enter data. If unchecked, it does not pop up, perhaps because the user is familiar with how we want data to be entered.

(It is always polite to include such help windows as well as the option of preventing them from appearing. Hence the presence of the checkbox.)

```
<HEAD><TITLE> Giving some Help </TITLE>
<SCRIPT>
// BODY onLoad - set the helpdate field to null
function init() {helpdate = null; } //EoFn
// auto help on date field
function autohelp(obj2, file) {
  if ((obj2.help.checked == true)
  && (helpdate == null))
    helpdate = window.open(file, null,
                "width=370,height=270");
} // EoFn
function checkdate(obj2){
   if ( (obj2.date.value.length == 8)
      &&(obj2.date.value.indexOf("/") == 2 )
      &&(obj2.date.value.indexOf("/", 4) == 5))
      { obj2.submit1.value =
             obj2.submit1.value.toUpperCase();
       return true;        }
```

```
      else { alert(obj2.date.value
             + " is not valid.");
          obj2.date.value=""; obj2.date.focus();
          return false; }
} // EoFn
</SCRIPT>
</HEAD>
<BODY onLoad="init()">
<B>Enter your date of birth.</B>
<FORM NAME="dateform"
      onSubmit="return checkdate(this)"
      ACTION="mailto:j.shelley@ic.ac.uk"
      METHOD=post>
<TABLE WIDTH=80%>
<TR><TD WIDTH=35%>Auto Help?</TD>
<TD><INPUT TYPE="checkbox" NAME="help"
          CHECKED></TD>
<TR><TD WIDTH=35%>Enter date: dd/mm/yy
<TD><INPUT TYPE=text SIZE=10
          NAME="date"
 onFocus="autohelp(this.form,'datehelp.htm')">
<!-- datehelp.htm is passed as an argument to
   the dummy argument file in the autohelp()
   function. -->
<TR><TD COLSPAN=2 ALIGN=center>
<INPUT TYPE=submit NAME="submit1">
</TABLE>
</FORM>
<ADDRESS>length-Ex34.htm</ADDRESS>
</BODY>
```

Notes:

1. When the document is loaded, the init() function is invoked which simply sets a variable *helpdate* to null:

```
helpdate = null;
```

We did not use the var keyword with helpdate, thereby making it a *global* variable so that other functions can make use of it. The JavaScript keyword null is a special value that indicates 'no value'. So what purpose does it serve in our code?

Notice that the *autohelp()* function tests to see whether variable `helpdate` equals *null*. If it is true (and the checkbox is checked) then a window is opened displaying the help file `datehelp.htm`.

```
function autohelp(obj2, file) {
  if ((obj2.help.checked == true)
      && (helpdate == null))
    helpdate = window.open(file, null,
                    "width=370,height=270");
} // EoFn
```

`datehelp.htm` has been passed to the dummy argument `file`. (It would be more sensible, of course, to create the HTML document at the client-side rather than force the browser to retrieve it over the Internet, as shown in Exercise 18, page 101.) Note, also, that it is the *onFocus* event handler which causes the function to be executed.

```
<TD><INPUT TYPE=text SIZE=10
           NAME="date"
 onFocus="autohelp(this.form,'datehelp.htm')">
```

We have made the `help` checkbox element to be in the *checked* state when the page is first loaded:

```
<TD><INPUT TYPE="checkbox" NAME="help"
           CHECKED></TD>
```

So when the user clicks into the `date` text box (giving it *focus*), the *autohelp()* function is invoked. We have left it to the user to uncheck the checkbox before clicking into the `date` box if he/she does not need any help.

When the `datehelp.htm` window is closed, a value is returned to *helpdate* which is not *null*. Therefore, when a user focuses on the date box again, the autohelp() function will fail because *helpdate* is no longer equal to *null*. This approach assumes that having read the help once, the user does not want it popping up each time the date box is focused on. It also prevents infinite looping (see below).

But more important, it also prevents some browsers from being caught in a loop which will cause the help window to keep coming up so that the user cannot do anything else. Netscape fails completely when this occurs and simply keeps on showing the help window again each time the window is closed. Internet Explorer does something similar.

This is one of the dangers of using the *onFocus* event handler. It is easy to get caught up in an *infinite* (ever repeating) loop. We then have to use Windows Task Manager to end the application. In the above code, assigning a value to *helpdate* which is not *null*, is one way of preventing the *onFocus* event handler from repeating for ever. There are other ways, for example, by putting in a button which when clicked will close the window as discussed in Exercise 18, page 106.

3. In the INPUT text element called *date*, this.form is used as an argument which is passed to the *autohelp* function via the *onFocus* event. It is now a reference to the form in which the date element is contained, namely, the form NAMEd dateform. Therefore:

this.form is equivalent to document.dateform

```
<INPUT TYPE=text SIZE=10 NAME="date"
 onFocus="autohelp(this.form,'datehelp.htm')">
```

If we had used this by itself, it would refer to the element text box - date. If you look back to the *autohelp* function, it is testing to see whether the checkbox called *help* is checked or not. *help* is one of the other form's elements but not the text element called *date*. By itself this would refer only to the text box *date*. But by passing this.form as an argument to *autohelp*, we can specify any of the elements in the form dateform.

In the following, obj2 will be replaced by this.form

```
function autohelp(obj2, file) {
    if ((obj2.help.checked == true) ...
```

and is equivalent to:

```
    if ( (this.form.help.checked == true) ...
```

which is equivalent to:

```
if ((document.formdate.help.checked == true) ...
```

We could have used the above, but the idea is get you familiar with using the *this* keyword and to know how to use it correctly.

4. As the program stands, there is nothing to stop a user entering the following into the `date` box and the form would be submitted quite happily: `aa/bb/cc` or even `dd/mm/yy` - the latter not being beyond the capability of some users. Likewise, `55/34/99` would also be accepted.

You can now begin to see that checking even a simple form is not trivial and involves much painstaking effort on the part of a thorough programmer. When I began teaching programming several decades ago, it was always important to point out to students that a working program is about 10% of the final code, error checking comprises some 60% and the other 30% is in-line documentation - explanatory comments within the code.

Exercise 35: *Combining it all together (see page 211)*

We shall create an application form for a mountaineering post. Applicants have to be in the age range of 18 - 35. We could also have allowed a user to make three mistakes when entering data into the date of birth box. If they exceed this, we would not permit them to submit the form - assuming that they would inevitably pose a threat to anyone on a climbing trip. (Try it yourself in Test 13.8). Here is the code and comments follow.

Tip: These scripts are now beginning to get quite large. A common approach for many programmers is to begin by creating the basic HTML bit by bit and to keep viewing it in a browser to make sure that it is working correctly. Once the HTML is correct, then the scripts can be added one by one, viewing and testing each one in the browser and gradually building up to the grand finale. It is asking for trouble if you write all your scripts and expect them all to work first time. Do one, get it right and then do the next.

```
<HEAD> <TITLE>Mountaineering Application Form
Ex35. </TITLE>
<SCRIPT LANGUAGE="Javascript">
   //sets the focus on to the fullname box.
function setfocus() {
  document.mountain.fullname.focus();} //EoFn
// check for empty strings
function isempty(obj) {
  if (obj.value == "") {
    alert("The " + obj.name
        + " field must be completed!");
    obj.focus();
    return false; }   // End of IF
 /* whichever return is met will close the
    function. Only one will be encountered.*/
    return true;
}  // EoFn isempty
// check age in 18-35 range
function checkage(objage,lowage,highage){
 userage = objage.value;

if ((userage < lowage) || (userage > highage))
   {alert("Sorry you are either past it or "
         + "too young! ");
    objage.value="";
    return false; }
 else { return true;
    } // EofIF
} //EoFn checkage

function checkdata(f) {
// check all details
  alert("Details are being checked before"
      + " being sent off.");
  if ( (isempty(f.fullname))
        && (isempty(f.email))
        && (isempty(f.postcode))
        && (isempty(f.age))
        && (checkage(f.age,18,35))
     )  // end of the conditions to test
```

```
{ f.send.value = "Details Sent.";
        alert("You will be notified via your"
            + " e-mail address within"
            + " the next 20 days.");
        f.submit();}
   else {
        alert("Sorry Details cannot be sent.") }
} //EoFn
</SCRIPT>
<BODY onLoad="setfocus()" >
<CENTER>
<FONT SIZE=3 FACE="ARIAL">
3 Mountaineering Posts Available</FONT>
</CENTER>
<IMG SRC="images/Mountain.gif" ALIGN=right>
<TABLE>
<FORM ACTION="server.cgi"
      METHOD="post" NAME="mountain" >
<TR><TD>Full Name:<BR>
<INPUT TYPE=text SIZE=25 NAME="fullname">
<TR><TD>E-mail address:<BR>
<INPUT TYPE=text SIZE=25 NAME="email">
<TR><TD>Post code<BR>
<INPUT TYPE=text SIZE=25 NAME="postcode">
<TR>
<TD>Age:<BR>
<INPUT TYPE=text SIZE=10 NAME="age">
<TR>
<TD><INPUT TYPE="button" VALUE="Send Details"
     NAME="send"
     onClick="checkdata(this.form)">
</TABLE>
</FORM>
<ADDRESS>Mountain-Form-Ex35.htm</ADDRESS>
</BODY>
```

Notes:

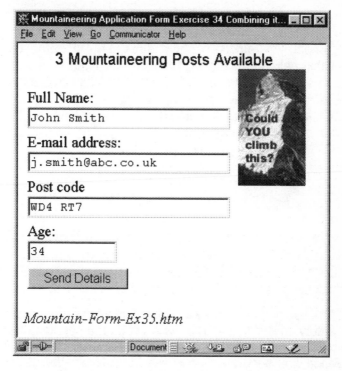

1. This code deserves careful study. The focus is set on the *Fullname* box via the *onLoad* event handler in BODY.

```
<BODY onLoad="setfocus()">
```

2. Note that there is *one* function - `isempty()` - which tests to see whether the *fullname, e-mail, postcode* and *age* text boxes are empty. In Exercise 30, we had to do a separate `if` test for each one. By using the `this` keyword we are now able to reduce the amount of typing and the size of the script.

13: **Further Form Validation**

In the following:

```
onClick="checkdata(this.form)">
```

`this.form` is passed as an argument to the dummy argument of function `checkdata(f)`. In turn, this function calls the *isempty()* function four times. Each call passes one of the INPUT object names: `fullname`, `email`, `postcode` and `age` along with `this.form`. The latter will replace the dummy argument `f`.

```
if ( (isempty(f.fullname))
        && (isempty(f.email))
        && (isempty(f.postcode))
        && (isempty(f.age))
        && (checkage(f.age,18,35))
    )
```

The above is worth looking at closely. Remember that `this.form` is equivalent to `document.mountain`. Thus: `f.fullname` becomes `this.form.fullname` which becomes: `document.mountain.fullname`

3. The user's age is checked twice. Once to see whether it is empty, and, if it is, the *focus* is put on the offending text box so that the user can begin to type in straight away. A second and separate test is used to see whether it lies within the given range. So, `age` is checked by two different functions: *isempty()* and *checkage()*.

4. The *isempty()* function checks whatever text box is passed to it as its argument. If it finds no data, that box will have its focus set and the function will return *false*. If the box is not empty, it merely returns *true*. By returning *false*, any one of the `if` statement's conditions in the *checkdata()* function will fail causing the entire if-condition to fail. Remember that when using the logical AND (&&), all tests must be true for the whole condition to prove true.

5. Although we have not done so in our code, we could check that at least an @ symbol appears in the e-mail address. We have to hope that the rest is correct since there is a limit to what can be tested.

Here is how we could have tested for the @ symbol:

```
if ( (isempty(f.fullname))
   && (isempty(f.email))
   && (checkmail(f.email.value,f.email))
.............. etc .... // end of if

// check that at least @ appears
function checkmail(emailvalue,emailobj) {
   if (emailvalue.indexOf("@") == -1)
     { alert("Are you sure this is a proper
             e-mail address?");
      emailobj.focus();
      return false;
        }
   else { return true;} // EofIF
} // EoFn
```

In the above code, we pass two arguments to *checkmail()*. The first (f.email.value) passes the *value* of the email object, in other words, whatever the user has typed in as the e-mail address. f will be replaced by this.form.

The second passes just f.email so that we can put the *focus* back on to it.

All these arguments get a bit confusing. But if you trace it through, it should make sense. It begins with:

- checkdata(this.form) which is invoked by the *onClick* handler when the send button is clicked
- in the declaration of function checkdata(f) this.form will be substituted wherever the dummy argument f appears

■ the above *checkdata()* function calls other functions and its dummy argument f (which is really this.form) will be substituted for those functions' dummy arguments.

In other words, this.form is passed to one function which passes it to another, and so on.

What we have learnt

In this chapter we have looked at various tests which can be carried out on data entered into forms. You should be able to appreciate how painstaking this can become. Much of a programmer's work is not so much creating a script which works but in testing for all possible errors which users can generate. We have not exhausted the possibilities by any means.

The *indexOf()* method was introduced to show how characters or phrases can be found in text strings. If not found, then -1 is returned which can be trapped via an if statement and appropriate steps taken.

We have seen how to use this. Not only does it cut down the amount of typing (and typing errors), but it can reduce the amount of code by using one function to work on different elements of a form.

When using *logical* operators, brackets are required around each expression in the if statement.

The *length* property can be used when we need to force users to enter a fixed number of characters.

Test: Chap 13

13.1 In the following, which are comparison operators and which are logical operators? && <= == ||

13.2 In the following string:

```
astring="The Owl and the Pussycat went to
sea"
```

how would you find the second occurrence of the lowercase:

a) 'w'
b) 'o' ?

13.3 What are the following: - event handlers, methods, user defined functions, objects or properties?

indexOf()
length
myfunction()
onChange
onFocus
onSubmit
submit()
this

13.4 What value is returned by *indexOf()* if its argument is not found in the given string?

13.5 Can you send form-data via e-mail (mailto:) using the submit() method?

13.6 What does *focus* mean?

13.7 When we were testing for two words, we decided to search the string for a space. If it were found, we assumed that there were two words. However, what is to stop a user from entering one word followed by a space? This would meet the requirement of our test but would still be incorrect. How could you test for this type of error?

[Hint: one way could involve the use of the *length* property.]

13: Further Form Validation

13.8 Add some extra code to Exercise 35 which will prevent the form from being submitted if a user makes more than three attempts to submit his/her application.

[Hint: It is quite simple and involves adding one to a count each time the checkdata function is called.]

FOURTEEN:

Animating Images

In this section we shall see how to animate *gif* images. There are some excellent packages around which will do much more but there is something we can all try and have a little amusement at the same time. It also saves having to install and learn new programs when we can do simple things more quickly in JavaScript.

Images can be animated by repeatedly displaying a series of individual images in quick succession, just like cartoons and films. To achieve the effect, we make use of the following JavaScript features:

- the *image* object
- *pre-loading* images
- *arrays* and *for* loops
- *setTimeout*() and its companion *clearTimeout*()

We shall examine each of these in relation to Exercise 36.

Exercise 36: *Animating Images*
Basically, we have five separate images, each of which is displayed in quick succession for a period of 500 milliseconds (½ second). They can be *gif* or *jpg* files.

Animate-1-Ex36.htm

The secret is to store the images in an *array* and then to extract each one in quick succession and display it for a certain number of milliseconds. But before we talk about arrays, we can look at a simple approach.

The Image object
We start off by displaying the first image when the page is being loaded: `<IMG SRC= "Love-0.gif">`

By repeatedly assigning different images to the SRC attribute of the above image tag, via JavaScript code, we can animate the images. The *src* is a property of the image object. So we need to create a new image object so that we can get to its *src* property and assign an image.

(We had to do the same with the Date object, in Chapter 11, when we needed to manipulate the various Date methods. Objects have methods and properties. But some objects, such as the image object, have no methods, only properties. Some objects have event handlers, some do not. We shall look at one of the image object's event handlers later.)

A new image object is created by the *new* operator which we have already used when creating new Date and String objects.

```
image1 = new Image()
```

Now that we have a new image object, we can get to its *src* property and assign any image to it:

```
image1.src = "Love-1.gif"
```

The following would create five image objects and assign an image to each one via its *src* property:

```
// create the image object
image0 = new Image()
// assign an image to its src property
 image0.src = "images/Love-0.gif"

// repeat for the rest
image1 = new Image()
 image1.src = "images/Love-1.gif"
image2 = new Image()
 image2.src = "images/Love-2.gif"
image3 = new Image()
 image3.src = "images/Love-3.gif"
image4 = new Image()
 image4.src = "images/Love-4.gif"
```

14: <u>Animating Images</u>

Pre-Loading images
We obviously do not want all five images to be displayed on the Web page when the page is being loaded. Neither do we want to force the browser to have to travel over the *Internet* to fetch each image each time we want to re-display a new image. It would take forever!

The trick is to load and store all the images *before* the page is displayed so that whenever we want to use them, they can appear instantaneously. This is called *pre-loading*. Pre-loaded images are stored safely by the browser inside the computer's memory until they are needed.

How is it done? Simply by putting the code on page 223 within <SCRIPT> tags within the <HEAD> tags of the document. It is that simple.

As the browser reads the code in the <HEAD> of the Web page, it will fetch each image and store them safely away in a *cache* memory, ready to be accessed when required.

However, the above code is clumsy. What we need is some simple mechanism whereby we can more easily refer to each image. This is done by the use of an *array*. We have not covered arrays so far, but they form an important part of any programming language. We shall have to digress for the moment to discuss arrays and then return to our exercise to see how an array can help us to extract each image from the cache memory.

Lists or *Arrays*:
All of us make lists from time to time:

- shopping lists
- a list of people to send wedding invitations to
- tasks to perform, etc.

In a shopping list, each item is different but they are all related to what we need to buy. Each person in our wedding list is different but they are all related in that we want to invite each one to a wedding.

A shopping list would look something like the following:

JavaScript has *arrays* which are, in effect, lists of individual items all related in some way. When loading Web pages, a browser creates many arrays. For example, all our images are stored in an *image array*. (We are going to make our own.)

1. Butter
2. Milk
3. Cat food
4. Kettle descaler
etc...

All the forms we use are likewise stored in a *form array*. There is an array for storing all our hyperlinks when using the anchor tag. Indeed, the string text, *'The Owl and the Pussycat went to sea'*, used in `indexof-1.htm` on page 196, would be stored in a *string array*. Each character, including spaces, is numbered according to its position in the array. That is how JavaScript is able to find out where a character is and what its index is so that it can return its position.

In the above shopping list, we could refer to *Cat food* as being the third item in the list. The 'w' of 'The Owl' would be in the sixth position in the string array, index number 5!

Arrays play a fundamental role in programming. From the earliest days of computing, it has been the means whereby programmers can store related information inside a computer's memory and whereby they can refer to or find one item in the list as opposed to any other. It is a simple yet effective way for programmers to keep track of where they have stored their data. Variables also store data but they contain only a *single* item. An array is used when *many* items need to be kept together.

This is precisely what we need to do with our images. Store them altogether in an array and then access each one separately for display.

Unlike us, browsers and JavaScript begin storing items at zero rather than one. These numbers are called *indices* and each index number refers to one of the elements in the array. Each index is enclosed in *square brackets* after the array name. Thus, the first of our five images could be referenced by the following:

theImages[0] to refer to Love-0.gif.

As a page is being loaded, the browser keeps track of all the images it loads in an internal array. As it loads each one, it is stored in the position it occupies on the Web page. Thus, the first image is loaded into an image array at index 0, the second into index 1, etc. So what has this to do with animating our Web images?

Since it is not sensible for us to interfere with the browser's internal image array, we first have to create our own array. We can then store the images in this array and manipulate them using the index number. Here is how an array is created.

theImages = new Array(5);

We use the *new* operator and the *Array* object to create an array which we have called theImages. The Array object specifies how many locations of memory to set aside for the array. We have five images, so we want an array with five locations. I have called the original images: Love-0.gif to Love-4.gif. *theImages* array would look like:

Contents of `theImages` **Array**	Index
Love-0.gif	[0]
Love-1.gif	[1]
Love-2.gif	[2]
Love-3.gif	[3]
Love-4.gif	[4]

But how do we store each of the images into our own *theImages* array? By a simple assignment statement.

```
theImages[0].src = "Love-0.gif"
...
theImages[4].src = "Love-4.gif"
```

However, and this is the important bit, each element in the array must be made into an *image object*, so that we can refer to its *src* property. This is how it is achieved:

```
<HEAD>
<SCRIPT>
//Preload images to be animated
// first create an array to hold our five images
theImages = new Array(5);

// now make the first an image object
theImages[0] = new Image()

// then assign an image to its src property
 theImages[0].src = "Love-0.gif"

// repeat for each element in the array
theImages[1] = new Image()
 theImages[1].src = "Love-1.gif"
theImages[2] = new Image()
 theImages[2].src = "Love-2.gif"
theImages[3] = new Image()
 theImages[3].src = "Love-3.gif"
theImages[4] = new Image()
 theImages[4].src = "Love-4.gif"
</SCRIPT>
```

What we are doing is to make each array element an image object so that we can specify what its *src* property should be. But rather than repeat all of the above (ten lines of code in total), we make use of a *for* loop and reduce our code to three lines.

(Note the use of the concatenate *operator to join the digit to the name of each image using the* for *index variable* i *.)*

```
for (i=0; i<5; i++) {
    theImages[i] = new Image();
    theImages[i].src = "Love-" + i + ".gif";}
```

We can refer to this array by using the array name and an index value within a *for* loop. This is an extremely efficient yet short piece of code. Note how the *for* loop's index variable, i, is used not only to refer to the array index but also to the digit in each image name. We have now pre-loaded all our images into an array from which we can retrieve them when required.

setTimeout()

The last thing we need to look at is a mechanism for repeatedly displaying the images. This can be done with *setTimeout()*, a method of the window object. (This method can be assigned to a variable which can then be used by the *clearTimeout()* method. See *Notes* below.)

```
abc = setTimeout('expression', delaytime)
```

The *expression* is a string containing JavaScript code which will be executed after the *delaytime* has elapsed. The latter must be in milliseconds.

In the following, when the browser meets the <IMG> tag, the *onLoad* event handler invokes the animate() function after a set time has elapsed. Essentially, this function assigns a new image to the *src* property of the image object named animation.

```
<IMG NAME="animation" SRC="Love-0.gif"
    onLoad="setTimeout('animate()', delay)">
```

We now have all the elements required to write our code which will animate our images.

Exercise 36: *revisited*
We shall now examine the following code in detail and, draw together all the points we have discussed.

```
<HEAD><TITLE>Amimating Gifs </TITLE>
<SCRIPT LANGUAGE="Javascript">
delay = 500; imageNum=0;
//Preload animated images
theImages = new Array(5);
for (i=0; i<5; i++) {
   theImages[i] = new Image();
   theImages[i].src = "Love-" + i + ".gif";}
// End of pre-loading
function animate() {
//assign another image from the image array
 document.animation.src =
             theImages[imageNum].src;
 imageNum++;
 if (imageNum > 4) {
     imageNum = 0;
    } // EofIF
 } // EoFn animate()
function slower() {
delay = delay + 100;
 if (delay > 4000) delay=4000;
} //EoFn slower()
function faster() {
delay = delay - 100;
 if (delay < 0) delay=0;
} //EoFn faster()
</SCRIPT>
</HEAD>
```

```
<BODY>
<B><TT>Do you believe in Love at First sight?
</TT></B><P>
<IMG NAME="animation" SRC="Love-0.gif"
    onLoad="setTimeout('animate()', delay)">
<FORM NAME=form1>
<INPUT TYPE=button Value=Slower
    onClick="slower()">
<INPUT TYPE=button Value=Faster
    onClick="faster()">
</FORM>
<ADDRESS>Animate-1-Ex36.htm</ADDRESS>
</BODY>
```

Notes:

1. As the page is being loaded, the browser will execute the <SCRIPT> code in the HEAD. This begins by assigning values to the delay and imageNum global variables and then creates an array with five elements.

```
delay    = 500;
imageNum = 0;

//Preload animated images
theImages = new Array(5);
```

The *for* loop which follows causes our images to be pre-loaded into this array by creating an image object for each element and assigning one of the five images to the object's *src* property. Note how succinct this piece of code is.

It is also worth noting how the *concatenate* operator is used to add the image digit (0, 1, .. 4) to each image name: Love-*0*.gif, Love-*1*.gif, etc., by using the *for* loop's index variable i. A neat use of the *for* loop.

```
//Preload animated images
theImages = new Array(5);
```

- 226 -

```
for (i=0; i<5; i++) {
    theImages[i] = new Image();
    theImages[i].src = "Love-" + i + ".gif";
}
```

The three functions, *animate(), slower()* & *faster(),* are stored away by the browser for later use.

2. In the BODY we display the first image. Since most HTML elements (tags) are JavaScript objects, the <IMG> tag is, therefore, an object which has a *src* property. This tag also has an *onLoad* event handler.

It is this handler which calls the *setTimeout* method which, in turn, calls the *animate()* function after a delay time of 500 milliseconds - ½ a minute.

```
<IMG NAME="animation" SRC="Love-0.gif"
    onLoad="setTimeout('animate()', delay)">
```

Remember that the delay time has been set in the <SCRIPT> tags of HEAD: delay = 500;

3. The *animate()* function assigns one of the images held in the image array to the *src* property of the document's animation image object. Initially, this will be the one associated with index 0 since imageNum was set to zero at the start of the script.

```
document.animation.src =
            theImages[imageNum].src;
imageNum++;
```

Variable imageNum has 1 added to it, using the *increment* operator.

The next piece of code tests to see whether imageNum is greater than 4, since the five images in the image array are numbered 0 - 4. If true, its value is reset to zero so that the five images can be re-displayed in sequence. If imageNum is not greater than 4, nothing happens. In either case, the function will then stop.

So how does the *animate()* function become invoked for a *second* and *third* time, etc? We can appreciate that it is automatically invoked when the Love-0.gif image is first loaded when the browser displays the Web page.

Well, every time a new image is being loaded via the *animate()* function, the <IMG> tag's *onLoad* event handler will be triggered again. Follow through the code to prove this.

4. We have added a *slower* button and a *faster* button. These have event handlers which call the *slower()* function and the *faster()* function respectively.

```
function slower() {
delay = delay + 100;
 if (delay > 4000) delay=4000;
} //EoFn slower()
```

The above function simply increases the delay time by 100 milliseconds each time the *slower* button is clicked.

```
function faster() {
delay = delay - 100;
 if (delay < 0) delay=0;
} //EoFn faster()
```

The above function subtracts 100 milliseconds from the delay time at each click of the faster button. But, we need to make sure that it does not fall below 0. (Note how the omission of brackets around the if code, makes for difficult reading. Not good practice!)

5. Finally, we have **not** been courteous and allowed the user to stop the animation. We should include one if we do not wish to drive our readers mad. This is left as a Test

exercise for you to complete. You will need to use the *clearTimeout()* method which works as follows:

```
clearTimeout(setTimeoutID)
```

It takes one argument and will cancel the execution of the *setTimeout()* code. Recall what we said earlier: that the *setTimeout* could be assigned to a variable. That variable is what is used as the argument for the *clearTimeout()* method.

```
onLoad = "stopit = setTimeout( 'code',
                                delaytime)"
....
...  clearTimeout(stopit)
```

Area Hot Spots

In the above, we have created some hot spots which when clicked will change the image to another season, as shown on the next page. Also, note how we display some text for a few seconds - "Click on a season." - and then hide it again using the window object's *setTimeout()* method. The text was created as an image file, *ashtext.gif*.

The *Ash Tree* through the Seasons

Winter

Spring Time

Summer Time

Autumn

Autumnal Season

ash-tree.htm

I got rid of the image-text by replacing it with an empty image. The user has clicked the Autumn *hot spot* to change the image to the Ash tree in Autumn. Here is the code.

```
<head>
<title>Ash Tree through the Seasons </title>
<script language="Javascript">
function change(season) {
   if (season == "winter") {
    document.img1.src="images/winter-tree.gif";
   } //EofIF
  if (season == "spring") {
   document.img1.src = "images/spring-tree.gif";
   } //EofIF
  if (season == "summer") {
   document.img1.src = "images/summer-tree.gif";
  } //EofIF
  if (season == "autumn") {
   document.img1.src = "images/autumn-tree.gif";
  } //EofIF
} //EoFn change()
```

```
function showit() {
document.hideimage.src="images/ashtext.gif";
setTimeout('hideit()',3000);} // EoFn
function hideit() {
document.hideimage.src="images/notext.gif";
} // EoFn
</script>
</head>
<body onload="x=setTimeout('showit()',2000)">
<h2>The <i>Ash Tree</i> through the Seasons</h2>
<img src="images/notext.gif" name="hideimage">
<table width="100%">
<tr> <td width="40%">
<img src="images/area-ash.gif"
     border="0" usemap="#ashtree">
</td>
<td width="50%">
<img src="images/winter-tree.gif"
     name="img1">
</td>
</table>
<a name="stay"> </a>
<map name="ashtree">
<area href="#stay"
      alt="The Winter Look"
      shape="rect"
      coords="150,46,203,55"
      onclick="change('winter')">
<area href="#stay"
      alt="The Spring Look"
      shape="rect"
      coords="123,66,225,73"
      onclick="change('spring')">
<area href="#stay"
      alt="The Summer Look"
      shape="rect"
      coords="125,90,227,100"
      onclick="change('summer')">
```

```
<area href="#stay"
      alt="The Autumn Look"
      shape="rect"
      coords="159,113,239,123"
      onclick="change('autumn')">
</map>
<address>ash-tree.htm</address>
</body>
```

Note:
When the page has been loaded, the *setTimeout()* method calls *showit()* after 2 seconds. This function re-assigns a new image to the one named `hideimage`. The trick was to place an empty image, called `notext.gif`, when the page was first loaded after the heading. This was simply a transparent gif image of a given size. The same size image was given some text and saved with the name `ashtext.gif`. It was necessary to have both images the same size to prevent the web page jumping in size.

What we have learnt
We have seen how to animate images by repeatedly displaying a series of images in quick succession. We have seen how useful an array can be to store images so that we can refer to any one of them using the array's *index* number and that the numbering begins at zero.

We discovered that browsers store many HTML elements in internal arrays (forms, anchors, images, strings, and so on). The idea behind these arrays, is that when the browser needs to refresh the screen, it has all the information it requires.

Images to be animated should be pre-loaded so that when they are required for animation they can be accessed instantaneously without the need to travel over the Internet to retrieve them.

The *for* loop proved to be an efficient programming tool for assigning images to an array. We saw that its index variable can be used to refer to any one of the array's index numbers.

Using the window's *setTimeout()* method allowed us to control the time for each displayed image. It has a companion method, *clearTimeout()*, which can stop the execution of the *setTimeout()* code.

Now that we understand how the `setTimeout()` function works, we can use it to create a live clock. Try it yourself first in Test 14.5 and then look at my attempt in the Test-Answers Chapter.

Jargon

array: this is an internal storage area in the computer's memory where data can be stored and retrieved when required. It is part of the core language of JavaScript 1.1.

User defined arrays are created by using the *new* operator and the *Array* object.

```
arrayName = new Array(10)
arrayName = new Array("fire", "water",
                      "earth", "wind")
```

When an array is created, all the elements are initially set to *null*, unless you assign values as in the second example above. Any element of an array can be referenced in either of the following ways - the 4th element in both cases:

```
arrayName[3]
arrayName["wind"]
```

cache: a special area of memory where application programs store data for their own use.

pre-load: loading, for example, images before the Web page is fully displayed. It is sometimes convenient to load images prior to animating them.

Test: Chap 14

14.1. Add an extra button which will allow the user to stop the animation in Exercise 36. [Hint: Where will the *clearTimeout()* method have to be placed?]

14.2 What steps are involved in order to assign a new image to the *src* property of an image array object? [Hint: you should have three steps.]

14.3 There are three types of brackets used in JavaScript code: { } [] and (). Give an example of when each one is used.

14.4 How many ways can you get a window, which you have created and opened, to close itself?

14.5 Use the `setTimeout()` function to create a live clock. [Hint: We need to use this method so that the clock can be updated every second - 1000 milliseconds.]

— — — — — — — — — — — — — — — — — — — .

GIF - JPEG - TIFF Images

Browsers can display images provided they are in one of two formats, `.gif` or `.jpeg`. If you are interested in:

- which format to choose
- why they were invented for Web pages
- what is the ideal image size
- why some pictures lose quality
- what are *interlaced* gif images

then read on.

We begin with Internet speeds in order to explain why these formats were invented.

Speed v. Size of a Web Image File
The overall size of a Web document is an important factor
to keep in mind when creating it since this will affect how
long it takes to load. An HTML page usually consists of
two elements. The basic HTML code plus any JavaScript
and, secondly, images files. The HTML source code is
usually minute compared to any graphic file which that
page has to load. The source code could be 1K but an
image could well be 25+K.

At present most of the Internet community[1] still connects
via a 28.8K bytes per second modem from their homes.
You would be forgiven if you thought that, at that speed, a
50K byte Web page complete with image files would take
about 2 seconds to load. Unfortunately, a 50K byte Web
page is not sent in a continuous stream of bytes as one
single unit. A small fraction is sent (typically 256 bytes) but
the next fraction may not arrive until several seconds later
depending on the amount of traffic the host server has to
cope with. (See the Bibliography for a reference text on
the Internet and the WWW.)

It is recognised that a Web page of more than 50K bytes
takes an unacceptable time to arrive and display on the
average client screen. The ideal size for a Web page is
about 25K byes (it is really the *arrival* time that is the
important consideration).

What we discuss next is the size and format of the image
files which a browser has to load.

Scanning Images
Let us suppose that we scan a photograph which we want
to display on our Web page. After scanning the original,
the computerised picture must be saved as a separate file.

---

[1]   If you are working within a company Intranet using high-speed
direct lines, it may be a different matter.

But in which format do we save it? If you thought *gif* or *jpeg* you would be wrong. Many scanners cannot save in these formats. The best format to save it in, and one which is supported by most scanners, is TIFF (*Tag Image File Format*). Why? Because it is an industry standard. Almost all programs, except browsers, can read an image saved as a TIFF file; Word, PowerPoint, Excel and all image programs, for example, PhotoShop. The latter is another industry standard used by over 90% of professionals to touch up images.

Having improved our original photograph via one of the image processing programs, that program will then offer us the choice of saving the image in either *jpeg* or *gif* format.

TIFF, JPEG & GIF image formats

Most scanners can save an image in TIFF format - *Tag Image File Format* - to a very high quality. However, the resulting files (with `.tif` extensions) can run into megabyte sizes, far too large to transmit over the Internet. So, to transfer these files over the Internet, they have to be *compressed* (reduced in size) by using various Web encoding techniques. The image program will do this compression for us.

When HTML was developed, it was known that users would not tolerate the time taken for TIFF files to load. Therefore, two other image formats were especially devised for use on the Web: *GIF* (Graphics Interchange Format) and *JPEG* (*Joint Photographic Experts Group*), the latter having a `.jpg` extension on PCs.

GIF

Originally devised in 1987, Graphics Interchange Format files have a `.gif` filename extension. It is a format which all graphical web browsers can recognise. It is especially useful if the graphical image is a logo, an icon or a banner, where there is little variation in colour detail. It can store black-and-white, greyscale and colour images, although it is limited to 256 colours per image. It is also useful when *transparent* images are required. This allows any background colour on the web page to show through the transparent areas. It also allows for *interlacing*. Usually, images are built up pixel line by pixel line starting at the top and working to the bottom. Interlacing is a technique whereby groups of lines are displayed, interspersed throughout the image, so that the entire image is seen in more and more detail giving the viewer an overall 'picture' of the image from the outset.

It works as follows. When the entire image is decompressed, it is scanned in four passes resulting in four groups of scanned lines. In Table 14.1, we have 20 rows. It is a small image but it will illustrate the procedure.

1st pass:	every 8th line starting with row 0
2nd pass:	every 8th line starting with row 4
3rd pass:	every 4th line starting with row 2
4th pass:	every 2nd line starting with row 1

JPEG

Joint Photographic Experts Group is a format especially designed for storing photographic images. Its file extension is `.jpeg` or `.jpg`. It has a 24-bit colour depth and should be used when a high level of colour and detail must be preserved, for example with photographs.

Generally, speaking, JPEG format is better than GIF for photographic images. The quality is better and through its more sophisticated compression techniques the resulting files are smaller than an equivalent GIF version.

When saving an image in JPEG format, some image programs allow a *progressive* option to be chosen. It is the equivalent of the GIF interlaced format.

Row #	Interlace Pass			
0	1			
1				4
2			3	
3				4
4		2		
5				4
6			3	
7				4
8	1			
9				4
10			3	
11				4
12		2		
13				4
14			3	
15				4
16	1			
17				4
18			3	
19				4

Table 14.1: Interlacing passes

PNG

The last format we shall mention is the Portable Network Graphic (.png). Like GIF, it allows for transparency, interlacing and image compression. It has better colour quality than GIF so why have I given up on using png images? The problem is that Navigator and IE show the colours differently. The same image often looks much darker in IE than in Netscape, to the extent that the detail becomes blurred. Try it out and make up your own mind.

LZW - GIF's compression technique

A GIF file contains the image data in a compressed format. The browser 'unpacks' the file before displaying it. The compression technique used to create a GIF file is called LZW (from *Lempel* and *Ziv* who did the early research work at the Sperry Corporation and their colleague *Welch* who perfected it - initially to make more efficient use of hard discs).

LZW is a dictionary based data compression technique. The image is examined for patterns which occur repeatedly within it. A dictionary of these patterns is built up and a short code used for each pattern. Whenever the same pattern occurs again the code is substituted. This effectively compresses the file. When the file is decompressed by the browser, the real data is re-substituted for the code.

The decompressed file is an exact copy of the data before it was compressed. This is called a *lossless* compression because the original file does not lose any of its original data. Although the following is a simplification, let us suppose that there is an area of 20 red pixels, this could be coded as 20R. Another area of 20 red pixels could be coded as 20R so that three bytes (one for each character 2-0-R) rather than twenty bytes could be used.

LZW compression works best for images with regular large patterns or long runs of identical colour, for example, company logos, icons and buttons. However, for colour photographs where pixel colours change frequently and unpredictably GIF files will not compress well and would result in large files, hence the JPEG format.

JPEG compression

Colour photographs can be reduced to a tenth or fifteenth of their original file size when saved in JPEG format. The process is known as a *discrete cosine transform* and the result is a frequency map represented as a cosine wave. It gets worse! ` :) - *quantization coefficients* are involved. If this turns you on, I suggest you find further information from the web. But the end result is a loss of some of the original data - called *lossy*, unlike GIF files which are *non-lossy* or *lossless*.

GIF v JPEG

When you have a choice, which format should an image be saved in? It is a question of compromise in certain cases.

GIF files are *lossless* in that they do not lose any of the original image data. JPEG files are *lossy* since during the quantization stage of compression some data is thrown away and cannot be re-constituted.

GIF is restricted to 256 colours whereas JPEG can support 16 million. However, the latter will not reproduce well on a monitor which can only display 256 colours.

GIF files can be interlaced, JPEG files cannot. (However, there is a variant of JPEG - *JPEG Tile Image Pyramid*, JTIP, which can appear on a screen as a wave of successively detailed renderings. This is known as *progressive JPEG*.)

GIF files should be used for images which contain largish areas of the same colour, for example:

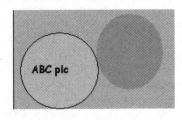

GIF files can be *transparent*, JPEG files cannot (for the time being). The 1989 revision of the GIF format - GIF 89a, allows pixels to be defined as transparent.

Colour photographs which typically do not have large areas of the same colour but are *continuous* in colour should be saved in JPEG format. As an example, I saved one photograph in both GIF (245Kbytes) and JPEG (44K). The JPEG reproduced slightly better on both the monitor screen and printer and was a much smaller file. The GIF proved larger since it had no large re-occurring patterns which could be compressed efficiently into a dictionary.

Dithering

The most noticeable difference among computer systems (*platforms*) is colour. However, we can easily adjust for this. Most colour computers today can display at least 256 different colours, often thousands and even millions of colours. This number is determined by the type of computer, the size and resolution of the monitor, and the amount of video RAM (VRAM) built into the computer. Most current computers can display millions of colours.

A computer's colour palette is simply all the colours it can display on the screen at one time. Imagine an artist painting a landscape. Let's say he/she has 256 tubes of paint, each a unique colour. If a colour is needed that is a little different from any tube colour, two or more of those tubes can be used to mix and create the needed colour.

When a computer mixes two or more of its colours to create a new colour, it's called *dithering*. The computer screen puts dots, called pixels, of the colours from its palette on the screen, very close together, hoping to fool your eye into seeing one uniform colour.

Unfortunately, this does not always work as planned. Often these dithered graphics will look so grainy the pixels become too obvious. Computers with more colours are more likely to have the exact colours needed and can simulate additional colours more closely, so the dithering becomes less noticeable. But it is not even that simple! ☺

Each of the main three platforms (Mac, PC, and UNIX) has its own unique palette of 256 colours. The Mac and PC platforms share 216 colours of the 256-color palette, but the UNIX palette has far fewer shared colours. So your graphic might look great on your PC, but it will look all dithered on a Mac if you use colours other than the ones shared by the Mac palette.

It's a good idea to consistently make use of the 216 shared Mac-and-PC colours, to avoid dithering on at least those platforms.

Transparency

Transparency allows one of the colours in an image (including black and white for B&W images) to become transparent. This allows the background colour to shine through. This can be seen in the previous illustration.

Every image is contained within a rectangular border. In order to hide this box and allow the background to show through, we need to make the background transparent.

Without a transparent background, the image's border box will be seen unless it happens to be the exact colour of the background, which is unlikely to be the case.

14: <u>Animating Images</u>

FIFTEEN

Further Programming Statements

In this section, we shall examine some other aspects of the JavaScript programming language. It will not always be possible to give practical examples of their use, so it is left to the reader to note the syntax and to use them should the need arise.

Loop statements
We have seen the *for* loop, but there is also a *while* loop. Loops are used to repeatedly execute a block of code until a certain condition is met. In addition, the *break* and the *continue* statements can be used within loops.

while statement
This repeats a loop as long as a specified condition evaluates to true. It looks like the following:

```
while (condition) {
   ... statements to perform
       while the condition is true ...
} // Eof While
... the carry on statement ...
```

When the condition becomes false, the statements within the loop stop executing and control passes to the statement following the loop, the *'carry on statement'* above.

The condition is tested the first time the *while* loop is encountered. If it is *true*, the loop statements are executed. When the closing curly bracket is encountered, the condition is tested again to determine whether to repeat the instructions.

The main difference between the *for* loop and the *while* loop lies in where the *initialise*, the *condition* and the *increment* statements are placed. In the *for* loop all three are contained within the round brackets:

```
for (initialise; condition-to-test; increment)
{ statements }
```

In the *while* loop, they are typically placed as follows:

```
    initialise;
    while (condition-to-test)
    { statements to be executed;
      increment; }
```

Warning: *Without an increment statement within the body of the while loop, it could be possible to loop for ever, an* infinite loop.

Example 1: The following *while* loop iterates as long as n is less than three:

```
x = 0;
n = 0;              // initialise control variable
while( n < 3 )  // condition
{   n++;            // increment -     n=n+1
    x += n;     // shorthand for:   x=x+n
} // EofWhile
```
... the carry on statements, if any, e.g.   ...
```
    alert("X has become " + x)
```

With each iteration, the loop increments n and adds that value to x. Therefore, x and n take on these values:

After the first pass: n = 1 and x = 1
After the second pass: n = 2 and x = 3
After the third pass   n = 3 and x = 6

After completing the third pass, the condition n<3 is no longer true, so the loop terminates.

Example 2: *An infinite loop:* Make sure the *condition* in a loop eventually becomes false, otherwise, the loop can never terminate. The statements in the following *while* loop execute forever because the condition never becomes false. A Boolean operator, true, has been used.

```
while (true) {
          alert("Hello, world"); }
```

The condition statement of the *while* loop can be any JavaScript code which can be evaluated to true or false.

do-while loop

This has been included in JavaScript 1.2. You need to specify: <SCRIPT LANGUAGE="Javascript1.2" >.

The main difference between the *while* and the *do-while* is that the latter will always execute the loop instructions at least once, simply because the test for the condition is made at the *end* of the loop rather than at the *start*.

```
do
{statements to be executed}
while (condition);   // semi-colon is required!
... the carry on statements ...
```

Example:

```
var i = 1;  // initialise
do {
  document.write(i + "<BR>") }
while (++i <= 10);   // increment and condition
```

There are a few oddities here in the syntax. The *do-while* loop must end with a semi-colon because unlike the *for* and *while* loops which begin and end with curly braces, the *do-while* construction is not set up in the same way. The *do* marks the start, the *while* marks the end.

Also, note the succinct way in which the increment *and* the condition are both contained within the while() making use of the increment operator.

There are not many situations where you always want the instructions in a loop to be executed at least once. So, all in all, it is a feature which is seldom used. Note that in some versions of Navigator 4, the *continue* statement (see below) causes an error when used in a *do-while*.

break statement

If a *break* statement is encountered within a *for* and *while* loop, it will always transfer control (what instruction to execute next) to the statement after the loop. Again, the situations when it might arise are few, but they do occur from time to time so it is worth knowing about.

It is usually found embedded within an *if* statement, thus:

```
function test()
  { var i = 0;        // initialise while
    while (i < 10) // while condition
  { if (dothis() == false)
      {
          alert(i + "Hallo! from IF.");
          break; // exit while loop ─────────┐
      }                                        │
    else                                       │
      { alert("Hallo! from ELSE.");            │
        repeat_something();                    │
      } // end of if & else                    │
    i++; // the increment for while            │
  } // end of while                            │
  document.write("Now for your big break!"); ◄─┘
} // EoFn test
```

Should the *dothis()* function return *false*, the *break* statement will terminate the *while* loop which, as the code stands, will write out the message: "Now for your big break!"

If it returns `true`, the *else* section is executed and i will be incremented. This forces the *while* statement to test its own condition again and as long as i<10 the *while* code will be repeated.

continue statement

The *continue* statement behaves differently to the *break* statement when used in a *for* or *while* loop. It does not exit the loop but will repeat the loop with a new iteration. Like the *break* statement, its syntax is a single statement:
`continue;`

When the *continue* statement is met, it stops the current iteration and the next iteration begins. However, note the following:

In a *for* loop, control is passed automatically to the increment before testing the condition.

In a *while* loop, control is passed straight to the condition, so *you have to make sure* that the control variable has been incremented.

Here is an example of the use of the continue statement. It is often employed to control the flow of functions. I have kept it as simple as possible to enable you to follow the logic. In practice the functions would be more complicated. What we want is to keep a track of how many goods someone has ordered and to display the total when they have finished their 'shopping'.

Note the use of the *continue*, *break* and *eval()* statements.

```
<HEAD>
<TITLE> Total items ordered </TITLE>
<SCRIPT>
function shopping() {
 totitems = 0;
 i=0; // initialise while condition
  while (i<20) { // no shoppaholics wanted    ◄────┐
   more=confirm("Do you want anything else?");      │
    if (more == true)                               │
     { domore();                                    │
       i++;                                          │
       continue; // do they want more goods?───────┘
     }
    else
     {
     alert("You are now at the Checkout.")
     } // EofIF
   doreport(totitems);
      break;  // stops while repeating    ─────────┐
  } // End of While                                 │
 alert("Thank you for shopping at SADA.")  ◄────────┘
} // End of shopping()function

function domore() {
 x = prompt("How many items?", "");
 thisitem = eval(x); // converts text x to a number
 totitems = thisitem + totitems;
 return totitems;
} // End of domore() function

function doreport(totitems) {
alert("You have ordered: " + totitems
       + " items.");
} // End of doreport()function
</SCRIPT>
</HEAD>
```

```
<BODY>
<h3>Fill Up your shopping basket</h3>
<form method="" action="">
<input type="button"
        value="Add to shopping basket."
        onClick="shopping()">
</form>
<ADDRESS>while-continue.htm</ADDRESS> </BODY>
```

Notes:

1. When the button is clicked, the shopping() function is invoked. This sets the total number of items to zero; initialises the *while* control variable and enters the while loop.

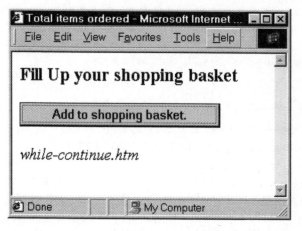

2. We have restricted the number of times the loop can repeat to prevent shoppaholics going too far.

3. The if statement tests to see whether more items are required, if *true*, the domore() function is called, the control variable is incremented and we continue with the while loop.

4. When the `if` becomes false, the `else` will display an alert box effectively saying that the bill will be calculated.

5. In either situation above, the `doreport()` function is invoked. This displays the total number of items. The *break* statement will be executed when the `doreport()` function has finished. If we did not have a *break*, the *while* loop would repeat again and again, for 20 times, even though the customer did not want any more items.

6. `domore()` issues a prompt box asking the customer to enter the number of goods required (in practice this would function would perform other tasks such as displaying a list of goods, and so on.) The number entered is stored in variable `x`, but remember that it will be a piece of text. Thus, we have converted it to a numerical value via the `eval()` method and stored it in `thisitem`. We add this to the total items already purchased.

7. The `doreport()` would of course calculate the goods bought and ask for payment details, etc.

8. Notice that no variable is preceded by the `var` keyword so that they are global in scope (see page 119).

Making more Decisions
else .. if
So far, we have used the `if` statement and sometimes used it in conjunction with the `else` statement. The latter will execute when the `if` block proves to be false. These allow for one of *two* actions to be performed. But suppose you have more than two possibilities? You then need to make use of the `else-if`. For example:

```
n = prompt("Enter a value in range 1-4.","")
if (n == 1)
  { alert("You entered 1.") }    // #1
```

```
else if (n == 2)
 { alert("You entered 2.") }      // #2
else if (n == 3)
 { alert("You entered 3.") }      // #3
else if (n == 4)
 { alert("You entered 4.") }      // #4
else
 { alert("Value " + n
        + " not in range." ) }   // #x
```

Note that the last statement is an *else* by itself. This is used to state what to do when *none* of the previous conditions has been met.

The Conditional Operator
Here is a strange beast which you may not wish to use but you may come across it in someone else's code. It has three parts and is the only ternary operator in JavaScript. It is a shorthand way of writing simple `if` statements.

```
x > 0 ? x*y : x*z
```

The first part must result in a Boolean value, usually the result of a comparison expression: `x > 0` but it could be something returned by a function.

If the result is true, the second part after the ? is executed: `x*y`, otherwise, the third part, after the colon, is executed: `x*z`
Here is the corresponding `if` statement :

```
    if (x>0)
     x*y;
    else
     x*z;
```

The switch statement
This is another decision making feature much loved by earnest programmers. However, it may prove useful to the

rest of us and, you never know, you may see it in some other script. The general syntax is:

```
switch (expression) {
  case x₁:
     .. code ..
   break;
  case x₂:
     .. code ..
   break;  and so on until...
  default:
     .. code ..
   break;
}  // Eof Switch
```

When a *switch* is executed, the *expression* is computed and then a case label is searched for which matches the expression's value. We have used x_1 and x_2 as the case values.. The case label consists of the keyword `case` followed by a *value* and ending with a colon: `case x₂:`

The values may be integer or real numbers, strings and Boolean values. They **cannot** be objects, arrays or functions. So this confines its possible uses.

When a match is found, the code within that *case* is executed. When the *break* statement is encountered, the whole process stops. (Note the semi-colon after *break*.) If a match is not found, the special *default* is used. Its code will be executed until the *break* is encountered. If the *default* is not present, the entire block of the switch code is skipped. Note that curly brackets enclose the entire switch code and that the `default` must not contain the keyword `case`.

Assume you need to check what number a user has entered, via a prompt box, within a given range; let us suppose the range is 1-5. Depending on the value, a given function needs to be invoked.

```
userdata = prompt("Enter a number in the"
                  + "range 1-5, please.", "");
usernum = eval(userdata);
switch (usernum) {
  case 1: // if 1 do this
     one();
     break;

  case 2: // if 2 do this
     two();
     break;

  case 3: // if 3 do this
     three();
     break;

  case 4: // if 4 do this
     four();
     break;

  case 5: // if 5 do this
     five();
     break;

  default: // if not in range, do this
     alert("Naughty!")
   break;
} // End of Switch
```

Notice that we converted the text typed into the prompt box to a number using the `eval()` method. However, we could have kept it as text and simply changed the case value to text:

```
case "1":, case "2":, etc.
```

A few really weird things!

The C programming language was developed by programmers for programmers. We all like to take shortcuts and programmers are no exception. What follows are some of the weird shortcuts developed for C and transcribed to JavaScript.

The increment & decrement operators
postfix `i++`
equivalent to `i = i+1` but takes place *after* some other action.

prefix `++i`
equivalent to `i = i+1` but takes place *before* some other action.

Try out the following:

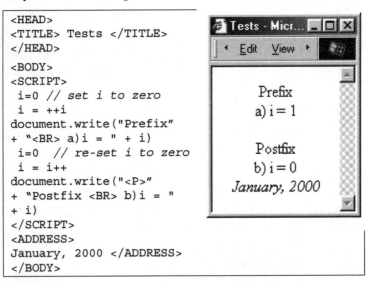

```
<HEAD>
<TITLE> Tests </TITLE>
</HEAD>
<BODY>
<SCRIPT>
 i=0 // set i to zero
 i = ++i
document.write("Prefix"
+ "<BR> a)i = " + i)
 i=0  // re-set i to zero
 i = i++
document.write("<P>"
+ "Postfix <BR> b)i = "
+ i)
</SCRIPT>
<ADDRESS>
January, 2000 </ADDRESS>
</BODY>
```

Notice how the variable `i` is set to zero in both a) & b). However, the prefix version in a) adds 1 to `i` and then proceeds with the rest of the script, whereas the postfix version in b) does not increment `i` until the same statement is met again.

Any variable name can be used, but due to the strong influence of Fortran i is the most commonly used variable in arithmetic programs, not x, surprisingly! (In Fortran i is an *integer* variable name, x is a *real* variable name.)

prefix decrement --j *& postfix decrement* j--
Behaves like the increment but subtracts one from j. It is not used much, but could be useful when working backwards through an array.

Multiple assignments: *i = j= k =89;*
Here, 89 is assigned to k, which is assigned (now having the value of 89) to j which is assigned to i. It might be worth remembering.

It is also useful to be aware that a for loop can take several initial and incremental statements but each must be separated by a comma:

```
for (j=1, p=3; j>=30; j++, p++) { ... }
```

Event handlers may also have multiple statements but each statement requires a closing semi-colon:

```
onClick= "one(); two(); three();"
```

Save time with these assignment statements:
You may come across this use in someone else's script, so it is necessary to be aware of them.

a += b is equivalent to: a = a+b
a *= b is equivalent to: a = a*b
a %= b is equivalent to: a = a%b

If you have not met the *modulo* operator before, it returns the remainder when the first value is divided by the second an integral number of times. a %= b

Thus, 5 % 2 results in remainder 1
    17 % 3 results in remainder 2

15: **Further Programming**

Condition

When using a conditional test in an `if` or `for loop`, the following is permissible:

```
if ( (a+b) == x) {.. do when true ..}
```

So too is this, where the return value of a function is used:

```
<SCRIPT>
function test(){ return 5; } // EoFn
.......
if (test() == 5)
  { document.write("test() returned 5") }
</SCRIPT>
```

This can turn your condition tests into powerful features.

Do Nothing

Do you remember that statements usually end with a semi-colon? In many languages, there is a 'do nothing' statement which, in JavaScript, is just the semi-colon by itself - ; - usually called the *empty statement*. It seldom has any practical value, but it can be the source of errors. What will the following *if* statement do in this careless piece of code?

```
x = 1;
if ( x == 1 ); // Oh my! End of IF
document.write( " x = 2");
document.write( "<BR> x <> 2");
```

Absolutely nothing! It is perfectly valid and it illustrates how careful the programmer must be. If you are not fully awake, you may inadvertently slip in the odd semi-colon.

Both of the *document.write* methods will be executed. But the *if* does nowt!

Finally, let us look at two other event handlers which may prove to be of use at some time.

onAbort event handler
In the following, an alert message appears when a user aborts the loading of an image (for example by clicking the browser's *Stop* button.)

```
<IMG NAME="verybig" SRC ="hugeimage.jpg"
 onAbort= "alert('You did not finish loading'
    + ' the image. Pity, it was very good.')"
```

onReset event handler
A reset event occurs when a user clicks the reset button. If the associated *form* has an *onReset* event handler, the JavaScript code will be executed.

```
<FORM NAME= "tosubmit_or_not_tosubmit"
 onReset="alert('Defaults will be'
                 + ' restored!')"
 onSubmit="alert('It is too late now!')">
<INPUT TYPE=submit VALUE="Send off form.">
<INPUT TYPE=reset  VALUE="Clear form."
        onClick="confirm('Are you sure?')">
</FORM>
```

Note how the *reset button* can take an `onclick` attribute, whereas the *onReset event* belongs to the *form* tag.

Test Chap 15:

15.1 How many types of *repetition* loops can you think of?

15.2 In an `if` statement which employs `else..if`'s, what is the purpose of the lone `else` statement?

15.3 What is the main syntactical difference between the `for` loop and the `while` loop?

15: <u>Further Programming</u>

15.4 What is this feature known as: `--j` ?

15.5 What is the difference between a variable which is *undefined* and one which has the *null* value?

SIXTEEN

Objects - Their Properties & Methods

We have mentioned several times that JavaScript has three parts to its language:

- the core language
- client side additions
- server side additions

Chapters 9 & 15 considered the core of the JavaScript language. These allow us to create programs which can:

- perform calculations using arithmetic operators
- decide which instruction to execute next (*if-else*)
- repeat a block of instructions (*while, for* loops)

Like all programming languages, JavaScript includes variables, arrays and operators. But JavaScript has something more!

Client and server additions to the basic core language allow the programmer to manipulate browser (client) features and server features. The bulk of this book has looked at the client-side features of JavaScript. It is here that the *objects* exist.

Client-side (and server-side, of course) JavaScript is an object oriented, some would say object based, programming language. That simply means that the programmer works with objects.

16: <u>Properties & Methods</u>

In this chapter, we shall concentrate on objects and their properties, methods and event handlers. Not all objects have all three, some have no properties only methods, others have properties but no methods. Some have properties and event handlers. It is time to sort out which object has what. But first, what are objects?

What are Objects?
In everyday life, objects abound - kettles, doors, chairs, cars, yea, even computers. Let us take the *car*.

We have to become somewhat philosophical here. There is no such 'thing' as a *car* or a *chair*. When I was studying Philosophy, I was surprised to be told this. But the blow was softened this way.

We all have a *concept* of a car but, as such, it does not exist as a physical entity. What does physically exist is a *particular instance* of a car. This means that a given instance of a car must have certain *properties*, such as a colour, a make, a model, and so on, as well as behave in a car-like manner. It must do 'car-things', such as move forward, reverse, move faster or slower, turn corners, stop. These comprise its functionality - the things motor cars do. You can think of many more.

When a new model is exhibited for the first time, we know it is a car although we have never seen it before. This is because it has the properties and behaviour common to our *concept* of a car. But we would not expect it to do 'non-car like actions' such as the washing-up or decorating the house.

That is enough philosophical discussion. How does this apply to JavaScript? We start with objects.

The client-side aspects of JavaScript allow us to manipulate the objects associated with a browser. We cannot use objects just by themselves because they do not exist. But we can refer to and, therefore, manipulate given *instances* of an object, which can and do exist.

Let us suppose that I want to change the colour of the document background. The object is `document`, by itself we can do little with it, but by specifying its `bgColor` property, I can refer to something which can exist, thus:

```
document.bgColor = 'lightblue'
```

The above assigns a lightblue colour to the document's property *bgColor*. One of the basic chores for a JavaScript programmer is to learn what properties, if any, each object can have.

What about an object's functionality? What can it do?

The document object can be asked to output a message by giving its *write() method* something to write out. Thus:

```
document.write("Here is a message.")
```

So the document object not only has properties but also methods. A *method* is the formal term for *function*, what an object can *do*, what *actions* it can perform. One of the things the document object can do is to write something out to the current page via its *write()* method, as shown above.

JavaScript programmers, therefore, have to know what, if any, methods (actions, functions) each object can take. In the table on page 334, we see that the *document* object has 4 *methods* and 8 *properties*. (There are in fact some 19 properties.)

Here is a more complicated example, whereby a property itself may become an object in its own right and as such may have its own properties and/or methods. In the following, the document object's *form property (form1)* is specified. HTML FORMs are properties of the document object. Forms, as we know from our knowledge of HTML, have INPUT elements of various kinds, textboxes, radio buttons, etc. These are the properties of the Form object rather than the document object.

```
document.form1.text1.focus();
```

Here, the document object's *form* property (form1) has become an object because a reference is made to one of its properties, the INPUT element NAMEd text1. In turn, text1 becomes an object because a reference is made to one of its methods, the *focus()* method.

This serves as a typical example of how a programmer sets the focus on to a particular instance of an object's property. What I want to do is to set the *focus* onto an INPUT element named text1. To do so, I have to specify the object of which text1 is a property. Well, text1 is a property of the form object, named form1 which happens to be a property of the document object.

Once you can appreciate what is going on in the above, you are well on your way to understanding what object oriented programming is all about and how it works. Note how each object/property is separated from its higher level by periods (full stops). This is the required syntax for writing object oriented statements.

Here is another example:

```
firstname = document.form1.text1.value
```

The *document* object is being made to reference its form1 property which in turn references its own text1 property. Because form1 is being made to reference its property (text1), form1 has to become an object, although it is also a property of the document object. So some properties can also be objects.

Likewise, in order to reference the `value` property of `text1`, the latter becomes an object although it is also a property of the `form1` object. The value is then assigned to a variable `firstname`. And that is what objects and their properties and methods are all about.

I admit I was confused at the start of my JavaScript experience. I could accept that an HTML form could be a property of the document object. "Ok! then it is a property." The confusion came when some book I would be reading would suddenly call it an *object*. "But I thought this was a property not an object." I would wail!

It comes down to the context in which something is used.

```
firstname = document.form1.text1.value
```

In the above, `text1` is used in two ways. First, as the property of the `form1` object. Secondly, as an object with its own *value* property.

In the tables which follow, we shall be specifying something along these lines:

window is an object which has a *document* property. So we latch onto the idea that document is a property, but in the next breath we shall state that document is an object with its own properties such as forms, bgColor, the <A> tag, etc.

window, in fact, is the only object we have seen so far which is not a property of anything else. It is a top-level object.

Event Handlers
So what are event handlers? They are neither properties nor methods. They are *attributes* of certain HTML tags to which a programmer can 'attach' some JavaScript code. Pure object oriented languages such as Java or C++

cannot manipulate HTML tags. This is something unique to JavaScript and was the reason why it was invented.

These attributes, such as *onClick*, *onMouseOut*, *onLoad*, are recognised only by the later versions of browsers - Internet Explorer 4 and Netscape 3 or higher. The event handlers were added to version 4 of HTML.

```
<BODY onLoad = "myload_function()">
```

This is why we separated event handlers from methods and properties in Appendix A. *onSubmit*, for example, is an event handler associated with the FORM tag. The fact that a form is a property of the document object and that it is also an object with its own properties is a separate matter.

What objects does client-side JavaScript possess?
Our next step is to see what browser objects are available to JavaScript.

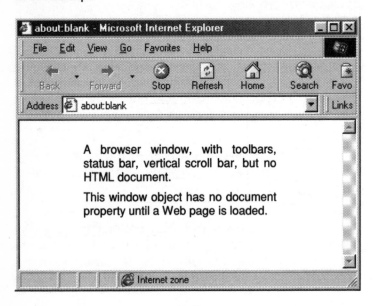

A browser window, with toolbars, status bar, vertical scroll bar, but no HTML document.

This window object has no document property until a Web page is loaded.

There is one main object, namely *window*, the window in which the browser program is displayed. What is shown within this window, apart from the various toolbars, scroll bars, etc., will be an HTML document. That document will then become the property of the window object.

The window object:

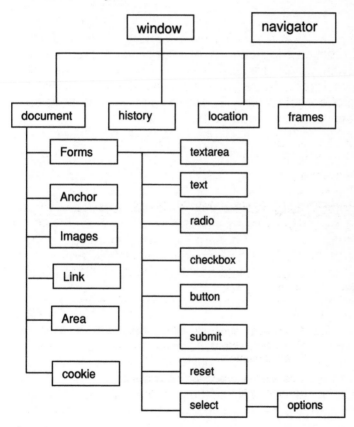

Figure: 16.1 Objects and their properties

There is a hierarchy of objects, with the window object as the master object at the topmost level. From Figure 16.1, we can see that window has four properties: document, history, location and frames. In turn, the document has several properties of its own: form, anchor, images, etc. form has its own properties: textarea, text boxes, radio buttons.

navigator is another object which, like *window*, does not belong to any other object. It provides information about the browser being used. We show two examples on pages 270 and 271.

In one of the tables in Appendix A, we summarise the various objects used in this text and list their properties and/or methods. It is not exhaustive but shows those features which are most commonly used.

In the following, we introduce the history and location objects. A detailed use of these objects is beyond the scope of this text since they are used to navigate through various sites users have visited or would wish to visit. To control such an exercise is non-trivial. However, we can illustrate their use and provide some simple examples of when they may prove useful to us. When shall then look at the navigator object.

history Object
The history object is a list of URLs which a user has visited. It is equivalent to clicking the GO menu in Netscape or the History button in IE. This is the list which is used by browsers when we click their *Forward* and *Back* buttons. Its use is limited but it can enable you to replace the current page with a new page. Using the history *back()* and *forward()* methods mimics the browser's Forward and Back buttons.

history Properties	
current	specifies URL of the current history entry
length	reflects the number of entries in the history list
next	specifies URL of the next history entry
previous	specifies URL of the previous history entry

You can reference the history entries by using the history array. These entries are *read-only* and cannot be changed by JavaScript code. Thus, **this is not permitted:**

```
history[0] = "http://isp.mine.com/"
```

history Methods	
back()	go back to a previously visited URL
forward()	go forward to a previously visited URL
go()	go to a particular previously visited URL
toString()	method of all objects. It returns a string representing the specified object

Examples:

`history.back();` performs the same action as clicking the Back button

`history.back(-2);` performs the same action as clicking the Back button *twice*

The following code determines whether the string 'micro' occurs in the first entry in the history array (index 0). If it does, *myfunction()* is called.

```
if (history[0].indexOf("micro") != -1)
{ myfunction(history[0])}
```

location Object

This object contains information about the current URL. It has several useful methods and properties but these are best left until you gain much more experience with JavaScript. You will need to be aware of the full details before using this object. However, here is one simple thing we can do. We shall invite a user to enter a URL and get our code to go to that Web site.

```
<HEAD>
<TITLE> Using the Location Object  </TITLE>
<SCRIPT>
function jumpto() {
window.location.href =
                    document.form1.userurl.value;
}  //EoFn
</SCRIPT>
</HEAD>

<BODY>
<FORM method="" action="" NAME="form1">
<INPUT TYPE=text NAME="userurl" SIZE=60>
<INPUT TYPE=button VALUE="Go for it!"
       onClick="jumpto()">
</FORM>
</BODY>
```

The *location* object is a property of the *window* object. In the above, we have used the `href` property of the *location* object. You need to include the `http://` protocol.

navigator object
This object contains information about the version of the browser being used. Here are two of its properties.

navigator Properties	
appName	specifies the name of the browser
appVersion	specifies version information of the browser

Examples:

The following displays the name of the browser:

```
document.write("The name of your browser"
                + " is " + navigator.appName)
```

Netscape displays:
```
The name of your browser is Netscape
```

Internet Explorer displays:
```
The name of your browser is Microsoft
Internet Explorer
```

By assigning the value of navigator.appName to a variable, you could find out which browser your reader is using and perform an appropriate action for either case.

```
x = navigator.appName
if ( x.indexOf("N") == 0) {
  do the Netscape thing ... }
else if (x.indexOf("M")== 0){
  do the Microsoft thing ...          }
else {
    document.write("Get yourself a life!") }
```

A *switch* could be useful here!

```
browsername = navigator.appName
switch (browsername) {
  case "Netscape": // do the Netscape things
     alert("Netscape is being used.")
     break;

  case "Microsoft Internet Explorer":
     // do the IE things
     alert("IE is being used")
```

```
      break;
   default: // if not in range, do this
      alert("Why not use Netscape or IE?")
      break;
} // EofSwitch
```

In the following code, we shall also print out the *appVersion* of the browser running on a Windows system:

```
<BODY>
<SCRIPT>
document.write("The name of the browser is "
             + navigator.appName
             + " and the version is: "
             + navigator.appVersion )
</SCRIPT>
<ADDRESS>appname.htm </ADDRESS>
</BODY>
```

Here is what Microsoft will display:

```
The name of the browser is Microsoft Internet
Explorer and the version is: 4.0 (compatible;
MSIE 4.01; Windows NT)
```

Here is what Netscape will display:

```
The name of the browser is Netscape and the
version is: 4.5 [en] (WinNT; I)
```

SEVENTEEN:

Cookies

New Material covered in this Chapter

- ASCII
- CGI
- document.cookie
- escape() and unescape()
- expires=
- lastModified
- substring()
- toGMTString()

In this final Chapter, we shall look at *cookies*. A cookie is a small piece of data - text information - which a Web server can store on your hard disc with the aid of your browser. It provides a browser with a 'memory'.

Suppose you request a particular Web page from some site. That site can include a cookie along with the Web page. The cookie will be stored temporarily by your browser on your hard disc so that should you re-visit the site, the cookie's information can be retrieved by your browser. Typically, the cookie's stored data is sent back by the browser to the server site which can then process the data. But that entails server-side JavaScript which is not within the scope of this text. However, we can do some things at the client end with a stored cookie, for example:

- to find out whether someone has visited the page before
- to remember a user's name

- to inform a user that the page has been modified since it was last viewed
- to note any preferences a user may have
- to add items to your shopping cart as you shop on-line

If you think about it, it is clearly more efficient for each individual browser to store such information rather than to expect the Web server to store all the information when there could well be thousands of visitors each day.

We must not get carried away with cookies. Despite all the hype, they have their limitations, as we shall see later, and are somewhat crude. The examples below will work with Netscape and behave similarly with Internet Explorer. However, there are some differences between the two main browsers. Netscape stores all its cookies in a single file called `cookie.txt` on PCs (see page 292 for Unix and Mac platforms). Internet Explorer stores each cookie as a separate file. The latter browser can only write cookies using scripts loaded from a server. Whereas, using Netscape, you can create the examples below at the client end.

Popular concepts and rumours about what cookies can do have reached mythical proportions, frightening the wits out of all and sundry. But since cookies store only text, they cannot contain programs sent by the server. Therefore, our files can neither be destroyed nor compromised. Cookies cannot damage our computers nor snoop around our hard discs. They can only identify a web user and send back short pieces of information. Information about where you come from and what pages you have visited already exists on the server's log files. Cookies simply make it easier to find this data. So let us be more relaxed about them.

To use cookies to their full potential is more of a server task, beyond the scope of this text. They were originally designed for CGI programming at the server side. The Common Gateway Interface, CGI, is the traditional protocol for transferring data stored between a browser and web servers. This data can be either cookies or information submitted by our readers via FORM elements.

However, we shall look at a few of the things we can do at the client-side, using JavaScript. We shall create cookies and store them on our readers' hard discs and if our page is revisited, our JavaScript code will redeem our cookies.

Cookie attributes
cookie is a property of the document object:
`document.cookie` and can take various attributes:

`expires=`	which specifies the cookie's lifetime
`path=`	specifies sub-folders where cookies are stored
`domain=`	the Web server's domain (e.g.: www.abc.com)
`secure`	unlike the others, this attribute takes a Boolean value of true or false.

By default, cookies are insecure and travel over insecure Internet connections, using the standard HTTP protocol. If the *secure* value is true, the cookie is sent via HTTPS connections or some other secure protocol.

With the exception of the *expires* attribute, the others require a knowledge of how a web server is set up and relates more to server-side JavaScript. So we shall not discuss them further. The one we shall consider is: *expires=date of expiry.*

Apart from the `expires=` attribute, a cookie requires a name and a value. The *value* of the *name* is the text to be stored, but can contain just a limited amount of information. See page 290.

Exercise 37: *Setting and retrieving a cookie*

In this exercise, we shall store a cookie on the user's browser and then read it back and display it in a text box.

```
<HEAD><TITLE>Cookie Set & Get</TITLE><SCRIPT>
function setcookie(){
var cookdate = new Date();
cookdate.setTime(cookdate.getTime()
                + 1000*60*30); // plus extra ½-hour
document.cookie = "Cookiea=My A
Cookie.;expires=" + cookdate.toGMTString();
} //EoFn setcookie
function getcookie() {
var cookstring = new String(document.cookie);
var cookname   = "Cookiea=";
var startpos   = cookstring.indexOf(cookname);

if (startpos != -1) {
   document.form1.cookvalue.value =
        cookstring.substring(startpos
                       + cookname.length);

   }
else
 { document.form1.cookvalue.value =
                       "Cookie not found!";

 }  //EofIf
} // EoFn  getcookie
</SCRIPT>
</HEAD>

<BODY><CENTER>
<FONT size="+2">
<B>Creating and Retrieving a Cookie</B>
</FONT>
<FORM method="" action="" NAME=form1>

<INPUT TYPE=button NAME=setcook
```

```
        VALUE="Create the Cookie"
        onClick="setcookie()">
<INPUT TYPE=button NAME=getcook
        VALUE="Retrieve the Cookie"
        onClick="getcookie()">
<INPUT TYPE=text NAME=cookvalue SIZE=15>
</CENTER>
</FORM>
<ADDRESS>cookie1.htm </ADDRESS>
</BODY>
```

Notes: This exercise introduces the basic use of cookies. All the exercises work for Netscape. Not all behave similarly in Internet Explorer.

1. First we set up three FORM elements. A button to create the cookie, a second button to retrieve it and a textbox to contain the cookie's information. All this is contained within the <BODY> tags. We have seen how to do this many times now.

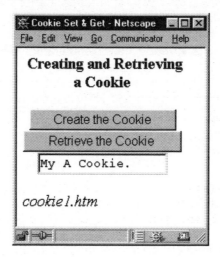

2. When the user clicks the *Create cookie* button, it calls our *setcookie()* function.

```
function setcookie(){
var cookdate = new Date();
cookdate.setTime(cookdate.getTime()
                             + 1000*60*30);
document.cookie =
            "Cookiea=My A Cookie.;expires="
            + cookdate.toGMTString();
} //EoFn setcookie
```

We create a new instance of the *Date()* object since we are going to set an expiry date using the `expires=` attribute. If this attribute is left off, the cookie is automatically deleted when the user closes the current Netscape session. If it is included, the cookie will persist until the date specified by the expiry attribute. Such cookies are known as *persistent cookies*.

We shall set the expiry date at ½ an hour after the page is first loaded. Typically, this would be a week, a month or a year. But we need a short time in our example since we would like to check that it has 'disappeared'. We set the ½-hour expiry time using the *setTime()* and *getTime()* Date methods. The idea behind this is that when the page is next loaded the cookie will be available provided the expiry time has not passed.

```
var cookdate = new Date();
cookdate.setTime(cookdate.getTime()
                           + 1000*60*30);
```

We have assigned to `cookdate`, the current date plus an extra half-hour. The plus here is the arithmetic operator:

```
1000 milliseconds*60 = 1 minute * 30 = ½-hour
```

The next step is to assign text information to the cookie.

```
document.cookie =
  "Cookiea=My A Cookie.; expires ="
          + cookdate.toGMTString();
```

We have given a name to our cookie, *Cookiea,* and supplied the information it will contain: *My A Cookie.* The expiry time is concatenated to the above using the *expires* attribute. Its value is the current time + a ½-hour which we previously gave to cookdate.

The expires attribute requires that its value is in GMT format. So we have set cookdate to this format using the *toGMTString()* method of the *Date* object. It is necessary to convert a date or time to a string since cookies are text based files.

That is it! We have created a cookie with a string text "My A Cookie" which will expire after ½-hour.

3. A second button allows us to retrieve the cookie and simply display its contents in the textbox named *cookvalue.* The important thing we need to know is that the cookie property does not allow you to *read* or *display* the attributes. You can *set* the attributes but you cannot read them. So when we eventually read the cookie, the only part which can be read is the cookie *name* and the *value* after the name, but not the expires attribute. That is handled by the browser.

```
"Cookiea=My A Cookie."
```

We can read the *name* and what follows but nothing else.

```
function getcookie() {
var cookstring = new String(document.cookie);
var cookname   = "Cookiea=";
var startpos   = cookstring.indexOf(cookname);
```

```
if (startpos != -1) {
    document.form1.cookvalue.value =
      cookstring.substring(startpos
                           + cookname.length);
      //addition not concatenation
}
else
  { document.form1.cookvalue.value =
                        "Cookie not found!";
  } // Eof if..else
} // EoFn  getcookie
```

We need to retrieve the cookie text into a string so that we can manipulate it. Consequently, we first create a new instance of a String object which we have called `cookstring` and then assigned to it the value of the *document.cookie.*

```
var cookstring = new String(document.cookie)
```

Another important point is that `cookstring` will contain *all* the cookies that apply to the current document. In Netscape, each new cookie is appended to the one *cookie* property which stores *all* the document's cookies.

We shall have to search this list for our cookie, hence the need to give it a unique name. To do so, we assign the cookie name to the variable `cookname`. Note the inclusion of the equals symbol after the name.

```
var cookname = "Cookiea="
```

Next, we find the index position of our cookie using the *indexOf()* method.

```
var startpos = cookstring.indexOf(cookname)
```

In the following, we test for whether *indexOf()* returned -1 using the 'not-equal to' comparison operator (`!=`). If this is true, then the method has returned the starting position of our cookie. In other words, it has found our cookie.

```
if (startpos != -1) {
    document.form1.cookvalue.value =
            cookstring.substring(startpos
                        + cookname.length) }
```

It is now a simple matter to assign the value of `Cookiea` to the value of the text box `cookvalue` using the *substring()* method of our string instance `cookstring`.

substring() method
We have not met the *substring()* method before, but here is our chance. It is a method of the String object.

```
mystring.substring(from, to)
```

It returns the specified substring of the string using the index positions of the arguments *from* and *to*. If the *to* is not present, it is optional, the rest of the string is returned. In our example, we have found the starting position of `Cookiea` and we add the length of the cookie name to it to provide the *from* argument using an addition operator (it is not the concatenate operator). Since we have no second argument, the rest is returned.

4. Finally, we add an *else* clause to determine what to do if the cookie is not found:

```
else
  { document.form1.cookvalue.value =
                    "Cookie not found!"
  }
```

We simply write out a message into the text box saying that the cookie is not found.

These are the new features which we have used here.

- `toGMTString()`
- `substring()`
- `document.cookie`
- `expires=`

Exercise 38: *You have been here before!*
In this exercise, we shall create a cookie which will store a visitor's name typed into a text box. If the person returns within a specified time, we shall be able to welcome them by name. It works fine in Netscape but not for IE.

Notes
When the page is loaded, we search for the cookie. If it is not found, the first illustration below will be displayed. We have supplied a text box for the user to enter his/her name. When OK is clicked, a cookie is created which will store the name. We allow the user to delete the cookie.

If it is found, because they return within a given time, the cookie is found and will display the second illustration.

```
<HEAD>
<TITLE>Cookie 2 Welcome</TITLE>
```

```
<SCRIPT>
var cString      = new String(document.cookie)
var cHead        = "Name1="
var cstartpos    = cString.indexOf(cHead)

if (cstartpos!= -1) {
var cName = cString.substring(cstartpos
                              + cHead.length)
 document.write("Hello, " + cName + "!") }
else
 {document.write("Please enter your name "
                + "and click OK ...")
document.write("<FORM NAME=form1>")
document.write("<INPUT TYPE=text NAME=cName "
               + "SIZE=40>")
document.write("<INPUT TYPE=button"
     + " VALUE='OK' onClick='storename()'>")
document.write("</FORM>")
} //EoIF/Else
function storename() {
var cDate = new Date()
cDate.setTime(cDate.getTime() + 60*30*1000)
document.cookie = "Name1="
          + document.form1.cName.value
          + ";expires=" + cDate.toGMTString()
} // EoFn  storename()
function delcookie(name)
{ document.cookie = name
      +"=;expires=Thu,01-Jan-70 00:00:01GMT"
      + ";";
  alert("Cookie gone!");
} //EoFn
</SCRIPT>
</HEAD>
<BODY><H3>Welcome Cookie</H3>
<FORM NAME=delcook>
<INPUT TYPE=button NAME=delbutton
```

```
        VALUE="Delete Cookie"
        onClick="delcookie(cHead)">
</FORM>
<ADDRESS>cookie2.htm </ADDRESS>
</BODY>
```

We start off as before, being careful to place the 'search for cookie' code in the <HEAD> so that it is the first thing to be done as the page loads.

```
var cString    = new String(document.cookie)
var cHead      = "Name1="
var cstartpos  = cString.indexOf(cHead)
```

If the cookie is found, we do this:

```
if (cstartpos!= -1) {
var cName = cString.substring(cstartpos
          + cHead.length) // + = addition
 document.write("Hello, " + cName + "!")
}
```

If it is not found, because it is a first time visitor or the expiry date has passed, we display an invitation to enter a name and click OK.

```
else
 {document.write("Please enter your name "
               + "and click OK ...")
document.write("<FORM NAME=form1>")
document.write("<INPUT TYPE=text NAME=cName "
               + "SIZE=40>")
document.write("<INPUT TYPE=button"
     + " VALUE='OK' onClick='storename()'>")
document.write("</FORM>")
} //EoIF/Else
```

The OK button, when clicked, will invoke the *storename()* function. Remember that this button will appear only when the cookie is not found.

```
function storename() {
var cDate = new Date()
cDate.setTime(cDate.getTime() + 60*30*1000)
document.cookie = "Name1="
     + document.form1.cName.value
     + ";expires=" + cDate.toGMTString()
} // EoFn  storename()
```

Notice how the value stored in the cookie called Name1 is the value of the text box NAMEd cName. We have also set the expiry time to ½ an hour. This expires= attribute will not be 'readable' except by the browser's internal program. Again, we have to use the *toGMTString()* method.

Within the <BODY> tags, we have set up a button which when clicked will delete the cookie. The standard way to delete a cookie is simply by re-setting its expiry date to a date prior to the current date.

```
function delcookie(name)
{
document.cookie = name
     +"=; expires=Thu,01-Jan-70 00:00:01GMT"
     + ";";
alert("Cookie gone!");
} //EoFn
```

To avoid too much effort, we have set the expiry date by hand in the required GMT format:

```
Weekday, dd-mm-yy[yy] hh:mm:ss GMT
```

for example: Mon, 18-Dec-1996 17:45:56 GMT

Notice that a semi-colon is used after the *name* value and after the expires= value.

Finally, we display an alert box informing the user of the deletion.

17: Cookies

Exercise 39: *This page has changed since your last visit*

In this last exercise, we shall set a cookie to the last modification date of our page. When a user revisits the page, we shall compare the cookie date with the current visit's *modification date*. If the page has been modified in the meanwhile, we shall inform the user. This makes use of the *lastModified* property of the document object.

lastModified

It is a read-only string which contains the date and time a document was most recently modified. It is derived from the HTTP header data sent by the web server.

Web servers are not required to provide last-modification dates for the documents they hold. When they do not, JavaScript assumes 0 which translates to the date of midnight, January 1st, 1970 GMT. Consequently, we need to test for this situation. For the moment, we shall assume that the last modification date has been sent.

```
<HEAD><TITLE>Cookie 3 Modification</TITLE>
<SCRIPT>
document.cookie = "ModVern=" +
             escape(document.lastModified);

var allcookies = document.cookie;
var pos = allcookies.indexOf("ModVern=");

if (pos != -1) {
// 8 is length of cookie name plus equals symbol
   var start = pos + 8;
   var end = allcookies.indexOf(";", start);
   if (end == -1) end = allcookies.length;
   var value = allcookies.substring(start,
                                    end);
   value = unescape(value);

   if (value != document.lastModified)
    document.write("This document has changed
              since you were last here.");
} // EofIf
```

```
</SCRIPT>
</HEAD>
<BODY>
<B> Modified Page Cookie</B>
<SCRIPT>
document.write("This page was last modified"
             + "on: " + document.lastModified)
</SCRIPT>
<B>Here is the rest of the Web page!</B>
<ADDRESS>cookie3.htm </ADDRESS>
</BODY>
```

Notes:

Our cookie is called `ModVern` and is assigned the last modification date.

```
document.cookie = "ModVern="
             + escape(document.lastModified);
```

Since cookie values may not include semi-colons, commas or *whitespace* (tabs and extra spaces), we need to use the *escape()* function.

escape()

It is a global function in client-side JavaScript and is not associated with any object. It creates and returns a new string which contains an encoded version of its argument. The original string is not changed. All spaces, punctuation, accented characters and anything else which is not ASCII letters or numbers are converted (encoded) into the form: `%xx` where `xx` is the hexadecimal number preceded by % which represent the ISO-8859-1 (Latin 1) code for the character.

For example: `!` has the Latin 1 code of 33 in decimal and `21` in hexadecimal. A space is hexadecimal `20` and a comma is hex `2C`. Thus:

```
escape("Hello, World!")
```

would yield the new string:

`'Hello%2C%20World%21'`

The purpose of *escape()* is to ensure that the string is portable to all computers and across all networks, regardless of whatever character encoding they support. They must, however, also support the American Standard Code for Information Interchange (ASCII). This is important in the case of cookies being transmitted over the Internet.

Use *unescape()* function to decode an escaped string.

```
<SCRIPT>
mystring = "Hello, World!"
Estring = escape(mystring)
document.write("The escaped version:")
document.write("<BR>" + Estring)
//... and sometime later ...
document.write("The unescaped version:")
document.write("<BR>" + unescape(Estring))
</SCRIPT>
```

The rest of the code should be easy to follow since we have used similar coding in the previous two examples.

In the following example, we use the *lastModified* property at the end of a web page to display the date of the last modification. This saves having to remember to update your Web pages after each modification.

```
<SCRIPT>
document.write("This page was last modified"
           + " on: " + document.lastModified)
</SCRIPT>
```

Finally, here is some code which can test whether the web server has included the last modification date.

```
// get date
lastmod = document.lastModified
// convert to milliseconds to compare with 0
lastmoddate = Date.parse(lastmod)

if (lastmoddate == 0){
  document.writeln("Last Modified: Unknown")
else
  document.writeln("Last Modified on:  "
                                  + lastmod)
} // EofIF
```

Notes:

lastModified returns a date in this format:

mm/dd/yy hh:mm:ss - 02/08/00 10:35:02

It needs to be converted to milliseconds via the Date.parse() method to compare it with zero. Remember, that 0 is assumed when a *lastModification* date has not been sent by the server. You would also need to add some extra code if you wanted to display the date in *dd/mm/yy* format, as discussed in Chapter 11.

Cookie Limitations

We have already seen that the *lastModified* property depends upon the web server and is beyond our control. But there are other limitations. Cookies are intended for storage of small amounts of text for a limited period of time. Web browsers are not required to store more than 300 cookies in total. That covers all the web pages which are downloaded. They are also not required to store more than 20 cookies from any one web server (for the entire server, not just for your page). They are limited to a maximum of 4Kbytes of data per cookie.

Browsers can be instructed to refuse cookies by their users. It is not an automatic affair.

Bearing in mind the small amount of text-data a cookie can store, the number of cookies browsers can store and that users can refuse to accept cookies, we should be moderate in their use.

JavaScript Security
Loading a Web page with JavaScript code could cause security problems and seriously damage your computer unless precautions are taken. Early versions of client-side JavaScript were plagued with security problems mainly related to e-mail. Scurrilous code could be written to send messages on behalf of a user.

The simple way to make users' computers safe from JavaScript programs is to prevent client-side JavaScript from having any means of writing to or deleting files or directories on the client's computer. Therefore, JavaScript has no File object and no file access object. Our computers are safe.

Client-side JavaScript can load URLs and send form data back to a web server, as well as CGI scripts and e-mail addresses. But it cannot establish direct contact with other hosts on the Internet. This means that a JavaScript program cannot use a client's machine as a platform to crack passwords on other machines. This is especially important if the JavaScript program has been loaded over the Internet and through a *firewall* - a means of preventing unauthorised access to a network.

Imagine a network heavily protected with a firewall and then a Web page is loaded with a JavaScript program which then has the means of reading the other servers inside the company's Intranet. To prevent this, JavaScript has not been given any mechanism for making contact with other servers from a client base.

The browser's history file (a record of your previously visited sites) and bookmarks remain private and outside the realm of JavaScript. Otherwise, a program would be able to view your sites of interest and report back to the host server. You could then be bombarded with unsolicited e-mail or worse. Some companies pay good money to get hold of such information to plague you with sales pitches. Likewise, your e-mail address remains private unless you wish to send it.

JavaScript cannot examine other open windows such as a Word document or an Excel spreadsheet. Just think about the implications of this if JavaScript could begin to examine and return all the contents of any of your open files.

Client-side JavaScript just has not the capability of loading other files from your hard disc, closing open windows which are not browser windows, deleting files and being a general nuisance. It is also unable to open new windows within the browser's scope which are less than 100 pixels in size. This prevents scripts from opening windows that a user cannot easily see and which might contain scripts which are still running after the user thinks they have stopped.

Cookies are safe because they cannot contain code. So our computers are safe from hacker-crazed cookies, for the time being! In any case, a browser can be set up to prevent cookies from being accepted. The cookies file can be deleted by users and to do so should be a harmless exercise.

The Windows system stores cookies in a `cookies.txt` file; Mac systems store cookies in a file named `MagicCookie`, and for Unix systems the file is called `cookies`. These files can be read by any editor.

Web servers sending cookies cannot find out anything about your computer, let alone do any damage.

Finally, information sent via FORMs should *always* be checked *again* at the server end. We already know enough JavaScript to be able to ask users to enter their credit/debit card details and to substitute our own address in place of the user's address for the delivery of the goods they have just paid for. Hmm! that's a pity.

EIGHTEEN:

Common Errors

When writing program scripts, it is all too easy to make mistakes. Here are some JavaScript errors which I, my students and you will make. They are worth taking to heart since you will reduce the amount of frustration you will otherwise endure. Programming requires a clear mind which we, as humans, cannot always command. We create a script which does not work. The main difference between the novice and the experienced programmer, is not that the latter never makes a mistake but when they do they can find the error more easily. Such experience comes from practice.

Netscape and IE will offer some help. In the case of Netscape, you must type in `javascript:` in the location box. The colon is important otherwise you will simply call up the Netscape home page.

General tip:
When possible, create the HTML code first and make sure that it works. Then add your scripts preferably one at a time, testing each one as it is added. This approach will at least confine any error to the last script or function added. Should you write all the scripts and then run the programs, it will take much longer to identify any rogue errors.

Common errors
1. Opening & closing curly brackets missing from functions and controls such as `if`, `else`, `for`, `switch`, etc. Marking the end of such features with a comment will help to identify missing brackets: `// EofFn` - `//EofIF`.

18: <u>Common Errors</u>

2. Forgetting the end script tag: `</script>` - I do it all the time.

3. Pressing the *Enter* key between quoted strings. The Enter key is taken to be the end of a statement.

4. Misuse of single and double quotes:
```
document.write("Here is the text')
```
and: `onClick = "alert("Type this out")"`

should be: `onClick="alert('Type this out')"`

5. Mistaken use of the three types of brackets: `[ { (`

6. Confusing JavaScript interCapped words where case *is* significant with HTML attributes which are *not* sensitive:
`bgcolor` (HTML) with `bgColor` (JavaScript)

7. Forgetting correct case and spelling:
`maths.round` instead of `Math.round`

8. Using one = for equality rather than two ==
```
if (x = 1) instead of if(x == 1)
```

9. When using logical operators, forgetting to put expressions in their own brackets:
```
if ( (exp1) || (exp2) )
```

10. It is not good style to put a space after function name:
`function fred ()`

Many browsers will tolerate this, but it is not correct syntax.

11. Very common is the misspelling of names:
```
var lastname = document.form1.surnam.value
................                 ⇕
<input type="text" name="surname">
```

and to use the wrong case for your variable names: `Lastname` instead of `lastname`.

12. Although permissible, you are asking for trouble if a variable name is the same as the value of the attribute *name*:

var **surname** = document.forml.**surname**.value
. . . .
<input type="text" name="**surname**">

13. There are a number of reserved words in JavaScript which cannot be used as variable names and function names: `case, default, delete, new, switch, this, var` are but a few.   `var new = 456` is wrong!

14. Mistaken *scope* of variables (page 119). When the `var` keyword is used, the variable becomes *local* to the function in which it is contained and will not be recognised by any other function.

15. If, like me you tend to use Word 97, then the `<FORM>` tag should contain *method* and *action* with *name* being the third attribute when used. Otherwise, Internet Assistant will have a fit and crash the program. There is no such problem with Notepad. See page 57.

16. Be careful about where you position your functions and especially the position from which they are invoked. You should place all your functions within the `<HEAD>` tags. Here is an example:

```
<HEAD><TITLE> Live Clock  </TITLE>
<style>
input {color:red; font-size:9pt;
      background-color:#DBC47C;}
body  {background-color:silver;}
</style>
```

```
<SCRIPT LANGUAGE="Javascript">
function showtime()  {
   var digital=new Date();
   var hours=digital.getHours();
   var minutes=digital.getMinutes();
   var seconds=digital.getSeconds();
   var ampm="AM" ;
  if (hours>12) {
       ampm="PM";
       hours=hours-12;   // 12-hour clock
       } //EofIF
  if (hours==0) {
       hours=12; } //EofIF
  if (minutes<=9){
       minutes="0"+minutes; } //EofIF
  if (seconds<=9) {
       seconds="0"+seconds;} //EofIF
 document.Tick.Clock.value = hours + ":"
   + minutes + ":"  + seconds + " " + ampm;
 setTimeout("showtime()",1000);
  } // EoFn showtime
</script>
</HEAD>
<BODY>
<h3>Tempus fugit</h3>
<SCRIPT LANGUAGE="Javascript">
showtime()  // a big mistake!
</SCRIPT>
<form method="" action="" name="Tick">
<input type="text" size="12" name="Clock">
</form>
The script should GO HERE or as onLoad in body
so that the entire page is loaded before it is
invoked.
<ADDRESS>John Shelley <BR>
</BODY>
```

If the script tags which invoke `showtime()` are placed where I have put them, what do you think will happen?

The page is loaded and the function is stored away safely. The browser meets the invocation to `showtime()` and immediately executes it. This function has the following statement:

`document.`*`Tick.Clock`*`.value = hours + ":"`

But the point is, that *Tick* and *Clock* have not yet been met by the browser because it has not reached the `<form>` and `<input>` tags which use the names *Tick* and *Clock*. Therefore, it will tell you that it has met *undefined* objects.

However, if the script tags are placed where I have suggested or the `showtime()` function is used as the value of the `<BODY>` onLoad event, then they will have been encountered by the browser. The onLoad in the body elment will only take effect once the entire page is loaded.

Do you notice how small the text is within the time box (it is 9pt) and that I have managed to colour the background of the text box? How was that done? By the use of style sheets. It cannot be done by using HTML. Here is the style sheet (CSS - cascading style sheets). You can lift this and use it in your own pages provided you are using version 5 or 4 of IE and Netscape respectively.

```
<style>
input {color:red; font-size:9pt;
       background-color:#DBC47C;
       font-family:verdana;}
body  {background-color:silver;}
</style>
```

It must be placed within the `<HEAD>` tags. It simply states that all input elements will have a font-size of 9 points, coloured red with a background colour of brown and use the Verdana type face. (*Netscape cannot recognise the background colour style for input elements.*)

The other style states that the background colour of the document is to be silver.

CSS is very easy to learn, although its syntax is different to HTML and JavaScript. There is a book in the Babani series, "XHTML and CSS explained" which will explain how to use style sheets to create desk top publishing style web pages. For example, overlapping text:

Answers to Tests

Test: Chap. 2

2.1 *What are <SCRIPT> tags used for and where can they be placed?* [See also error 16, page 295.]

Browsers expect to find JavaScript code enclosed within a pair of opening and closing <SCRIPT> tags.

They can be placed anywhere, although it would not be sensible to place them before the opening <HEAD> tag. Otherwise, they can be placed:

- between the <HEAD> tags
- between the <HEAD> and <BODY> tags
- between the <BODY> tags
- after the </BODY> tag - not recommended!

The actual position of the <SCRIPT> tags within the <BODY> tags will determine where they will take effect.

2.2 *Do the <SCRIPT> tags form part of HTML or JavaScript?*
Part of HTML version 4.

2.3 *Is* document *an object or method?*

document is an object. *methods* are things we can do to objects.

2.4 *Is writeln() an object or method?*
write() & *writeln()* are methods of the document object.

2.5 *What is the main difference between write() and writeln()?*

Effectively none. In Netscape, both methods write to the *View source code* window. *writeln()* will append a new line after the message has been output, *write()* does not. In both cases, only the message is seen, not the JavaScript source code. Internet Explorer uses Notepad to view the source code so that it will be displayed exactly as it had been typed in the original.

2.6 *Can you have more than one pair of <SCRIPT> tags in the same HTML document?*

There is no limit to the number of pairs of <SCRIPT> tags used.

2.7 *What would the following display on a Web page:*

```
document.write("Hallo there.",
                "My name is Joe.")
```

| Hallo there.My name is Joe. |

There would be no space before the 'M' of 'My'.

2.8 *What is the formal term for what is enclosed within the round brackets in the above code?*

Multiple arguments each separated by a comma.

2.9 *When would you need to add:*
LANGUAGE="Javascript1.2" to an opening <SCRIPT> tag?

It would be required if you wished to use features found only in JavaScript version 1.2.

2.10 *How are multiple arguments separated?*

By commas, except for the last one.

Test: Chap. 3

3.1 *Does the alert() method belong to the* document *or* window *object?*

To the window object.

3.2 *In the following, should the message displayed by the alert box be in double or single quotes?*

`onClick = "alert ( the message )"`

Should be: `onClick="alert('Message')"`

Because the value of the *onClick* attribute must be surrounded by quotes *and* we have used double quotes, only single quotes can be used to surround the message. Using two different sets of quotes allows the browser to recognise the opening pair of one set and the opening pair of an inner set of quotes. Otherwise, it would take the opening of the second set as the closing of the first set.

3.3 *What is the JavaScript term for the* onClick *attribute?*

An event handler.

3.4 *What type of value does the* onClick *attribute take?*

JavaScript code.

3.5 *When a user clicks on a button, what is this called in JavaScript?*

An event.

3.6 *In OOP languages, what is the formal term for* bgColor *in the following?*

`onClick = "document.bgColor = 'lightblue'"`

It is a *property* of the document object.

3.7 *In the above, would it matter if* bgColor *was typed as* `bgcolor` *or* `BGCOLOR`?

Absolutely! JavaScript is highly case sensitive. It can recognise only *bgColor* and no other variation, unlike HTML where case is not significant.

3.8 *What value will z have after the following code is executed?*

```
z = 1; z = z + 3;
```

The variable z will contain 4 (1+3).

3.9 *In the above code, is + a concatenate or an arithmetic operator?* An arithmetic operator.

3.10 *What could happen in Netscape when a window is re-sized?*

When a page is re-loaded to fit a newly sized window, the source code may well be an earlier version which Netscape has fetched from its *cache* memory. If this re-displayed page contained JavaScript errors which you have subsequently corrected, Netscape will re-display the earlier version with the uncorrected errors. This does not happen with Internet Explorer.

3.11 *Is onClick an attribute or an event handler?*
It is an attribute of the HTML <INPUT> tag and an event handler in JavaScript.

Test: Chap. 4
4.1 *In the code for Exercise 9c what is the* declaration *and what is the* invocation *of the function* yourname()?

Invocation: the value of the *onClick* event handler:

```
onClick = "yourname()"
```

Declaration: function yourname() { .. code .. }

4.2 *How many functions can be placed within a single pair of <SCRIPT> tags?*

Any number, there is no limit.

4.3 *How many syntax errors can you find in the following?*

```
onclick  "function abc{}'
```

Four: It should read: `onclick="abc()"`

- `onclick` attribute should have an equals symbol after it. The case of *onclick* is immaterial since it is part of HTML, not JavaScript
- wrong mix of double & single quotes
- wrong type of brackets used - should be round brackets not curly
- the *function* keyword must not be included

4.4 *The prompt dialogue box can take two arguments. What purpose does the second serve?*

The second argument is a string quote which is used to replace the word 'undefined' when the prompt box is displayed.

4.5 *What would the following write out?*

```
sum = 1.5 + 2;
document.write("The sum is: " + "sum");
```

```
The sum is: sum
```

Enclosing the variable `sum` in quotes turns it into a quoted string which will be displayed literally. To print out the contents of the variable `sum`, it must *not be enclosed* in quotes.

4.6 *When would you want to use an* alert, *a* confirm *and a* prompt *pop up box?*

alert: when you wish to display an informative message to a user

confirm: when you want a user to confirm (OK) or cancel (Cancel) something *prompt*: when you want the user to type something in and to capture what has been typed

4.7 *You cannot use multiple arguments in the alert() method. What device must you use when you wish to display some text as well as the contents of variables?*

You will have to make use of the concatenate operator which will convert the arguments into a single argument.

4.8 *In the following code, in what order would the browser display the information on the screen?*

```
<HEAD> <TITLE> .. a title .. </TITLE>
<SCRIPT>
function yourname(){
  x = prompt("What is your name?");
  confirm("Did you say your name is "
          + x + "?");
} // EoFn
</SCRIPT> </HEAD>
<BODY>
<H4> Here is a Prompt</H4>
<FORM>
<INPUT TYPE="button" VALUE="Tell me your name."
        onClick="yourname()">
</FORM>
<ADDRESS>PROMPT-Ex9c.htm </ADDRESS></BODY>
```

The way the code is written would mean that the heading in the <H4> would come first, then the FORM button, and finally the contents of the <ADDRESS> code. The prompt box would appear *only* if the user clicked the Form button. Once the prompt box was OK-ed, the confirm box would appear.

4.9 *What type of arguments can the write() method take?*

So far, we have seen that it can take string quoted text and HTML tags as well as variables.

Test: Chap. 5

5.1 *How can you find out what a user has typed into a prompt box?*

By assigning to a variable what has been typed in and then passing that variable as an argument to a function. The function can then perform tests on the argument's *data* to determine what it contains.

5.2 *Why are arguments useful?*

Via arguments, data can be passed to a function for processing. The data can be 'captured' from text or prompt boxes or entered as fixed data by the programmer. The same function can process different data each time it is invoked.

5.3 *To what object does the* `sqrt()` *method belong?*

To the Math object.

5.4 *Is the Math object part of core or client-side JavaScript?*

It is part of core JavaScript.

5.5 *Give one main reason for giving an INPUT element a name attribute.*

By giving a name to an INPUT element, such as a text box or radio button, it can be referred to individually and manipulated in some desired way.

For example, what a user types into a text box can be assigned to a variable:

```
x = document.form1.calculator.value
```

In order to 'capture' the value of the text box NAMEd `calculator` above, it was given a unique name, thus:

```
<INPUT TYPE="text" SIZE="12"
       NAME="calculator">
```

5.6 *If you only have one Form and wish to refer to it via JavaScript code, does it still need to be given a name attribute?*

Yes. Names are the means by which JavaScript can refer to a form and many other HTML elements.

5.7 *Why must an invoked function include the function call operator - () - rather than just the function name?*

How else could JavaScript differentiate between a variable name and a function name? It is precisely by using the function call operator that JavaScript can recognise a call to a function. Characters not enclosed in quotes and which do not include the function call operator are taken to be variable names.

If you think about this, you can see that computers use very simple cues (syntax) to make distinctions between one thing and another. This is why computers will never be able to make up jokes which rely on very subtle use of words or their sounds.

Teacher to a class on their last day at School:

"Remember this! The world is your lobster."

> The Prime Minister of Australia is on an official visit to New Zealand. On the way from the airport, he is amazed at the lush vegetation of the countryside after his own dried and scorched land. He turns to his host, the PM of New Zealand and asks:
>
> "How do you keep your country so green?"
>
> To which the New Zealand PM replies, "I don't tell them anything!"

Test: Chap. 6

6.1 *What is a dummy argument and why is it useful?*

A dummy argument is a 'dummy name' given to an argument and which is used throughout the function's declaration. When the function is invoked, it is passed a real argument, typically a variable containing data. This real argument is substituted for the dummy argument during the execution of the function.

6.2 *For the following :* 5 + 4 * 2 + 3

a) *What result would be given by a* computer?
    4*2 = 8; 8+5 = 13; 13+3 = **16**

b) *What result would be given by a* pocket calculator?
    5+4 = 9; 9*2 = 18; 18+3 = **21**

6.3 *Why are comments used by programmers?*

To annotate JavaScript code. Typically, comments are used to explain what the code is doing. It is useful to others who have to understand your code and even to the *author* of the code when it is revisited at a later date. Comments are also used to mark the end of functions and control statements such as *if* and *for* (see Chapter 9).

It is not unusual for even experienced programmers to spend quite some time trying to work out what a particular piece of their own code is trying to do when they have not looked at it for several months.

6.4 *How do you create a single line comment in JavaScript?*

Use a double forward slash:

```
// here is a single line comment
```

6.5 *How are multiple line comments created in JavaScript?*

Use: /*   .. comment .. */

```
/* here is one line of a comment
   and here is a second line. */
```

6.6 *How many errors can you find in the following?*

```
function dothis(sqroot)
 x = Maths,sqrt(squroot);
 document.write("The square root of: "
                  + squroot + " is: " + x)
}
```

1. there is no opening curly bracket to mark the start of the function's code
2. `Maths` should be `Math`
3. replace comma with a period: `Math.sqrt(sqroot)`
4. mis-typed argument name: `sqroot` not `squroot`

Test: Chap. 7

7.1 *Can the HTML <IMG> tag be a property of the document object?*

Yes. In fact the document object can take many HTML tags as properties: <IMG>, <A>, <AREA>, <FORM>, etc.

7.2 *How can one image be replaced by another image in JavaScript?*

By assigning its *src property* to another image file:

```
document.img1.src =  "image2.jpg"
```

This involved having previously named the <IMG> tag so that it could be referenced as a property of the document object.

`<IMG `**`NAME="img1"`**` SRC="original.gif".. >`

7.3 *What happens in Netscape if the image which replaces another is of a different size to the one it replaces? Will the same thing happen in Internet Explorer?*

Netscape assumes that any image which replaces another has the same dimensions as the first. If not, the second is forced into the same space as the one it replaces. This will cause distortion.

This does not happen in Internet Explorer.

7.4 *Can the onMouseOver event handler be used with a text box INPUT element?*

No, more is the pity. It is only used with the <A> tag.

7.5 *With which HTML tags are the onMouseOver and onMouseOut event handlers usually associated?*

The <A> tag and the <AREA> tag.

7.6 *What user event will an onMouseOut event handler trap?*

When the user moves the mouse out of an image (or text) enclosed in <A> tags with an onMouseOut event handler attached.

Test: Chap. 8

8.1 *How many arguments does the* window.open() *method take?*

Maximum 4, minimum 1.

argument 1: which file to open into the new window
argument 2: used with the target attribute of FORM
argument 3: specifies the new window's features
argument 4: used with the browser's History - seldom used

It must contain at least the first argument, even if this is empty, in which case a blank window would open:

```
window.open("")
```

8.2 *You want to use the first and the third arguments of the window.open() method. Is it still necessary to include the second argument?*

Yes. Even when an argument is not used or required, its position in the order of the arguments must still be 'filled in' even if this is a pair of *empty* quotes, such as shown in the next answer where no file has to be opened. In this question we need to insert null as the second argument.

8.3 *In the following code, why is* null *not in quotes?*

```
var win = window.open("",null,
    "height=400 width=500 status=1
     resizable=yes status=0");
```

It is a special value indicating 'no value'. If it were in quotes, it would be taken to be the name of a target attribute, the purpose of the second argument.

8.4 *Why was it necessary to assign the new window object to the variable win in Exercise 18 &19, but not in Exercise 17?*

In both Exercise 18 & 19, we wanted to write HTML tags along with text to the new window via the *document write()* method. We could not simply use:

```
document.write("HTML etc..")
```

since this would write to the existing window, not to the new window. This is because *document* is the property of the currently open window. In order to write to our new window, we need to create a new window object (*win*) and use the *document.write()* property of this new window. To do this we assign the new window to a variable - *win*:

```
var win = window.open("... arguments ... ")
```

We can now use this variable to specify what to write to the new window via its own document property.

```
win.document.write( " the HTML code")
```

8.5 *What do you think would happen if* window *rather than* win *were used in the* removewindow *function for Exercise 19?*

```
function removewindow() {
   window.close()
}  // EoFn
```

The main window would be closed instead of the newly created window. But we want the window called `win` to be closed, therefore, we have to use `win.close()`.

Test: Chap. 9

9.1 *What are the four basic features of any programming language?*

- creating, storing and moving data
- input and output of data
- making decisions
- repeating instructions

9.2 *What is an integer number and what is a real number?*

Integer: a whole number with no decimal places; e.g. 124.

Real: a number with decimal places; e.g. 1.23, 1.0, 0.54.

9.3 *How can you capture, for subsequent processing, what a user has typed into a text box or a prompt box?*

Assign it to a variable and perhaps pass the variable as an argument to a function. For example:

```
function abc(){
   x = document.form1.text1.value} // EoFn
```
or:
```
x = prompt("Type something.")
....
onClick="user_entry(x)"
```

19: <u>Answers to Tests</u>

9.4 *Give one example of where case is not significant and one where it is?*

Event handlers are part of HTML and their case is not significant, therefore, *onclick* and *onClick* are both valid.

Whereas, *Math* is part of JavaScript and, therefore, case is significant. Likewise for *round(), for, if, bgColor,* etc.

9.5 *What is happening in the following code?* `var x = 1;`

The variable `x` is being created (*declared*) and assigned the value 1.

9.6 *What is happening in the following code?*

`if (x == 1) { ... }`

The value of `x` is being *compared* to integer 1. If *true*, the code in curly brackets will be executed. If *false*, the code will be ignored.

9.7 *According to its syntax, an* if *statement can execute only a single instruction. How do you make it execute more than one instruction?*

Multiple statements can be 'converted' into a 'single' statement by enclosing them in curly brackets so that they become a *compound* statement.

9.8 *What do the following do?*

i) `++i` this is called the *prefix increment* operator. The increment variable `i` will immediately be incremented by 1 before any other instruction is executed.

ii) `k--` this is called the *postfix decrement* operator. The decrement variable `k` will have its value decremented by 1 but will not take effect until some other instruction is executed.

They are frequently used as increment or decrement statements within `for` loops.

9.9 *What will be written out by the* `document.write()` *method for the following?*

```
<SCRIPT>
var aBc = 12;
var abc;
document.write("Variable abc is: " + abc
              + "<BR>Variable aBc is: " + aBc);
</SCRIPT>
```

The following will be written out:

```
Variable abc is: undefined
Variable aBc is: 12
```

(The point of this test is to show that `aBc` is created and assigned a value, whereas `abc` is created and has not been assigned a value. It is therefore given the special value of `undefined`.)

9.10 *Look very carefully at the following code and work out what will be written out after the code has been executed.*

Note:

    (a) i = j = 12; is another shortcut, beloved by C programmers and now part of JavaScript, which assigns a value to more than one variable in one statement.

    b) IF statements can be nested as we see in the following.

```
i = j = 1;  // both i and j assigned value of 1
k = 2;
if (i == j) // i does equal 1 therefore true
  if (j==k)
    document.write("i equals j");
else
  document.write("i does not equal j");
                              // Oops!
```

i does not equal j will be written out. We have not used curly brackets and that is our undoing. JavaScript, and most other languages, stipulate that an else clause (block) is part of the *nearest* if statement. Despite the indenting of the original source code, the *else* belongs to: if(j==k). Since, this results in *false*, it is the accompanying *else* clause which will be executed and the message *"i does not equal j"* is written out.

In order to make this example less ambiguous and easier to understand, maintain and debug, use curly brackets, thus:

```
i = j = 1;   // both i and j assigned value of 1
k = 2;
 if (i==j)
  {   if (j==k)
       {document.write("i equals j");
       } // end of inner IF
  }
 else {
       document.write("i does not equal j");
       } // end of outer IF
```

This now makes it clear to both JavaScript and humans that the *else* is part of the outer if statement and will be executed when i does not equal j. Have you also noticed that since the logic is clearer, nothing at all will be written out. The *else* clause will no longer be executed because it has now been associated with the first if statement which results in true. This now tests to see whether j==k, which it does not. Consequently, the second if clause will not be executed, and, so, nothing more will happen.

This is an excellent example of how horrendous and tortuous nested if clauses can become.

9.11 *Why cannot a variable name begin with a digit?*

So that JavaScript can distinguish between a variable and a number. To make life easy for the people who programmed the JavaScript language, they decided that anything not enclosed in quotes or which did not have a function call operator appended to it would be either a variable, a number or a Boolean value. To make it easy to distinguish between them, they decided that anything starting with a digit must be a number (or should be). Anything starting with a letter, $ or _ (underscore) would be interpreted as a variable. A separate test for *false* or *true* would check whether the 'variable' was indeed a Boolean value. They were no fools!

9.12 *What will happen in each of the following?*
a) This one is correct.

```
<SCRIPT>
sum = 0;
for ( i = 1; i <= 10; i++)
   { sum = sum + i;   }
document.write("numbers 1-10 = " + sum)
</SCRIPT>
```

It sums the first ten numbers and prints out:

```
numbers 1-10 = 55
```

b) Incorrect *initialisation* of the loop variable

```
<SCRIPT>
sum = 0;
for ( i = 2; i <= 10; i++) // sloppy
   { sum = sum + i;   }
document.write("numbers 1-10 = " + sum)
</SCRIPT>
```

```
numbers 1 -10 = 54
```

This demonstrates how careful we have to be with the initialisation of the loop variable, i. Since it began at 2, sum does not include the first number 1. Hence, the result of 54. We cannot afford to be sloppy.

c) *sum* is undefined since it has not been declared prior to use.

```
<SCRIPT>
for ( i = 1; i <= 10; i=i+1)
   { sum = sum + i;   }
document.write("numbers 1-10 = " + sum)
</SCRIPT>
```

Internet Explorer and Netscape will pop up an error message saying *'sum is undefined'* and the loop will not proceed any further. The point here is that variables used in functions must not only be defined but also assigned some value as shown next.

d) A common error - *declared but no assignment*

```
<SCRIPT>
var sum;
for ( i = 1; i <= 10; i=i+1)
   { sum = sum + i;   }
document.write("numbers 1-10 = " + sum)
</SCRIPT>
```

This produces: numbers 1-10 = NaN

The variable has been declared but has not been assigned a value (in fact it has the non-numeric *null* value). Since it appears on the left-hand side and is therefore being used as though it had a numeric value, the loop will not work as expected. Remember that NaN is something returned by JavaScript to inform the user that arithmetic is being performed on a variable which does not contain a numeric value.

e) Another common error - *no comparison for the condition test, just an assignment*

```
<SCRIPT>
sum = 0;
for ( i = 1; i = 10; i=i+1)
   { sum = sum + i;   }
document.write("numbers 1-10 = " + sum)
</SCRIPT>
```

This program could cause your PC to hang. (Save all your work before you try this. You may need to re-boot your computer!)

The above program will loop indefinitely and not get beyond:

- assigning 10 to i
- adding it to sum
- incrementing i to 11
- and then re-assigning 10 to i
- for ever and ever, Amen!

Test: Chap. 11

11.1 *Try writing some JavaScript which will tell a user how long it has taken to load a page.*

(The combined code for test 11.1 and 11.2 is shown below.)

We need *two* times: a time when the page begins to load and a time when the page has finished loading. Subtracting the two times will yield the time taken to load. The start time is obtained by:

```
var today = new Date()
```

but note that the code is placed *before* the <BODY> tag so that we take the time just before loading begins.

The ending time is obtained by doing the same *after* or just *before* the closing </BODY> tag when the page has just finished loading.

```
nowtime = new Date()
```

The next step is to convert the two new date objects into milliseconds using the *getTime()* method and subtract them:

```
(nowtime.getTime() - today.getTime())/1000
```

and then divide by 1000 to convert into seconds.

11.2 *Write another piece of code to work out how many days are left to Christmas Day.*

Answers to exercises 11.1 & 11.2:

```
<HEAD><TITLE> Days to Christmas? </TITLE>
<SCRIPT>
// create new instances of the dates
var today  = new Date()
var xmas   = new Date()

xmas.setMonth(11)
xmas.setDate(25)

if (today.getTime()< xmas.getTime()){
  difference =
      xmas.getTime() - today.getTime();
  difference =
      Math.floor(difference / (1000*60*60*24));
  document.write("Only " + difference
        + "days until next Christmas Day! <P>");
}  // EoIF
</SCRIPT>
</HEAD>
<BODY>
<P>
<H3>Christmas and Loading Time</H3>
<IMG SRC="Xmas.gif">
<ADDRESS><B>Test-10.htm</B> </ADDRESS>
</BODY>
<SCRIPT>
```

```
nowtime = new Date();
document.write("It took "
  +(nowtime.getTime() - today.getTime()) / 1000
  + "seconds to load this page.");
</SCRIPT>
```

We need today's date and the date for Christmas day. We create two new date instances, and set the Christmas day instance using the *setMonth* and *setDate* methods:

```
var today  = new Date() // for current date
var xmas   = new Date() // for Christmas Day

xmas.setMonth(11)
xmas.setDate(25)
```

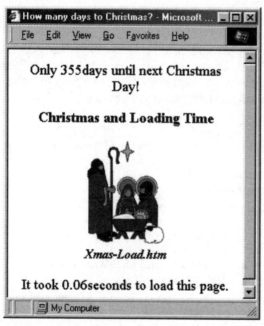

It is now a simple matter to subtract the two and to convert the result into days:

```
difference = xmas.getTime() - today.getTime();
difference = Math.floor(difference /
                               (1000*60*60*24));
```

We have used the `Math.floor` method to return the greatest integer less than or equal to a number. Thus, if you passed 45.95 to *floor*, it would return 45; pass it -45.95 it would return -46. We do not want parts of days.

We have also used an `if` statement to check that today's date does not start after Christmas Day. If it does then nothing is displayed

11.3 *Convert Exercise 24 to show how many* minutes *someone has been connected to their ISP.*

```
document.howlong.answer.value =
((connect_time/1000)/60)
```

This is a very simple matter of dividing the number of seconds by 60. Of course, we would also need to change the words *Secs* to *Minutes*. With more arithmetic you could even display minutes and seconds.

11.4 Try the following in both Netscape and IE.

```
<HEAD><TITLE> Using the date Object  </TITLE>
<SCRIPT>
// Enter your own date
mydate = new Date("18 Dec 1686")

var monthday = mydate.getDate()
var month    = mydate.getMonth() + 1
var day      = mydate.getDay()
var year     = mydate.getYear()
var fullyear = mydate.getFullYear()

document.write("<h3>Full Year Test </h3>")
document.write("Full year is: " + fullyear)
document.write("<DIV ALIGN= right>"
            + "day of the month =  "
            + monthday + "<BR>")
document.write("month =  " + month + "<BR>")
```

```
document.write("day =    "   + day + "<BR>")
document.write("year =   "   + year + "<BR>")
document.write("The date is: " + monthday
              + "/" + month + "/" + year )
// Get current date
var today     = new Date()
var monthdayx = today.getDate()
var monthx    = today.getMonth() + 1
var dayx      = today.getDay()
var yearx     = today.getYear()
document.write("<BR>Today's date is: "
              + monthdayx + "/"
              + monthx + "/" + yearx )
</SCRIPT>
</HEAD>
```

What do you observe for the year 1686 when using Netscape?

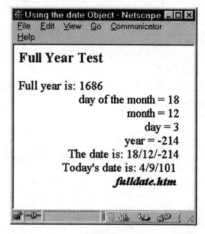

You should see a negative year in Netscape for 1686: (-214) and the current year as a positive value (101).

When getFullYear() is used, there is no problem.

IE writes out all the years 'correctly'. See illustration above for the Netscape version.

Test: Chap. 12
12.1 *Which HTML elements are allowed to take the* onChange *event handler?*

The *text* element and the *textarea* tags
12.2 *When is the* onChange *event handler triggered?*

Once a user has typed something into a text box and clicked outside that box.

12.3 *What do you see when the following is run?*
```
<head> <title> ... </title>
<script>
function abc() {x = 2;} // EoFn
</script>
</head>
<body>
<script>
  alert("Are you ready?");
  y = abc();
  alert("Y = " + y) // What value is variable y?
</script>
</body>
```

It says that Y is undefined. We need the `return` x to return the value of x at the point of invocation.

12.4 *A form may be submitted in any of three ways. What are they?*
- clicking on a *submit button*
- using the *submit()* method
- returning a non-false value to the *onSubmit* event handler

The last example will take effect once the submit button has been clicked and the code in the onSubmit event handler has completed its work. This code will return either a false or non-false value.

12.5 *To which object does the* submit() *method belong?*

It is a method of a named FORM tag which is a property of the document object.

12.6 *What function does the* submit() *method perform?*

It mimics what occurs when a user clicks the submit button. However, since it can be placed in a function, various validation tests should be performed before it is actually invoked.

12.7 onSubmit *is an event handler of which HTML tag?*

The FORM tag.

12.8 *What purpose does the* onSubmit *handler perform?*

It extends the behaviour of the more simple submit button. When the submit button is clicked the JavaScript code associated with the *onSubmit* event handler will be executed. Typically this is a function which validates the form's data. If the function returns anything but *false*, the form will be submitted.

12.9 *When does the* onSubmit *event handler send the form to a server?*

When anything other than *false* is returned such as either *true* or *undefined*. It will not send off the form when *false* is returned.

Test: Chap.13

13.1 *In the following which are comparison operators and which are logical operators?* && <= == ||

logical: && ||
comparison: <= ==

13.2 *In the following string:*

```
astring="The Owl and the Pussycat went to
sea"
```

how would you find the second occurrence of the lowercase:

 a) 'w'   b) 'o' ?

a) By setting the second argument of the *indexOf()* method beyond the first possible occurrence:

```
indexOf("w", 7)
```

b) As above, except that it will not be found since there is no second occurrence of lowercase 'o'.

13.3 *What are the following: - event handlers, methods, user defined functions, objects or properties?*

`indexOf()`	a method of the String object
`length`	a property of a string value typed into a text box
`myfunction()`	a user defined function
`onChange=`	event handler of text & textarea tags
`onFocus=`	event handler of the text and textarea tags
`onSubmit=`	event handler of the FORM tag
`submit()`	a method of whatever form object is referenced
`this`	none of the above. It is an *operator* which refers to the current object
`this.form`	a property of whatever *this* refers to

13.4 *What value is returned by indexOf() if its argument is not found in the given string?*

`-1`   which can be tested via an `if` statement.

13.5 *Can you send form-data via e-mail (mailto:) using the submit() method?*

Not for Netscape. For security reasons, `mailto:` `news:` and `snews:` protocols are ignored by the *submit()* method. You will have to use the *onSubmit* event handler or a simple *submit* button to do so, or make sure that only IE5 is being used on your intranet.

13.6 *What does focus mean?*

The *focus()* method puts the focus on to the text box which has become its object. This is equivalent to a user clicking into the text box so that he/she can type in text.

13.7 *When we were testing for two words, we decided to search the string for a space. If it were found, we assumed that there were two words. But, what is to stop a user from entering one word followed by a space but no second word? This would meet the requirement of our test but would still be incorrect. How could you test for this type of error? [Hint: one way could involve the use of the length property.]*

```
<SCRIPT>
function checkspace(){
userentry =
      new String(document.form1.namebox.value);
space1 = userentry.indexOf(" ");
totlength = userentry.length;
 if ( space1 == -1){
   alert("No spaces" + " " + space1)   }
  else if (space1 == totlength-1) {
      alert("Space at end but one word")   }
else{
    alert("Something follows the space.")
  } // EofIF
} // EoFn
</SCRIPT>
```

13.8 *Add some extra code to Exercise 35 which will prevent the form from being submitted if a user makes more than three attempts to submit his/her application. [Hint: It is quite simple and involves adding one to a count each time the checkdata() function is called.]*

The trick is to set a variable to zero in the <SCRIPT> tags within the HEAD of the document, *not* within the function itself! Use this variable in the *checkdata()* function and add 1 to it each time the function is called:

```
x = 0;
......
function checkdata(){
  x = x + 1;
  if (x > 2) {
   alert("Third time? No way!");
  }
  else {.. go ahead with the checks .. }
} // EoFn
```

This can be tested with an `if` statement and if it exceeds 2, then create an alert box informing the user that you cannot proceed with the registration.

Test: Chap. 14

14.1. *Add an extra button which will allow the user to stop the animation in Exercise 36.*

Simply add another button to the FORM with an *onClick* event handler which uses the *clearTimeout()* method. This will stop the animation by cancelling a timeout which was set with the *setTimeout()* method. However, the argument for the *clearTimeout()* method must specify which *setTimeout()* has to be cancelled.

```
<FORM NAME=form1>
.. etc..
<INPUT TYPE=button Value="Click to Stop!"
        onClick="clearTimeout(stopit)">
```

Consequently, we need to assign the original *setTimeout* method set in the <IMG> tag to a variable, `stopit`.

```
<IMG NAME="animation" SRC="Love-0.gif"
onLoad="stopit=setTimeout('animate()',delay)">
```

14.2 *What steps are involved in order to assign a new image to the* src *property of an image array object? [Hint: you should have three steps.]*

i) First we must create a new array of, say, five elements with the *Array()* object:

```
arrayabc = new Array(5) // using Array object
```

ii) Each element of the array has to become an image object so that we can manipulate its *src* property:

```
arrayabc[0] = new Image() // using Image object
.. etc ..
arrayabc[4] = new Image()
```

iii) Finally, we can now assign a new image file to each image object in the array:

```
arrayabc[0].src = "image0.gif"
.. etc ..
arrayabc[4].src = "image4.gif"
```

14.3 *There are three types of brackets used in JavaScript code:* {} [] *and* (). *Give an example of when each one is used.*

{} used to enclose the JavaScript code within a function, `if` or `for` loop:

```
if (test) { .. code ..}
```

[] used to enclose the index number of an array element

`arrayabc[3]` This would reference the *fourth* element!

() used to enclose the test for an `if` statement or arguments of a function: `function abc(arg1, arg2)`

14.4 *How many ways can you get a window, which you have created and opened, to close itself?*

Either by adding a button within the new window which executes some code to close it via an event handler. See page 106 and Exercise 18 for a fuller discussion.

Or, by using *onMouseOver* and *onMouseOut* handlers:

```
<SCRIPT>
function removewindow(){
 win.close()
 } // EoFn
function multselections(){
 win = window.open("wnd-2.htm")
 } // EoFn
</SCRIPT></HEAD>
<BODY BGCOLOR="D5EAff">
<B>Selecting Messages</B><BR>
<FONT SIZE=-1> Move your mouse over the phrase
to open a new window.</FONT>
 ... continue with paragraph ...
<BR>
<A HREF="" onMouseOver="multselections()"
          onMouseOut = "removewindow()">
<FONT SIZE=-1><B>Open new window
</B></FONT></A>
```

14.5 *Use the* setTimeout() *function to create a live clock. [Hint: We need to use this method so that the clock can be updated every second - 1000 milliseconds.]*

See page 295, error 16 in Chapter 16, for the full code.

Test: Chap.15
15.1 *How many types of repetition loops can you think of?*

for, while **and** do-while.

15.2 *In an* `if` *statement which employs* else..if's, *what is the purpose of the lone* else *statement?*

It supplies the code to be executed when all previous tests fail. Similar to the `default` case in a `switch`.

15.3 *What is the main syntactical difference between the* for *loop and the* while *loop?*

The *for* loop contains all three control statements within its round brackets:

```
for ( initialise; test; increment)
 { .. code ..}
```

Whereas the *while* loop contains just the conditional test, leaving it to the programmer to insert the other two where appropriate.

```
while (test) { .. code .. }
```

15.4 *What is this feature known as:* `--j` ?

It is called the *prefix decrement operator*. It will subtract 1 from `j` and continue with the rest of the code.

15.5 *What is the difference between a variable which is* undefined *and one which has the* null *value?*

An *undefined* variable is one which is being used but which has not been declared. Here `sum` has not been declared:

```
sumx = sum+1;
alert("Sum =" + sum);
```

In the following, `sum` *has been declared* but not yet assigned a value. Thus,

```
var sum;
sum = sum+1;
alert("sum =" + sum);
```

sum is declared but unassigned and if it were to be used, IE and Netscape would present an error message saying that sum is NaN. Since JavaScript first looks at the right-hand side of an assignment statement, sum is *undefined* but is being used for arithmetic. JavaScript will not add 1 to a variable in an undefined state and it would then result in being not-a-number (NaN)

On the other hand, assigning *null* to a variable means that it exists but has the special "no value - null" value. We can think of it as being empty, but it can still be used, thus:

```
var sum = null;
sum = sum+1;
alert("The value of sum is: " + sum)
```

would result in: The value of sum is: 1

When a variable holds the value *null*, you know it does not contain a number, a string, an object or a Boolean value. Remember this, it may prove useful one day.

Summary of JavaScript

Statement	Comment
break	exit a loop
case	which block to execute in a *switch*
comment	use // for single line; /* ... */ for multiple lines
continue	return and test condition in a loop
default	used in *switch* when all *cases* fail
do-while	loop executed at least once
else	executed when an associated *if* fails
else if	used in an *if* statement for multiple choices; it must end with an *else* statement.
for	repeat loop as long as condition is *true*
function	declares a block of code to be executed when invoked
if	decision making - conditionally execute code
return	return value of a function
switch	decision making feature using *case*
var	declares a variable and makes a variable local to the function in which it is declared
while	repeat loop as long as condition is *true*

Operators	Example		Equivalent
arithmetic			
+=	a += b	addition	a = a+b
-=	a -=b	subtraction	a = a-b
*=	a *=b	multiplication	a = a*b
/=	a/=b	division	a = a/b
%=	a%=b	modulo	a = a%b
^=	a^=b	exponentiation	a = a ^ b
logical			
&&	logical AND		
||	logical OR		
!	logical NOT		if a is true, then !a becomes false

Summary

Operators	Example	Equivalent
comparison		
<	less than	a < b
>	greater than	
==	equal to	
! =	not equal to	
<=	less than or equal to	
>=	greater than or equal to	

Miscellaneous	Comment
new	operator used to create new objects
null	special value meaning 'no value'
this	keyword used to refer to the object it is used with
undefined	special value meaning a variable has not been defined

Event	Associated with	Comment
onAbort	<IMG>	when user stops (aborts) loading image (e.g. clicking *Stop* button)
onChange	text or textarea element	user enters text, then clicks outside text box
onClick	button, checkbox, radio, submit buttons and also used with links	links refer to the <AREA> & <A> tags. The first is used for image hot-spots.
onFocus	button, checkbox, radio, submit and reset buttons, text and textarea	triggered when focus is put on to its associates. Notice that the event can result from the focus() method.
onLoad	BODY <IMG>	page/image must be completely loaded before the handler can be invoked
onMouseOut	used within links	reacts when user moves mouse out of a link
onMouseOver	used within links	reacts when user moves mouse over a link

Event	Associated with	Comment
onReset	FORM	automatically invoked when the reset button is clicked
onSubmit	FORM	automatically invoked when the submit button is clicked

Methods	Where used	
submit()	used within a function	performs the same action as the submit button
focus()	used within a function	performs the same action as though a user had clicked into a text box or a textarea box which has an onFocus event handler

Object	Properties	Methods	Event handlers
area	href pathname protocol target		onMouseOver onMouseOut onClick
button	name type value	blur() focus()	onBlur onClick onFocus
checkbox	checked name type value	blur() focus()	onBlur onClick onFocus
Date Date (cont)	prototype *(not covered)*	getDate() getFullYear() getHours() getMinutes() getMonth() getSeconds() getTime() getDay() getYear parse() setDate() setHours() setMinutes() setMonth() setSeconds()	

Summary

Object	Properties	Methods	Event handlers
		setTime() setDay() setYear toGMTString()	
document	area bgColor, fgColor cookie form image links title	open() close() write() writeln()	
form	action button checkbox length name radio reset select submit target test textarea	reset() submit()	onReset onSubmit
history	current length next previous	back forward go	
image	border height name src width		onAbort onLoad
link	href pathname protocol target		onClick onMouseOver onMouseOut
Math	E LN2 LOG2E PI	abs() acos() asin() exp()	

Object	Properties	Methods	Event handlers
	SQRT2 *(not covered)*	floor() log() max() min() pow() random() round() sin() sqrt() tan()	
navigator	appName appVersion mimeTypes plugins	javaEnabled taintEnabled	
radio	checked length name type value	blur() focus()	onBlur onClick onFocus
reset	name type value	blur() focus()	onBlur onClick onFocus
select	length name options type	blur() focus()	onBlur onChange onFocus
String	length	big() blink() bold() charAt() fontcolor() fontsize() indexOf() italics() lastIndexOf() small() substring() toLowerCase() toUpperCase()	

Summary

Object	Properties	Methods	Event handlers
submit	name type value	blur() focus()	onBlur onClick onFocus
text	name type value	blur() focus()	onBlur onChange onFocus onSelect
textarea	name type value	blur() focus()	onBlur onChange onFocus onSelect
window	document history location	alert() confirm() prompt() close() open() focus() setTimeout() clearTimeout()	onLoad onFocus

arguments: values which are passed to a function so that it can process (do something with) them.

array: an internal storage area created by the browser in the computer's memory where data can be stored and retrieved as and when necessary. It is part of the core language of JavaScript 1.1.

assignment statement: a piece of code which assigns a value on the *right* of the assignment operator (=) to a *variable* on the left of the operator: x = x + 1
Here, x is a variable which is incremented by 1.

block: refers to a group of instructions, for example, those repeated by a *for* loop or those executed when an *if* condition test proves true. They are also sometimes referred to as a *clause.*

cache memory: part of the computer's memory where some browsers store copies of loaded Web pages (and images) for quick access should that page need to be re-displayed after a user has re-sized the browser's window.

client-side: the user's browser. When a user wishes to obtain a web page, he/she sends off the request via the browser. The browser becomes the client of the request.

client-side JavaScript: those additions made to version 4 of HTML which allow us to manipulate the browser.

code: a term used for JavaScript instructions. In general, the terms *code, scripts* and *programs* can be used interchangeably to refer to a block or group of JavaScript instructions.

compound statement: many features execute single statements. But when more than one statement needs to be executed, the 'single' statement has to be converted into a *compound* statement by enclosing all the statements in curly brackets. The *many* effectively become *one*.

CSS: cascading style sheets allow pages to be displayed in near desk top publishing style, for example, overlapping text and images, letter and line spacing. In conjunction with JavaScript, text can be made visible or invisible when users cause mouse and click events to happen.

declaration: refers to the instructions inside a function's curly brackets. It declares what must be done when the function is called (invoked) from some other point in the Web page. It is sometimes known as the *definition* since it defines what the function will do.

distance learning: in the context of this book, it means presenting teaching material to users who are not sitting in a classroom but who have access to the WWW in order to learn. A web page could interact with the user via JavaScript.

dummy argument: an argument which is used within a function but which has no identity until the function is invoked by a function call. That call will have a real argument which is passed over to the function and used in place of the dummy argument.

dynamic HTML: those features of HTML version 4 which allow the content of a Web page to be changed. In this text we use JavaScript to alter a page's content. It can also be used with CSS.

event handlers: HTML attributes, such as *onClick* or *onChange*, with associated JavaScript code as their values. The code is executed when a user causes an event to happen.

events: things which users may do, such as move a mouse over a hypertext link, click on a button, change text in a text box.

flag: a common technique in programming is to give a value to a variable in order to discover whether something has happened or not (such as some data being invalid). This variable, often called a *flag variable*, can be tested to see which state it is in and react accordingly. Many programmers use the numeric values 1 and zero, but the Boolean values *true* or *false* may also be used.

focus(): a method which causes a text box or textarea box to be given *focus*. It is the same as if the user had clicked into the text or textarea box.

function: a function is a way of naming a section of JavaScript code which you wish to execute at your leisure. It includes the keyword *function*, a *name* and *round brackets*, plus the *code* to be executed in curly brackets.

identifier: another term meaning a *variable*.

interCapping: the use of Capital letters within a word e.g. bgColor.

invoke: a programming term used when we want to execute a function. The function *name* and the *function call* operator must be used:

```
onClick = "myfunction()"
```

ISP: Internet Service Provider

Glossary

JavaScript enabled: choose this option in your browser so that it will be able to execute any JavaScript code within SCRIPT tags.

link: JavaScript refers to the <A> tag and the <AREA> tag as links, since *both* can be used to load other web documents. Both tags may employ the *onMouseOver/Out* event handlers.

method: in object based languages, a *method* is a function, a short program, which does something to an object. Many objects have one or more methods. document is an object which has the *methods* write() and writeln().

object: in object orientated languages, programmers work with basic *objects*. Objects are manipulated by using their methods and properties. For example, the document object can have its background colour property changed by giving a colour value to its *bgColor* property.

onLoad: an event handler contained within the BODY or the IMG tags. When the page (or image) has been completely loaded, the event handler is automatically invoked and its JavaScript code executed.

onSubmit: an event handler within a FORM tag. Once the submit button is clicked, the JavaScript code associated with the handler is executed. Typically, it is used to validate form data. But it must have a return statement which evaluates to false to prevent the form from being submitted. Any other value will cause the form to be submitted, even an undefined value.

operators: a programming term for the various symbols used within a program statement, such as:
  * (multiplication) >= (greater than or equal to).

parentheses: brackets surrounding part of a calculation which you want to be computed before any other part.

pre-load: loading images, for example, before the Web page is fully displayed. It is sometimes convenient to load images prior to animating them.

property: most objects have properties which can change the object in some way.

quoted string: a string of characters enclosed in double or single quotes. The character string may consist of simple text and/or HTML tags.

reserved words: those words which have special meaning in JavaScript. Many have a fixed case and if the case is not preserved, they will not be recognised by JavaScript. Examples are: `if`, `else`, `for`, `alert()` (all lowercase) and `Math` with `M` in uppercase. Such words should *never* be used as variable names (identifiers).

return: all functions return a value when they have completed their work. It takes the Boolean value *true* or *false* or the *undefined* value. It is also possible for other values to be returned, in fact, any value.

scope: refers to where a variable is recognised. *Local* variables are recognised only within the function in which they were created. *Global* variables can be recognised by any other function within the same Web page.

script: a term used for JavaScript code.

server-side: the server which holds the web pages and any validating programs requested by a user's browser.

statement: each piece of programming code is known as a statement or, indeed, an instruction. It is akin to a complete English sentence or command. In JavaScript, each statement can end with a semi-colon.

submit(): a method which submits a form. It requires the name of the form as its object.

```
document.form2.submit()
```

It fails without warning if *mailto: news:* or *snews:* is in FORM's ACTION attribute. This is for security reasons.

syntax: the rules or syntax for constructing JavaScript code. Some examples are: including a full-stop between an object and its method; the correct use of case and interCapping; and the correct use of quotes.

transparent GIF: A GIF image can be made transparent so that the background shows through any transparent areas in the image.

undefined: a special value which is given to any variable or object or function call which has not been explicitly defined and assigned some other value.

UTC: Universal Coordinated Time.

variable: a programming term which refers to where a programmer has stored a piece of data in the computer's memory for later use. Variables can be passed as arguments to functions.

XHTML: HTML is not going to be developed any further. It will be superseded by eXtensible HTML. (The uppercase X is intentional.) It is based on XML.[1]

---

[1] For those who would like to learn CSS and XHTML and how the latter relates to XML see: "XHTML and CSS explained" in this Babani series by John Shelley.

Bibliography & Webliography

A full reference text of the JavaScript language would run into more pages than this text comprises. Here are some references which do provide such detail. They do not explain the language in depth but are meant more for the experienced JavaScript programmers, which you should be by now, and for those who wish to obtain complete information about the various features of the language.

JavaScript the Definitive Guide. 3rd edition or later.
Author: David Flanagan. Published by: O'Reilly.
Approximate price: £30.00

There are other texts around which you can explore at various bookshops.

Here are a few Web references which were active at the time of writing. Remember that sites come and go.

JavaScript References

(Some of the JavaScript code which you may come across will not actually work.)

Here is a good reference for JavaScript. Look at the cookies section.
`http://www.ozemail.com.au/~phoenix1/html/`

Try the following Netscape site and type in 'JavaScript' in the search box.
`http://www.netscape.com/`

Free 'cut & paste' scripts & e-mail group
`http://javascript.internet.com/`

Hot tips from the Doc
`http://www.webreference.com/js/`

Bibliography

For details about Charles Babbage, try:
```
http://www-groups.dcs.st-and.ac.uk/
~history/Mathematicians/Babbage.html
```

When sites are no longer active, you should use search engines to find the latest active sites. Here are two particularly useful ones. They will also lead you to find many other sites which will help you in your search for JavaScript material.

The Ask Jeeves search engine is a quick and useful resource:
```
http://www.askjeeves.com
```

or the Yahoo site at
```
http://www.yahoo.com
```

For details about XHTML & CSS

"XHTML & CSS explained"
Author: John Shelley.
Published by: Bernard Babani Books.
Cost: £7.99

For details about the Internet:

"Understanding the Internet"
Author: John Shelley
Published by: Bernard Babani Books.
Cost: £6.99

Index

Notes

Notes

Notes

Notes

Notes